Provincial Hinduism

PROVINCIAL HINDUISM

Religion and Community in Gwalior City

DANIEL GOLD

OXFORD

UNIVERSITY PRESS

OXFORD
UNIVERSITY PRESS

Oxford University Press is a department of the University of
Oxford. It furthers the University's objective of excellence in research,
scholarship, and education by publishing worldwide.

Oxford   New York
Auckland   Cape Town   Dar es Salaam   Hong Kong   Karachi
Kuala Lumpur   Madrid   Melbourne   Mexico City   Nairobi
New Delhi   Shanghai   Taipei   Toronto

With offices in
Argentina   Austria   Brazil   Chile   Czech Republic   France   Greece
Guatemala   Hungary   Italy   Japan   Poland   Portugal   Singapore
South Korea   Switzerland   Thailand   Turkey   Ukraine   Vietnam

Oxford is a registered trademark of Oxford University Press
in the UK and certain other countries.

Published in the United States of America by
Oxford University Press
198 Madison Avenue, New York, NY 10016

Material from two articles published in the *International Journal of Hindu Studies* was
reused here with permission of Springer Science + Business Media: "Internal Diasporas,
Caste Organizations, and Community Identities: Maharashtrians and Sindhis in Gwalior,
Madhya Pradesh" *IJHS* 11, 2 (August 2007): 171–90; and "Jai Gurudev in the Qasba: the
Ruralization of a Modern Religion" *IJHS* 17, 2 (August 2013): 127–52.

Much of an article published in the *Journal of Asian Studies* was revised for this book
with the permission of Cambridge University Press: "The Sufi Shrines of Gwalior City:
Communal Sensibilities and the Accessible Exotic Under Hindu Rule," *JAS* 64, 1
(February 2005): 127–150.

Thanks to OUP India for permission to publish in revised form most of a chapter
originally written for *From Ancient to Modern: Religion, Power, and Community in
India*, Ishita Banerjee-Dube, and Saurabh Dube, eds. (New Delhi: Oxford University
Press, 2009).

CIP data is on file at the Library of Congress
ISBN 978-0-19-021248-3 (hbk.); 978-0-19-021249-0 (pbk.)

Dedicated to the many in Gwalior who shared aspects of their lives with me over the years of this research and before. I miss you. Memories sometimes fade, but attachments linger.

Contents

On Hearing the Transliteration

THE TRANSLITERATED HINDI in the texts is mostly for specialists, so I have used a scholarly format—and for the sake of consistency have used it throughout the book. Thus, even those not trained in Indological niceties will come across it as they read. Frankly, I hope that most of those readers will be so engrossed in the book that they won't stop to think about how the transliteration is supposed to sound, and I would be happy if at this point they just skipped ahead to the text. Still, I feel obliged to offer some guidelines for those who would like to mentally hear the transliteration in a way that approximates how they might actually hear the Hindi speech it represents.

Vowels:

1. Long vowels sound like their equivalents in Spanish or Italian: *ā* represents "ah"; *ī*, "ee"; and *ū*, "oo."
   - *e* and *o* represent long sounds only: *e* is like the "ay" in "day" and *o* is always "oh" as in "oak" or "boat."
2. Short vowels are more or less as in English except that short *a* represents "uh" (think of the "a" in "about").

Consonants, in descending order of importance:

1. Perhaps the most important thing to remember is that *c* always represents the English "ch" in cheese (the hard English "c" is always represented by *k*).
2. Also importantly, an *h* after a consonant represents the aspirated version of the consonant, so *th* represents something like the "t-h" in "goat-herd," and *kh* something like the "k-h" in "black-heart." In English we don't regularly distinguish aspirated from unaspirated consonants and so don't always hear them clearly in Hindi. Just remember

not to think of *th* as resembling the initial sound of "thing" or *ph* as that of "photo" (for the latter, think u*ph*old).

3. ś and ṣ are both normally heard in English as "sh."

4. Underdotted *ṃ* indicates the nasalization of a preceding vowel.

5. English has no separate sounds for the underdotted *ṭ, ḍ, ṇ,* and *ṛ*—all pronounced in Hindi with the tip of tongue at the roof of the mouth. Nonspecialists tend hear these sounds simply as unusual variants of those represented by the corresponding plain roman letter in English.

Hindi words that are listed in the New Oxford American Dictionary are written without italics or diacritics. So are two other Hindi words that are used repeatedly in the text: *mandir* and *satsang.* Luckily, these two words would be transliterated without diacritics anyway.

Provincial Hinduism

Introduction

THIS IS A book about religious life in the Central Indian city of Gwalior at the turn of the twenty-first century. Gwalior, like most places, has an interesting history and culture of its own, aspects of which will unfold as the book progresses. But the dynamics of religious community there are also suggestive of those in other fair-sized Indian cities and towns, especially in the Hindi-speaking areas. These ordinary, midsized places have largely escaped the attention of ethnographically oriented writers on South Asian religion, who once mostly studied rural villages and then tended to turn their attention to outsized urban conglomerates: Bombay, Delhi, Bangalore, and a few other great cities—the "metros" of the Indian news media.[1] The demographic midrange of these less frequently studied, moderately sized urban places tends to put them as well in a cultural middle: no longer small-scale villages where rhythms remain largely agricultural and most people recognize one another, they don't yet exhibit the most extreme styles of Indian modernity apparent in the metros, where individuals are more easily liable to fall into anonymity and anomie. Their socioeconomic structures are characteristically urban—with markets, usually some manufacturing, and significant numbers of people engaged in government service and commercial enterprise—but, more so than the metros, they remain culturally integrated with their immediate rural hinterlands. Not national magnets, they serve as regional centers, with many of their inhabitants maintaining ties with natal villages or small towns not too far away. The pace of life is generally slower than in the metros and the culture more conservative—less directly impacted by global media flows and economic forces. South Asian varieties of global modernity certainly make themselves felt in these midsized places—as they increasingly do in villages as well—but, compared to the metros, these versions of modernity play out in more subdued registers. Here I write about traditions of religion and community as they have developed in a more moderately modern, provincial Indian city.

Although the term *provincial* was generally used by colonial-era essayists to encompass villages as well as smaller cities and towns, I am reserving the term for the more urban places lying distinctly beyond the boundaries of India's large cosmopolitan areas.[2] This sense of *provincial* actually corresponds more closely to the most common contemporary Western one, which normally suggests a sort of small-town cultivation—an incomplete, perhaps slightly skewed, assimilation of current cosmopolitan fashions and tastes. I mean it, however, without the implicit value judgment carried by the Western usage: indeed, from the South Asian provinces, the ways of the cosmopolitan elite in the metros can be seen as excessive—with some metropolitans apparently so taken with trends imported from outside that they lose sight of their own traditional moral bearings. While people in the provinces often respond positively to currents of change and are open to some innovations, many are also often attached to their local roots and don't like to move too far from them. While they, too, are sometimes fascinated by new fashions, many are also quite comfortable adapting them to local tastes. Similar sensibilities, to be sure, are also found among segments of the middle classes in the metros, but with the cosmopolitan extremes closer at hand, these sensibilities are likely to entail a greater tension in the balance between old ways and new. The provincials can seem more relaxed about it all.[3]

Their more relaxed attitude, further, can lead middle-class people in provincial cities to practice their Hindu traditions somewhat differently from their counterparts in the metros. Often with less demanding jobs and shorter commutes, they may have more time for religious practice, together with fewer urban alternatives to distract them from it. Closer to their rural hinterlands, proportionately more are likely to be familiar with older natal traditions and attached to them. Both cosmopolitan and provincial Indian modernities, of course, have room for large-heartedness and venality, narrow-mindedness and wisdom. Cosmopolitan India certainly offers intellectual attractions to the itinerant Western academic, but I personally feel more at home in the provinces. This is the India that I first encountered in Gwalior many years ago and with which I identify. When I use the term *provincial*, I mean it with affection.

My Gwalior Lives

In the autumn of 1968, I joined Gwalior's Government College of Education as a lecturer in English language pedagogy. I was part of a small group of American Peace Corps volunteers charged with disseminating the then-latest language teaching methods in Madhya Pradesh—India's "Central State" both literally and geographically. Also the biggest state in India before Chhatisgarh state was created out of its southeastern portion in the year 2000,[4] it was at the same time one of the least densely populated. Most M.P. cities are fairly distant from one another, without much of particular interest between them: the state was then, and with just a few exceptions still is, mostly passed over by tourists. Our group was dispersed through colleges in scattered urban areas, and most of us rarely had contact with one another or with any other foreigners to speak of. Alone in the Hindi-speaking heartland, I tried to make the most of my situation.

One of the ways I did this was to keep my eyes open for, and eventually find, a spiritual teacher (remember, this was the late 1960s). I'll write more about that guru, his successor-son, and their ashram toward the end of the book, presenting them in some detail in a long chapter on guru-centered traditions. At this point, I simply want to acknowledge the place of my relationship to the ashram community in the conception of this project and the more immediate research for this book. For both phases of the work it was crucial—although more so, I think, for the project's origins.

The research venture would certainly not have emerged as it did without my abiding sense of having a spiritual lineage rooted in Gwalior. This led to a continuing bond not only to the city itself but also to a particular group of devotees. Experiences with these devotees during my formative years in the city have necessarily colored my understanding of what it can mean to participate in a predominantly Hindu community. Those devotees were mostly middle-class urban folk from Gwalior itself and a few regional towns—teachers, office workers, and shopkeepers. There was also regular traffic to the ashram from the countryside, with frequent visitors from several villages in the area where the guru had made an impact; most of these visitors were at least sometimes actively engaged in an aspect of farming. There were, to be sure, a few who came from afar: an extended family from Delhi who were close to the guru, and a group of devotees from Rajasthan with their own sense of solidarity—but these were exceptions, keeping us aware that the guru's pull did in fact extend beyond our familiar turf. Although the ashram would later attract a much bigger and more regionally diverse following, during my early years in Gwalior, the community there had a distinctly local, provincial feel. This was the Indian world to which I first became (never completely) naturalized.

Most devotees, as might be expected, hewed to rather traditional social views. The vast majority were, like the guru himself, married householders also necessarily engaging with the everyday world. In doing so, they all—guru included—normally employed what were fairly conventional ideas at the time about such crucial matters as caste (a hierarchy to be taken seriously), marriage (to be arranged), and daughters' education (someone destined to be a housewife might not need too much). Although these ideas ran strongly counter to the liberal notions I cherished at the time, the close inner ties I developed for the guru together with my affection for my spiritual brothers and sisters meant that I couldn't simply dismiss the everyday understandings they took for granted. I had at least to try to make sense of the worlds in which their conventional ideas could seem reasonable, if perhaps not always equitable from my Western perspective. (This effort, by the way, I see as the beginning of my career as an analytic student of Indian religion.)

After extending my Peace Corps term to stay in Gwalior for several years as a devotee with a day job, I had certainly grown into the place—perhaps too much so. I felt my personal horizons, along with my sense of India, becoming *too* provincial—the term taken here in a narrow, less than positive sense. Encountering some visa problems and sensing it was time to leave Gwalior anyway, but not yet ready to return to the United States, I traveled for a year or so around the subcontinent—including Nepal and Sri Lanka—which I hadn't before felt motivated to explore. Eventually I went on to graduate school, where I became acquainted with a number of interpretive perspectives on South Asian civilization and the study of religion. These offered some new ways to think about my Gwalior experiences, but I didn't then at all feel like going back to the city for fieldwork. I had left it not so long before and wanted to get grounded in some different Indian worlds. So my research trips to India in the 1970s, 1980s, and early 1990s were based at other locations in the Hindi belt: Banaras and rural Rajasthan. I normally made visits to Gwalior on those trips, but they were personal ones. Although some of my earlier academic work had built on traditions first discovered at the ashram, I had followed those traditions out of their ashram context in different academic directions.

In the mid-1990s, however, it seemed time to return to Gwalior for research. Personally, I felt I had gained enough distance from the place, while, intellectually, a new and interesting field of study appeared on the horizon. With the economic liberalization that began in India at the beginning of that decade, the urban middle classes there had started to become a topic of broad interest in South Asia scholarship.[5] Religion scholars had already started exploring the topic's possibilities, but, as I soon discovered, mostly seemed to be investigating middle-class religion in the metros.[6] What about the religious life of all those middle-class people in more ordinary, not-so-big Indian cities, where experiences of Indian modernity were less intense? What about my own people at Gwalior, in the ashram and beyond? The idea came for a book on (mostly) middle-class religion in a midsized city in middle India. This was a project I could actually see myself carrying out! It took me, however, much longer to finish than anticipated.

I began in earnest in May 1997, with an eight-month stay, and didn't finish until well into the second decade of the next millennium. While in Gwalior on the first stay and on shorter, later trips, I lived at the ashram—now under the tutelage of the old guru's son, known to devotees as Maharajji. The ashram itself—a place less for rigorous routines of practice than for devotees to visit their guru—provided space to sleep and write, regular meals, and a community of old and new friends. This all made my life easier and more fulfilling. For research in the city outside the ashram, Maharajji and his devotees also offered a network of contacts that spread in many different directions. My connection with Maharajji, moreover, at the same time provided me with a public identity that was usually helpful. By the mid-1990s, Maharajji was a fairly well known (and generally well-liked) spiritual personage in town. My being seen as a popular guru's devotee of sorts gave middle-class Hindus a way to place me—and more often than not feel better disposed toward me than otherwise (or at least that is what I liked to think).

I handled my association with Maharajji differently in different situations. People I met directly through ashram contacts, of course, already knew me as someone in Maharajji's network, but these were just a small number of the people I ended up talking with over my many visits to Gwalior through the first decade of the new century and beyond. To most of those with whom I had serious research encounters during my explorations in the city, I introduced myself simply as an American researcher, frequently proffering them my business card with its university logo. At some point not too far into our acquaintance, however, people would usually ask where I was living, to which I would normally answer that I was staying at Maharajji's ashram. This answer, though—vague about

relationship—could mean anything from the guru's being coolly indul-
gent toward a foreign scholar to my being a devoted disciple (closer to the
truth). People rarely pressed further, and I let them make their own infer-
ences. Most people, I imagine, thought I was a newish devotee; the minimal implication was that at least I was respectful of religion and Maharajji
thought I was OK. In some situations, though, I would reply that I lived
over in Vinay Nagar, the large area on the north end of town where the ashram was located. I did this to avoid unnecessary explanations when I suspected my conversation partner might not know who Maharajji was—or
when I thought he or she might not think highly of Maharajji or any connection I might have with him. In the latter case, if the research relationship continued, more careful explanations would eventually be made.

Although I sometimes worked with assistants, more often I moved
through the city alone. Research help was most valuable during my first
visits, when I was finding my way again around the city—much bigger now than when I had lived there decades before. In the late 1990s,
moreover, the public transportation networks into Vinay Nagar were still
a bit spare. Giriraj Singhal, on whose motorcycle I used to ride pillion,
was a great help in doing an initial survey of city temples during my first
stay and discussing their results. He also, on another visit, helped follow some leads on home shrines to Sufi babas within his own Agrawal
community. A creative young research assistant who contributed significantly to some parts of the project in its early stages, he later moved
on to become a busy family man with a serious job and little time to
spare. I worked with a few other helpers over the years, but they ended
up mostly getting me around the city efficiently during limited stays.
By my last visits, however, this sort of help no longer seemed so important. Public transport into Vinay Nagar was by then fully developed,
and I could count on going out to the road and quickly finding a way
into town. Working alone, moreover, was often just as well: in many
social situations, the presence of even the best assistant can sometimes
be inhibiting, and some of the most fruitful ethnographic work often
begins by just hanging out.

The Progression of the Study

I talk about Gwalior as a midsized place, but for India, that means that it's
still pretty big, with 2011 census figures putting its population at well over a
million.[7] In planning a project about religious life in the city, then, I knew

I would have to be very selective. The proposal for the 1997 research focused on public religious establishments of different types: temples to be sure, but also religiously oriented service institutions and guru-centered establishments, both in their ways distinctively modern developments. On my arrival, however, as often happens in field research, I began to see other aspects of religious life that also seemed important and often more compelling. I ended up following these newer interests serially, in addition to my earlier focuses, through the 1997 stay and after. Although some of the threads I followed seemed particularly distinctive to local Gwalior culture, they all helped me discern some broad designs within urban North Indian religion generally. The resulting research did manage to encompass the temples, service institutions, and local and national guru-centered movements of the original proposal. It paid more attention than first planned, though, to elements of social and cultural identity that also play vital roles in peoples' religious lives: caste and communal sensibilities, ethnicity and class. The book has been organized into three parts, with much pertaining to the last-mentioned topics packed into the middle one.

Part I introduces the city of Gwalior and its public places of worship. The first chapter gives some historical background to the city as a prelude to discussing four old Hindu temples as they have developed through princely and contemporary patronage. From a discussion of these storied establishments on the outskirts of town, it turns to some much-frequented, centrally located temples that play current distinctive socioreligious roles. The rest of the chapter is based on the survey of neighborhood temples I did with Giriraj toward the end of 1997 together with some follow-up work undertaken alone in 2010–11. It explains some surprises presented by the survey's quantitative results and interprets a striking turn-of-the-twenty-first-century pattern of temple development that became apparent with the follow-up work thirteen years later.

Chapter 2 emerged from a surprise not with temples, but with the large number of at least occasionally active Sufi shrines that had long been in Gwalior but that I only began to notice with the beginning of deliberate research. Some of these were newly established, others had roots in distant Mughal pasts, while others were bound to the last, Hindu dynasty through story or ritual. All had substantial support from Hindu worshippers, and for quite a few this support was critical. In trying to explain these shrines' appeal to Hindus, I suggest some ways in which conventional sensibilities about the otherness of Muslims might play out in some Hindus' personal piety.

Part II explores some more and less familiar aspects of community life among working and middle classes. The third chapter examines neighborhood community in the working class area on a hill above Hippopotamus Street, which lay on the outskirts of the city during princely times. This area—with its narrow lanes, sometimes unusual shrines, and diverse population—began to intrigue me during our 1997 temple survey. A few of my middle-class acquaintances from the ashram discouraged me from frequenting the place—it had a reputation for being tough and dangerous—but I did anyway, meeting many friendly people of different castes and religious communities who lived in close proximity to one another. Most were rather poor, but some were clearly well on their way into the comfortable middle class or recently descended from it. Several spoke of the unifying effect of a fairly recent, short-lived movement of resistance to the razing of some illegal settlements at one of the area's edges, the story of which is narrated at the end of the chapter. Mostly, however, the chapter treats the intricacies of interpersonal relations against issues of caste, class, and Hindu and Muslim identity in an extended neighborhood mixed in all three respects.

Well-known issues of caste discussed in chapter 3 lead in chapter 4 to some issues of middle-class ethnic community, a topic less well studied but still vital for understanding the socioreligious dynamics of urban South Asia. Gwalior has sizable populations of Maharashtrians and Sindhis, immigrants from other parts of the subcontinent who have maintained their own language and aspects of the culture and religion of their places of origin. In fact treated as de facto castes in their Central Indian, Hindi-speaking environment, both communities have seen their internal social distinctions transformed from those common in their original homes—weakened in both cases, but along different lines. A more radical contrast between the two local ethnic groups, however, is evident in the ways in which their formal community organizations have developed, which stem both from social patterns indigenous to their old home regions and from their places in contemporary Gwalior society. At the same time, each group—from its own social niche—has managed to integrate aspects of its particular cultural traditions into the public religious life of the city.

Part III finally turns to the sorts of distinctively modern socioreligious establishments on which I had first planned to focus. Chapter 5, which deals with service institutions, began with an early visit to the Vivekananda Needam, a place I initially encountered at the beginning of my research, during the first years of its existence. The place interested

me then typologically as a large regional center for a national movement, the Vivekananda Kendra, headquartered at Kanyakumari in South
India: it would make a nice contrast both to a simple local branch of a
larger movement and to an institution with distinctive Gwalior roots.
Over the years of my intermittent research, the place kept drawing me
back—in good part through its environmentally innovative park-like site
outside town, increasingly attractive as its greenery grew in. When visiting in 2007, however, I found that its two leaders, a charismatic married
couple, had now left their national parent organization—to the dismay of
many in the local organization and others active in organized religious life
in town. Attempting to understand the split, I sought to investigate the
national Vivekananda Kendra more closely. Luckily, I met its then-current
local leader while visiting another a large local institution I had been following—the Ramakrishna Ashram, which propagates its own version of
Swami Vivekananda's Hindu reformist vision. The chapter juxtaposes
these three institutions' practical roles, physical spaces, and leading personalities in an attempt to explain a crisis that had led to a major local
institutional fissure and lasting personal wounds.

Chapter 6—treating guru-oriented establishments—is, with my personal situation in Maharajji's ashram, the most self-reflexive. The ashram
was the place I knew best and had undergone some interesting transformations over the decades, so it made sense to write about it. But my
personal involvement made perspective especially necessary, and it took
some time to identify an institution offering an apt comparison that
I would also be happy exploring. I finally decided to work with the devotees of Baba Jai Gurudev, who passed away not long after most of what
I say about him here was written.[8] He had (and still has) enthusiastic followers all over North India, and his movement, with an active Gwalior
branch, hadn't as yet garnered much scholarly attention. Although Baba
Jai Gurudev's following was on a much vaster scale than Maharajji's and
the two teachers had markedly different personal styles, they shared a
common guru-lineage—attenuated now by several generations—and thus
offered some related spiritual practices. Examining the two gurus together
could reveal the different socioreligious turns a lineage might take and
some ways in which spiritual practices can change.

I had started working with the Jai Gurudev group in Gwalior in 2007,
but hadn't actually started drafting chapter 6 until 2010–11, when I was
living in Jahazpur—a small town in Rajasthan where my anthropologist
wife, Ann Grodzins Gold, was starting a new field project. In Jahazpur

I was excited to encounter an active, welcoming congregation of Jai Gurudev devotees. I didn't have much community of my own in Jahazpur, and I was happy to find a group with whose specific scriptures and religious practices I was familiar. My religious identity in Jahazpur—certainly socially and to some extent personally—was less bound to Maharajji than it was while staying at his ashram in Gwalior, and I was able to participate in the Jahazpur group without much inhibition, appreciating Baba Jai Gurudev's spiritual persona. There were some awkwardnesses at times, but I did my best to be true to the devotees there and to represent them here in good faith. If this study has taught me anything, it is that in a globalized world religious identities—including my own—can be fluid and complex. Thus, as an afterword, I discuss some complexities of religious identity as they emerge in the moderately globalized, predominantly Hindu contexts of the study.

Readers, Informants, and Benefactors

Although the book builds from specific examples in a particular place, it is meant to have a broad audience. I hope that the ways in which the Gwalior particulars develop will be of interest to specialists, but the book is also meant to be accessible to college students and general readers without previous knowledge of Indian religion. General Indological concepts are reviewed when they need to be used, alongside any relevant historical background. I write as a historian of religion—attempting to understand the intricacies of peoples' inner lives as well as of their outward practices— but my method in the book is in good part ethnographic. I thus usually follow standard ethnographic practice in trying to protect the privacy of ordinary people with whom I have interacted as a participant observer, regularly giving them pseudonyms. I use people's real names, however, when I am discussing well-known local institutions with recognized leaders. I also normally use the real names of officers of moderately sized religious establishments: laypeople often take these positions in part because they relish a little fame and glory, and their identities are not secrets. In the few cases where I thought a figure at these establishments might be hurt or embarrassed, I refrained from using any name at all.

I did not systematically record interviews, although in more formal situations I sometimes carried a voice-recorder that I asked permission to use. Whether or not I recorded anything, I generally tried to make some notes immediately after any consequential conversation and write them up more fully in the evening. By 2004 I had actively started doing video work, and in interview situations would usually let the camera run and run until people had their full say. In the edited video productions that sometimes took shape, I only used short bits of their speeches; there was always much more left for analysis. (Video programs ranging from sixteen to thirty-five minutes that illustrate material discussed analytically in chapters 3, 4, and 6 are available at nominal cost from the Cornell South Asia Program: http://sap.einaudi.cornell.edu/publications.)

Funds for research in India were provided by the American Institute of Indian Studies, the Department of Asian Studies at Cornell, and the (unfortunately now defunct) Fulbright-Hays Program for Faculty Research Abroad. I am grateful to all who have supported those institutions when they could. Astute and sympathetic readings of the manuscript by Peter Gottschalk and especially by Jacob Copeman turned my attention to problems left to fix and new angles to explore. Such careful readers are not easy to find: I am grateful for their alertness as well as their understanding. Ann Grodzins Gold is always the first reader for all my prose. I appreciate her endurance and value her love.

PART ONE

A City in History with Temples and Shrines

I

Temples in the City

THE CITY OF Gwalior spreads out under a high and unusually long bluff, the site of a fort that commands the surrounding plains (fig. 1.1). A military prize near the geographical center of India, the fort was captured and recaptured over the centuries by diverse conquering dynasties. Together, they bequeathed to the city growing at the fort's base a multilayered culture still evident in its demography and architecture. The particular diversity of Gwalior's shrines and temples—in most ways not so different from those of other North Indian cities—derives from their distinctive cultural-historical landscape.[1]

The Chambal valley, in which Gwalior is located, is known for the straightforward martial manners of its Rajputs, who held the fort for much of its earlier history. The city's urban culture necessarily emerged out of the tough mores of its hinterland, which it still sometimes displays—but it generally managed to temper them, making a respectable place for itself in the history of Indian civilization. The last great Rajput leader, the legendary fifteenth-century Raja Mansingh, was recalled not only as a warrior and statesman but also as a patron of the arts. Responsible for much of the memorable palace and temple architecture on the fort, he was also a celebrated sponsor of musicians, who continued to flourish in the area. Aficionados of North Indian classical styles thus know the city as the place of the celebrated singer Tansen and the enduring Gwalior *gharāna*, a distinct musical lineage. With the city having developed as a regional center of culture and trade, commercial castes found homes there, including Jains, whose long presence in the vicinity finds testimony in monumental Jain sculptures carved into the side of the fort bluff. Sufis—including Tansen's famous master, the sixteenth-century Muhammand Ghaus—flourished in the region during Muslim regimes and Hindu ones, with active shrines

FIGURE I.I Gwalior fort from a nearby city street. Unless otherwise noted, all photographs are by the author.

to locally renowned and less well-known Sufi saints continuing to dot the cityscape. As the Muslim population in the urban area has proportionately decreased, these often serve a predominantly Hindu clientele.

The most distinctive layer of the continuing Gwalior culture, however, was inherited from the last princely rulers of Gwalior, the Scindias—a dynasty from the cultural region of Maharashtra to the south and west. Toward the end of the eighteenth century, Mahadji Scindia, one of the most astute political players of his day, came north to make the city the capital of an extended realm. In addition to their Maratha foot-soldiers and generals, the Scindias also brought Maharashtrian Brahmins to help administer their domains: Gwalior now appeared as the northernmost lasting outpost of the erstwhile Maratha empire, with a largely Marathi-speaking elite governing a Hindi-speaking North Indian populace. A significant Maharashtrian middle class still remains in Gwalior, maintaining its language, some distinctive religiocultural traditions, and a number of temples to divinities commonly worshipped in Maharashtra but not in the North.

Although the British also had a turn with the fort in the nineteenth century, they eventually returned it to the Scindias, who had proven to be valuable allies in the Rebellion of 1857 (known in colonial histories as the Mutiny).

During British times, the Scindias became wealthy rulers of an important princely state. Retaining much of their wealth in independent India, they also produced several successful politicians, for whom Gwalior remained a stronghold. Only with the turn of the millennium and the passing of the dynasty's two most politically prominent members has the practical influence of—and popular everyday fascination with—the Scindias begun to dissipate.[2] Eminently regal in its style, the princely regime developed Gwalior not only industrially but also architecturally, leaving an enduring legacy of cultural and religious monuments that many in the city still appreciate.

Four Temples on the Boundaries

Among the admirers of the city's visible religiocultural legacy was the late Ashok Mehra, whom I met at Maharajji's ashram in 1997. Like a number of people who regularly visited the ashram, Mehraji had diverse religious interests. In addition to his attraction to Maharajji and to a local Sufi baba whom he took me to meet, Ashok was also fascinated with the temples of Gwalior. From a Panjabi family settled in the city for several generations, he considered the place his home and didn't travel much, saying that it could take a lifetime to see all the religious riches in town. Indeed, for an extended experience of the urban divine, Mehraji didn't need to go to Banaras, North India's exemplary urban religious landscape;[3] he could find his sacred topography right there at home.

Mehraji's view of Gwalior, like the pilgrim's view of Banaras, was of a bounded place—which he saw set off by four large temples in the four directions. The pilgrimage places of the four directions (*cār dhām*)—seen in the broadest scale at the extremes of the Indian subcontinent—have long found local identifications among religiously imaginative Hindus.[4] So although Mehraji's inspired view of the city was unusual, it was probably not unique: certainly the vast majority of Gwaliioris did not see their city with a similar otherworldly gaze (though most Banarasis see their city largely as ordinary living space, too). One day Mehraji, whose inherited printing business did not at the time seem very busy, took me on a tour of these four temples—which all have some interesting stories behind them. Together with a fifth, which provides a short coda, they illustrate some ways in which the patronage of the old regime has shaped the monumental vistas of the city and how new forms of patronage and entrepreneurship are contributing to these vistas' transformation.

Princely Temples from Different Colonial Epochs

On the northern fringes of the city, on a magnificent site overlooking a small artificial lake and the surrounding areas of town, is the temple to Bhelsavali Mata, a goddess who directly evokes the Scindias' Maratha heritage (fig. 1.2). The image is one of Tulja Bhavani, understood to be the family deity of the legendary Maratha warrior Shivaji (as of many Marathas): she is said to have given him an invincible sword that helped enable his remarkable career.[5] The image was acquired in 1840 by a general named Govind Vitthal Parle when he conquered Bhelsa, near Bhopal, for the Scindia crown. I heard the story in 2007 from Govind Bhelsavali, who was then the temple's pujari—the person in charge of the ritual worship of an image.

The image of Tulja Bhavani had been kept in the treasury of Bhelsa's raja, said Govind, and Parle took it home along with the cash and valuables there as spoils of war. Giving the gold and jewels to his sovereign, he asked if he could install the goddess in a temple. Tulja Bhawani's main shrine is in Kolhapur, Maharashtra, Govind added, but that is far away; it's

FIGURE 1.2 The image of Tulja Bhavani that is known in Gwalior as Bhelsavali Mata.

FIGURE I.3 The great hall at Bhelsavali Mata. A relaxed man and woman hide the deity's image lit at back.

more comforting to see the goddess attached to the more familiar place where her image was found. So they call her Bhelsavali Mata, the Mother from Bhelsa—a name that can also evoke triumphant memories. In an era when the once-mighty Maratha military power had been largely tamed but was still within living memory, the installation of the goddess in the temple could represent its renewal in one of the still powerful Maratha states.

The temple complex built for the image in 1848 was a grand edifice, with a great hall below (fig. 1.3), another on the second floor, and a large courtyard bounded by small rooms. The temple still manages to give a hint of its old glory at Navratri, the annual autumn festival to the goddess that celebrates victory in battle. At that time—using 800 wicks and six kilos of butter-oil—two huge, tree-shaped receptacles for miniature oil-lamps are lit up, ideally in the presence of a distinguished personage (fig. 1.4). They shine high above the northern reaches of the city for hours.

During the rest of the year, however, Bhelsavali Mata is not so exciting and no longer sees a great deal of traffic. Not only does the Maratha-inflected martial tenor of the goddess have limited special appeal these days, but the temple is also out of the way for most people—accessible only through an area that is no longer so scenic, currently home to small workshops and a working-class population. The lack of broad regular attendance at the temple by worshippers of means is evident. Although the small shrine room is well maintained, the large hall surrounding it looked run-down during successive visits and was often used for household living space. People

FIGURE I.4 One of two giant oil-lamps at Bhelsavali Mata. The wicks at all its protuberances are lit at the festival of Navaratri.

sometimes lounged around the walls and once I found an unwell relative of the pujari lying on a cot. During the Scindia regime, the pujari explained, they used to get a regular stipend that covered all their expenses, but they don't anymore. They are on their own. As descendants of the founding general, the pujari and his family own the temple as private property.[6] They let out some rooms in the courtyard and get by mostly on the rents. The old pujari pointed to an upstairs hall and said he didn't know what it had been used for during the princely era: "the times have changed."

The times have changed less for the somewhat newer temple to Mandare Mata, built in 1873 on a small hill near the southern edge of the city. Throughout the year, it remains an impressive place. Off a main road going south in an area that is now clearly within Gwalior's urban traffic, it still looms high, with a broad staircase leading up to it, and is regularly maintained (fig. 1.5). Although only twenty-five years separate the origins of Mandare Mata and Bhelsavali Mata, these are divided by the failed rebellion of 1857 and the consolidation of British rule in the subcontinent.[7] Thus, while the stories of Mandare Mata's founding, like those of Bhelsavali Mata's, tell of a miraculous goddess, a raja, and a general, the tenor of these stories is different. For by 1873, even though in many parts of India rajas still held sway over their old territory, generals didn't have much opportunity to fight. The tales told here are not those of a victorious military man enshrining a conquering goddess, but of the religious and mundane pursuits of settled aristocrats.

Like the pujaris at Bhelsavali Mata, the pujaris here have been descendants of the founding generals, and the account of the temple's miraculous origins told by a pujari I met in 2008 stressed the close relationship of the general and the king. After the goddess announced her presence on the hill to the general in a dream and asked for a temple, he went to the maharaja, who suggested they investigate. Seeing an image of the goddess coming out of the ground, they decided a temple was indeed in order. The image is that of four-armed Kali slaying the demon Mahishasura,[8] but is commonly known by the family name of the general whose descendants continue to maintain it, Anand Rao Mandare.

For the maintenance of Mandare Mata, the raja provided rent-free lands adjoining the hill on which she appeared. Just a few acres, it was probably more important in earlier times than it is today, but it still provides wheat for feasts at the two annual festivals—the offerings at which, according to the main pujari in 2010, provide the bulk of the temple's income. Even

FIGURE 1.5 The stairs leading to Mandare Mata temple. Giving alms at a temple is considered virtuous.

though both Bhelsavali and Mandare Mata temples received princely support in state times, Mandare Mata received it in a form that lasted after
Scindia largess became more limited. Located in a classier, more accessible
area than Bhelsavali Mata, Mandare Mata draws about a hundred worshippers on Fridays, the goddess's days, and about twenty-five on ordinary days
(at Bhelsavali Mata the corresponding reported numbers are twenty-five
and "just a few," respectively). While at my visits to Bhelsavali Mata, I saw
mostly old stalwart devotees, a Friday visit to Mandare Mata revealed a
number of earnest young people offering ritual worship and vocal prayers.
With this kind of support, the pujaris don't have to rent out any rooms and
are able to maintain their living quarters at the back of the temple, leaving
the main hall clear. Thus the temple remains a stately place.

In addition to maintaining an air of courtly dignity, the temple also
plays in the imagination of a populace still fascinated by their former royals and the ways of these both grand and mundane. Instead of the pujari's
tale of how the goddess miraculously brought the king and his general
closer together, ordinary devoteess told me about how the temple figured
in the everyday aristocratic lives of the two. The maharaja, I heard, had
given his general some money to go to Kabul to buy a horse, but the general got sick and built the temple instead; the understanding raja then
told him he could just be a pujari. Others added that the general had the
temple designed in such a way that the maharaja, using a telescope, could
have a direct view of the goddess from his new palace.[9]

In contrast, then, to the rundown state but valorous legends of Bhelsavali
Mata, Mandare Mata presents a dignified visage but stories of somewhat
curious aristocrats. It is this later court culture of grandeur and gossip,
however, with which much of the Gwalior populace has remained capti-
vated long after the end of princely rule. Although the allure of the royals
is considerably less now than in the late-1960s local culture I first encountered, it hasn't entirely gone away—with those connected to the temples
of the old aristocrats still playing their own somewhat self-interested parts
in maintaining it. A teenage member of the Mandare family boasted that
Jyotiraditya Scindia, the present Maharaja who has followed his late father's
footsteps as a politician in the Congress party, often comes to Mandare
Mata at the spring Durga puja. And when I paid my respects at Bhelsavali
Mata shortly before Navaratri in 2007, Govind Bhelsavali informed me that
Jyotiraditya's aunt Yashoda Raje, following her mother's (and sister's) lead
in the rival Bharatiya Janata party, would be presiding over the great lamp-
lighting festivities. Returning there in 2010, the new mahant of six months,

Govind's younger brother Pramod, reported that in fact Yashoda Raje never showed up. Probably she had no plans to, and her imminent visit was just a hopeful idea in the mind of his predecessor. But it was an attractive one that piqued my interest, and I had almost believed it at the time.

Contemporary Patrons and Entrepreneurs

If the temples Mehraji highlighted at the northern and southern ends of the city were grounded in princely history, those at its eastern and western extremes show new vitality in the present, one having undergone major reconstruction and the other considerable recent expansion. While the princely temples demonstrate the benefits and limits of state patronage, these illustrate the crucial roles that can be played by capable, enthusiastic devotees and entrepreneurial shrine priests.

The temple to Shiva Gupteshwar, "Lord of the Hidden," is nestled on a high hill still well out of town off a main road heading west (fig. 1.6). It is an old site, built around a natural rock formation understood to be a Shivalingam, the form of Shiva as a stylized mound that suggests a phallus (a meaning of *lingam*).[10] Surrounding the Shivalingam is a nicely built but somewhat worn temple structure that seems to date from the days of Gwalior state. That and the long stairway leading up to the complex may well have once received princely support. But there was also much new construction at Shiva Gupteshwar, including a large hall and an extended

FIGURE 1.6 Gupteshwar temple in its wooded surroundings. It is approached by the stairs at left.

shrine to Lord Ram and his court—all put up by a contemporary temple committee. Its chairman, everyone we met at Gupteshwar seemed to know, was Devendra Gupta, reputed to be one of the richest men in town.

Gupta had a number of different business interests, including a local evening newspaper, a hotel, and a petrol pump, all bearing the corporate trademark Sudarshan, his mother's name. He kept his office, however, at his coal depot, which seemed to fit his rough-hewn persona. I went to visit him there one evening with my sometime research assistant Giriraj Singhal—a young man with a motorcycle and an interest in things religious—and found him sitting in a rumpled Indian tunic but wearing lots of gold. A plain-spoken man with a deep voice, he smoked through several cigarettes during the course of our conversation. Although he had to turn to business matters a couple of times while we were there, he came back to us quickly, clearly happy to discuss the temple and his devotion to it. The contrast between his alternate faces as the apparently hardnosed, gritty businessman and the ardent worshiper at the austere Shiva temple on the hill was striking but not particularly surprising. Many temples and religious movements in India and elsewhere find some of their most vital support from zealous enthusiasts who are also actively engaged in the world.[11]

Gupta eventually told us about how the temple first came to his attention, a narrative that sounded like a conversion story he had told many times before. Gupta had some land near the temple and was thus acquainted with it, he said, but hadn't really paid it much attention. Then one day returning by train from a business trip to Delhi, he had a dream. As soon as he arrived he "just had to go to the temple." Before then he had taken no interest in puja or other worship, but after performing a puja to Gupteshwar Shiva, he went daily for some time. Gupta was silent about the details of his dream, but it had obviously had a transformative effect on him and consequently on the temple site: he soon began renovations at the temple that have continued since.

As a place of worship, Gupta insisted, the site itself began with a natural rock formation stemming up from the earth, called a *piṇḍī*. "It came into being on its own," he said, and had been worshipped as a Shivalingam. Only the very tip of the *piṇḍī* was now visible, appearing as a rounded outcropping through the floor of the main shrineroom (fig. 1.7). It was surrounded by a flat copper representation of the customary *yonī*, "womb"—indicating Shiva's consort, Shakti. Because the rest of the *piṇḍī* was hidden *(gupt)*, some said, the temple was called Gupteshwara; others noted the similarity to its main patron's name. Gupta continued his narration: before the temple was built, cows used to graze on the hills; milk

FIGURE 1.7 Main shrine at Gupteshwar temple. Only the very tip of the *piṇḍī* is visible in the yoni.

would come from their udders and shower over the *piṇḍī*. (Pouring an oblation of milk over a Shivalingam—giving it a "milk bath"—is a common practice that is regularly carried out at the temple.) As with the *piṇḍī*, Gupta saw the temple itself shrouded in indefinite time. Just when the present temple came into being, he maintained, no one really knows, even if they say they do—a claim with which it is difficult to take issue.

While seeing the temple's origins as timeless, Gupta was clear about when renovations at the temple began: twenty-eight years before we talked to him in 2007, soon after his transformative train ride from Delhi. It was then that together with a few others he began some urgent repairs: the *piṇḍī* had collapsed from the bottom and needed substantial work. Although Gupta himself seems to have been a main mover at the temple ever since he became attached to it, he doesn't do everything singlehandedly. He works with a committee that regularly seeks donations. The committee welcomes offerings from the general public, and the number of names engraved in the new steps and flooring testify to many substantial individual donations. At the same time, the committee also seems to tap the professional contacts of its chairman. When Gupta talked about public building campaigns, he specifically mentioned some business communities—Maheshwaris and Sindhis—and spoke about raising hundreds of thousands of rupees for large projects using expensive materials such as marble. Funds are also needed for the temple's regular maintenance, pujaris' salaries, and *bhaṇḍāras*—feasts at special annual days. The biggest of these is at Shivratri, in the winter, and throughout the Hindu month of *Śrāvan*, during the July/August monsoon season, when, says Gupta, 20,000 people come each day. In *Śrāvan*, he adds, he "lives" at the temple—where, as chairman, he has a room. There are also occasional special functions: Gupta mentioned the visit a few days before of a well-known swami who had done an elaborate *abhiṣek*, a blessing ritual. Although the temple is crowded at these times, its distance for most people, outside the city limits and the regular urban transit network, helps keep it fairly quiet when nothing special is happening there.

For Gupta, this quiet has been part of the temple's continuing attraction: "You get a lot of rest and peace," he said; "your mind becomes completely cool." A number of new people, he added, have since started taking the temple as a particular place of spiritual refuge: "they go there and find peace." People in all stations of life, as we will see later in this chapter, go to temples to ask for things of this world—children, jobs, relief from sickness—and we do not know how far this has also been true for Gupta at Gupteshwar. But to us Gupta emphasized the temple's otherworldly aspects, repeatedly mentioning the spiritual calm the place gave him and the value of faith in the divinity even when times are good. For this vital man of affairs, the temple seemed to offer some psychospiritual balance. Since his involvement with the temple, Gupta told us, his existence has improved: "I peacefully make my life better." Even when people go to a temple with hopes of solving their worldly problems, it can also serve as a spiritual anchor.[12]

The temple to Kaila Devi, to the east of Gwalior's main urban center, is no longer so quiet, increasingly engulfed by the expanding city (fig. 1.8). The temple complex is large and includes the spacious main temple to Kaila Devi and a smaller one to Kunwar Maharaj—spoken of as her *upāsaka*, "worshipper"—a regional saint of the past with a shrine about 40 kilometers to the north.[13] Alongside these old structures, there is a recently constructed building housing a Ram Darbar, "Ram's court," as shrines to the main divine personages of the Ramayana are regularly called; and two new temples to the founding priest of the temple and his son. (The first of these new temples was being consecrated during a visit of mine in November 2010.) There is also a refurbished Shivalingam shrine. Although the shrine itself is small, it is distinguished by its location and mode of access. It stands in the middle of a large old stepwell called the Kaila Sea (*Kaila Sāgar*)—which has dried up within the last decade—and is reached by going down

FIGURE 1.8 Entering the Kaila Devi Compound.

the many steps and crossing a raised path over the grass that now grows in the seabed. It gives the old stepwell continuing religious life.

The Gwalior Kaila Devi temple—I was told by Sharad Sharma, an articulate member of the temple's priestly family in his early twenties—is "the little sister" of the main Kaila Devi temple in Karauli, eastern Rajasthan, a popular pilgrimage site in a culturally different region that is not so far away. The two temples were independent, however, without any historical relationship between them: the goddess can appear anywhere (in fact Gwalior has several other smaller Kaila Devi temples) and all her temples are different. What the Gwalior Temple has in common with the Karauli temple is its large size and, importantly, the presence of a medium who regularly gets possessed and responds to questions and requests from devotees.

Particulars of the possession events, of course, vary at the two temples. At Karauli, the goddess herself in her energy-form *(pavan-rūpī)* comes to the medium in the main temple every night.[14] In Gwalior, the medium comes only on Monday and is possessed by her "worshipper" Kunwar Sahib in his own separate temple in the Kaila Devi complex (fig. 1.9). It was Kunwar Sahib, not the goddess herself, who regularly came to the priest who developed the complex in the first half of the twentieth century. Through him, they say, the spirit was able to give babies to barren women and cure crazy people—phenomena frequently attributed to mediums at rural shrines. After this priest's passing, Kunwar Sahib has continued to possess one or another member of his family line, although not normally the same member designated as chief priest at the Kaila Devi temple and

FIGURE 1.9 The small temple to Kunwar Sahib, where weekly possession events are held.

head of the complex. Inevitable succession issues within a large family together with different personal aptitudes among its members has generated two distinct sacerdotal roles, with the head priest presiding over a spacious and well-maintained goddess temple and a medium who is possessed by Kunwar Sahib at the temple to its side.[15] In contrast to the temple at Karauli—a regional pilgrimage place that has itself long featured intense nightly possession events—Gwalior's Kaila Devi temple is the conventional center of a well-regarded urban complex that hosts a weekly possession event at a place distinct from the temple itself.

Although spirit possession remains common in parts of rural South Asia, in most of urban India the phenomenon remains on the fringes of religious respectability.[16] At Gwalior's Kaila Devi complex, however, Kunwar Sahib is found within an encompassing socioreligious environment that can offer ordinary middle-class people a sense of security. Certainly, what was expected of supplicants to Kunwar Sahib was made clear by two large signboards framing his temple's entrance, which were put up by the temple's service committee.

One signboard gives explicit rules for pilgrims' behavior during different phases of the multistaged possession event. After Kunwar Sahib descends on the medium, for example, people should not make noise or gossip idly, as that might cloud the medium's judgment. When offering garlands to the possessed medium, pilgrims shouldn't crowd but should quietly form a line. When offering prayers to Kunwar Sahib through the medium, a pilgrim should make just one request each time he comes, not come every Monday, and not repeat the same request. This is just a sample of twenty explicitly formulated injunctions, most of which are organized under five headings.[17]

The second signboard tells people whose wishes have been fulfilled through Kunwar Sahib and Kaila Devi just how to make offerings. Instructions include a listing of four shrines in the complex at which offerings should definitely be made (more are optional) and a reminder that liquor should be brought for Chamundi Devi, Bhairavnath, and Naharsingh Baba. The fried sweet cakes called *puās* ("from 250 grams to 1000 kilos, according to one's faith") should be brought for hungry poor children and dogs—animals generally seen as not particularly clean but favored by Bhairava, a powerful helper of Shiva. And even though feeding Brahmins is a virtue, those making offerings shouldn't bring their own Brahmins to feed: "one of the basic tenets of the temple is that the hungry person is a Brahmin" and it's important that all the poor people and sadhus who come in hopes of a meal be satisfied.

Even though these rules may not meet the most orthodox Brahminical norms, they are formal rules nonetheless. In attending the shrine—with its possessed medium, donations of liquor, and offerings to dogs—middle-class people might have to stretch beyond the bounds of their customary religious propriety, but they could do so in a defined and orderly way. For some attendees, then, the controlled Kaila Devi temple complex brought a potentially forbidding interaction with a spirit-medium into the realm of the performable. In doing so, it made the Kaila Devi temple distinctive, too. It was the temple's main special attraction.

Sharad spoke quite a bit about "attractions," using the English word in Hindi. In a city with no dearth of temples, attractions help an establishment stand out and draw attendees, which he called "pilgrims" (*yātrīs*). The Kaila Sea must have been a major attraction in the first years after it was finally constructed. Sooner resembling a medium-sized artificial pool than an ordinary stepwell, it still had water in it when I first saw it in 1997 and was a very welcome sight in the summer heat. The Shivalingam shrine and the bridge leading out to it (fig. 1.10), though, had not yet been built. Now that the water seems to have definitively gone ("a natural event," sighed Sharad philosophically), attendants have given more attention to the Shivalingam that currently stands in the dried pool's grassy bed—itself still an attraction, if not as impressive as the old watery Kaila Sea.

FIGURE 1.10 The Kaila Sea with the Shivalingam shrine at a time when the sea still had water in it.

The Ram Darbar was another new attraction, one with an unmistakable ideological component. With a major, still unresolved conflict erupting in 1992 over the site of a mosque built at what some Hindus see as Ram's birthplace, Ram became an emblem of a resurgent Hindu nationalism. We'll be examining this movement more fully in the next chapter as we try to understand some Hindu perceptions of Muslims. Here it is enough to note that since around the turn of the millennium, a Ram Darbar has often been one of the first new items to appear when a temple undergoes development. (We'll soon be seeing more new Ram Darbars at a number of city temples, large and small, in addition to the elaborate one already noted at Gupteshwar.) Not all ideas behind new attractions, however, emerge from rising politico-religious currents. Some attractions, for example—such as the recently constructed shrines to the founding priest at Kaila Devi and his successor son (fig. 1.11)—clearly appear to bolster the authority of the priestly lineage.

The founding priest at Kaila Devi, called Hiralalji, seems during his lifetime to have commanded considerable respect. People refer to him as a mahant, someone who runs a substantial establishment and carries religious authority, if not necessarily the spiritual weight of a personal guru. Although he may officiate at pujas, a mahant stands as a different sort of hereditary temple priest than those at Bhelsavali or Mandare Mata. Those are usually referred to simply as pujaris, make no claims to spiritual importance, and are sometimes not given much respect at all: I heard from two unrelated sources that the old pujari at Bhelsavali Mata had a drinking problem (which may have accounted in part for that temple's dilapidated condition under his stewardship). The priests at those two places are understood as descendants of aristocratic military men who happened to be devotees and were able to build grand temples. By contrast, people still speak of Hiralalji, who reigned at Kaila Devi for much of the first half of the twentieth century, with some awe. His physiognomy was remarkable, they say, with his arms so long that his hands came down to his knees. A man of practical skills, he was unusually proficient at reading animal tracks and could tell how many creatures of what kind were moving together. And his words, clearly, still bear weight: the instructions for making offerings at Kunwar Sahib, the signboard containing them explicitly states, come from Hiralal himself. In building temples to him and his son, his descendants

FIGURE 1.11 Shrine to Kaila Devi's founding priest, Hiralalji, with materials for its consecration.

seem to be creating a new line of "attractions" based on Hiralal's lasting spiritual authority and, implicitly, that of the priestly family itself.

Whatever their spiritual virtues, Hiralalji's descendants have a sense of ownership in the temple complex. Many live in houses in the compound and run the place through their senior member: although there is a committee of devotees supervising the Kunwar Sahib temple with its possession events, there is none for the main temple or the complex as a whole—the reigning mahant has the final word. In creating new attractions, the line of priests at Kaila Devi appear as entrepreneurs for their own establishment, attempting to keep it fresh in light of continuing new temple development in the area. Hiralalji himself, of course, also seems to have been something of an entrepreneur. Starting with an old image of Kaila Devi already there, he was able to capitalize on the reputation of the Karauli temple in Rajasthan to create a large complex. This entailed not only completely renovating the old Kaila Devi temple and building a new one to Kunwar Sahib from scratch but also constructing the Kaila Sea stepwell, a major project begun in 1924 and not finished until 1950. It took so long, I was told, because Hiralal built it from his own resources, but it's hard to believe that it didn't figure in fundraising efforts over the long term. Hiralal's descendants as entrepreneurs developing new attractions are in this sense following in his footsteps.

It is easy for outsiders in India and abroad to be cynical about temple attractions, but is it really such a bad thing to want people to come to your temple, particularly if you believe in the power of the divinity there? What's wrong with making some additions and improvements? Still, not all attractions—or at least forms of advertisement—are always welcome. The new pujari at Bhelsavali Mata, Pramod, who now keeps its main hall clear and marble floor polished, was most ambivalent when our conversation turned to some large new signboards visible from the street below. I was surprised to see them when revisiting the temple in 2010, especially remembering the run-down state of the place under Pramod's apparently troubled predecessor. Even though Pramod had made some other small-ish new additions, including a cement housing for an image of Bhairava off the steps up the hill, he frowned when mention of the new signboards came up: "it's not a sweet shop," he said. There was some scorn in his voice. It turned out the signboards had been donated a month before by a devotee who wanted to give the temple more public visibility. The new pujari had gone along with the idea, but now seemed to find them a bit crass.

Fears of crassness don't seem to bother the pujari at the Vaishno Devi temple down the road from Kaila Devi, in a patch of dry land still outside the urban bustle. Here, an elaborately constructed attraction seems to be the main initial draw. Vaishno Devi is the goddess at an extremely popular pilgrimage shrine in the Himalayan foothills, where she occupies a mountain cave approachable only by a cold, wet, narrow passage.[18] The Gwalior temple, like others in Haridwar and elsewhere, attempts to emulate the physical setting of the Himalayan Vaishno Devi through artificial contrivance. With no mountains to climb at hand, visitors to the Gwalior temple must instead climb up a steep ramp, traverse a little path, and then walk down into a narrow passage through which cold water is kept running; at the end of the path Vaishno Devi sits in an artificial cave.[19] The extent to which the Gwalior temple can evoke the trials and thrills of a Himalayan pilgrimage is questionable, but people still come, if sometimes just for the fresh experience. As a rickshaw driver who dropped me off there on one of my visits remarked, "It's a nice way to see a god; your feet will get wet." He was smiling, and mocking me a little, I think.

Despite its difference in style from Kaila Devi, the priest at Vaishno Devi, Lakshman Prasad, employed some of the same sort of entrepreneurial strategies as the Kaila Devi mahants. As with his artifice, however, he has taken them to greater extremes. Where Gwalior's Kaila Devi drew on the popularity of a shrine in a different, but nearby, region, the Vaishno Devi shrine looks to one of national scope. And the lineage reverence seems more exaggerated, too. As at Kaila Devi, the Vaishno Devi complex also contains a shrine to a spiritually accomplished forbear. There are some grounds for this: the site of the Vaishno Devi complex was originally the place to which Lakshman Prasad's father, after serving as a shrine priest in town, retired to meditate. But while Hiralalji at Kaila Devi seemed to have a following of sorts during his day, Lakshman Prasad's father's influence doesn't seem to have spread much beyond his immediate family. As a public place of worship, his son's shrine to him appears as a pious, hopeful stretch.

We nevertheless need to give Lakshman Prasad his due religiously. True, he inverts the dynamic between tradition and attraction found at Kaila Devi—beginning with an attraction instead of with traditional temple worship to which, as at Kaila Devi, attractions are added. Nevertheless, he still ends up offering devotees a vital version of traditional piety. However entrepreneurial his initial inspiration may seem, what he finally offers is most familiar: a powerful divinity who can help devotees in distress. He is emphatic about the workings of the goddess and frank about his devotees' motives. The goddess herself created the temple from nothing—"it's not in human strength to make," Lakshman Prasad repeatedly affirmed. She accomplished her goals by working gradually through her devotees: "Somebody sees there's a problem with space [and] slowly cement gets laid. . . someone brings a sack of wheat. . . someone sees that it's dirty and cleans." Devotees keep coming back because the goddess grants their wishes. No, said Lakshman Prasad, they didn't talk to him about what they asked of the deity—"Who tells anyone?"—but he knew that somebody wanted a child or someone else's child was sick. He saw this as instrumental to the shrine's development: people begin to have faith; they see their vows granted; they bring things—it's all the goddess's work. Through this process the devotees eventually added a shrine to Shiva—reached down a stony path through a faux-Himalayan cave (fig. 1.12)—and, in a sign of the times, a large and much more easily accessible Ram Darbar. The Vaishno Devi temple is nothing if not contemporary.

Perhaps this sort of attraction-oriented, artificial reduplication of a national Hindu site is the wave of the future, with a Mehraji of the next generation pointing to the wonderful Vaishno Devi temple as a boundary point of his city. But in Gwalior, at least, no such wave has yet fully arrived.[20] Although the Vaishno Devi temple has its own loyal devotees, it is normally much less busy than the Kaila Devi complex, with its more traditional charms. On a Monday in 2010, while Vaishno Devi experienced

FIGURE 1.12 Shiva in his faux cave at Vaishno Devi mandir.

just a few a visitors, Kaila Devi's place was humming. Although some devotees are drawn in by the novelty of a new site and then come back to make it grow, more prefer an old-fashioned temple that is regularly kept up to date. The goddess is equally accessible in each.

Presenting herself in old images but also able to create a shrine for herself from scratch, the goddess is a divinity with long pedigrees who can exercise power in a very practical way. Perhaps Mehraji saw her at the extremities of the city as a divinity who was protecting it, just as—perhaps more seriously—did the old Gwalior generals who built two of her temples. Certainly, Mehraji's inclusion of three goddess temples among his four urban boundary points reflects his own personal predilections, but these are consonant with widespread understandings about the goddess's powerful efficacy. As measured by the sheer number of sites dedicated to her, we found that she was by far the most popular divinity throughout the Gwalior urban expanse.

Divinities, Pieties, and Class

The Gwalior fort now looms above a rather diffuse, spread-out city. As new rulers conquered the fort, they organized settlements below it—sometimes at different spots. The old city at the base of the fort steps, known locally as Gwalior, was the seat of early Rajput rulers and later Mughal administrators. The Marathas settled with their retinue to the fort's southwest, in Lashkar, "the camp," a few miles away from the old city. The British cantonment was to the east, in Morar, then a separate village. These three hubs together now constitute the greater Gwalior urban area. Over the last decades, much of the once open space between the three has filled up with new development—some rather upscale for the region, such as City Center (near the area's geographic midpoint), which has housed boutique shops and, at least for a while, an espresso bar. The commercial core of the city remains the main bazaar in Lashkar, which has neither— maintaining instead its princely heritage with an imposing statue of the nineteenth-century maharaja Jayaji Rao.

The diverse spaces of this extended city have room for Hindu temples of many sorts.[21] Small shrines can seem omnipresent in the cramped lanes of old Gwalior and the byways of Lashkar. On the latter's larger streets stand many midsized, old, semipublic temples—some obviously once magnificent. Neat, new contemporary structures have been designed into the frequent residential colonies that have grown up in the spaces between the three urban hubs, where there has also been room for a monumental temple to the sun god built by the Birla industrial family. With the city's population greater than 90 percent Hindu, most residents perform some kind of ritual observance at least occasionally at one or more of these public places of worship.

The general Hindi term for a place of whatever size that houses a Hindu divinity is *mandir*. It can refer to temples large and small and to what we would refer to in English as shrines, images in small structures not really meant to hold people. Although anyone who has the money and space can build a mandir intended exclusively for his or her family circle, the term is most often used to refer to a detached or semidetached place of worship that is open to at least a section of a larger public. Although I will continue to write below about temples and shrines as appropriate, I will also start using the term *mandir*—particularly when I am using the term generically to refer to both temples and shrines and when it occurs in certain proper names.

In 1997, as I was starting this research in earnest, I thought it would be helpful to have something more than simply an impressionistic understanding of the diversity of the public Hindu mandirs in the city, so for several weeks in the fall I would hop on the back of Giriraj's motorcycle and we would survey selected neighborhoods. We endeavored to quantify the public places of worship we found according to some socioeconomic factors of the neighborhood and simple categorical questions that we could ask about each place of worship within it. The survey yielded some broad-stroked results about the patterns of neighborhood temples in the city, including the fact that the deity receiving the most attention across all economic classes was the goddess. But even before we began our survey, it was clear to us that many people preferred to go to temples that were not in their own neighborhood. Instead, they liked to go to other parts of town to visit deities they found to be particularly powerful or attractive or to listen to visiting religious speakers at a few central places that made a specialty of hosting them. Because they often replicate on a larger scale much of what goes on in the neighborhood temples and sometimes offer alternatives to them, understanding the appeal and workings of these central places can help put those in perspective.

Four Central Temples

Temples that drew people from all over the city tended to be largish complexes, like Mehraji's four *dhāms*—which, located in peripheral areas, also found support from people not living near them. A number of temples located in well-trafficked districts, however, are usually busier than those four and are in fact a more integral part of Gwalior's common religious landscape. In contrast to Mehraji's somewhat idiosyncratic vision of the temples marking the city's boundaries, these are mostly centrally located places that were all regularly mentioned when people were asked about the most important temples in town. Most of them serve much the same religious functions as neighborhood temples—ritual worship for both worldly and otherworldly aims—but have more powerfully attractive divinities and usually more elaborate and regular ceremonial. Of these I will treat two that are different enough from each other to offer some useful contrasts. In addition, two other temples have taken on special civic roles, presenting visiting speakers and religious performances to the general public.

Particularly Powerful Divinities

The temples to Kherapati Hanuman and Achaleshwar Shiva probably top the list of places drawing people from across the city. Why did people make cross-town journeys to offer the same sort of ritual worship they could do more conveniently at a neighborhood temple or home shrine? People from distant areas we talked to at the shrines gave different reasons for making the trip. The majority would talk about the power of the divinity there; we presume many of these visitors came with specific requests for him or her. Others stressed their devotional habit, coming regularly on the day of the week special to the divinity. The journey seemed to give a rhythm to their week, a small festive occasion to look forward to. We also heard about the ascetic virtues of actually making an inconvenient trip to attain the blessed sight of one's chosen divinity. (And certainly, Gwalior's transit network—which consists mostly of private, multipassenger vans with poor suspension—can be more than a little uncomfortable when the vans are packed.) Still, it didn't hurt the two temples' wide attendance that both were in fact readily accessible by public transport, if found in different sorts of locations.

Kherapati temple is located in one of those interstitial spaces between Gwalior's three centers, but it is in a close-in one between the old city and Lashkar. The temple is said to be old, its name meaning the lord (*pati*) of the *kherā*—a small settlement, usually something less than a full-fledged village.[22] In the late 1960s, when I first encountered Kherapati, the land around the temple was still mostly undeveloped. The small temple stood aloof from the encroaching construction, as if it were the lord of an old settlement that was no longer there. By the 2000s, however, all the land around was filled with middle- and upper-middle-class housing. Between the two eras, the temple underwent development, too. It is now a large complex with halls for shrines to other divinities, many bells, and rooms for some people who work there to live in. To approach the temple from the main road to the old city, one travels a path through a comfortable residential neighborhood (fig. 1.13).

The main Achaleshwar temple, by contrast, is built around a Shivalingam that juts out into the street in a busy commercial area. It never had much room for contiguous expansion and of necessity remains rather small by the standards of important city temples—about ten meters square. But it is usually quite busy. Regular worship proceeds daily, and on special occasions the Shivalingam there is bathed with Ganges water, sugar, honey, milk, clarified butter, and yogurt (fig. 1.14). During festival periods, religious stagings are held in the late evening, after the shops have closed. And on Monday, Shiva's day, traffic is sometimes obstructed by the crush of devotees.

FIGURE 1.13 Leaving Kherapati for town, the bicyclist heads into new middle-class development. Gwalior fort is in the background.

FIGURE 1.14 Making offerings to the Shivalingam at Achaleshwar temple.

FIGURE 1.15 Kherapati Hanuman, painted bright orange. Many old established shrines present Hanuman in an aniconic orange form.

Achaleshwar temple was built into the middle of the road, they say, because a Shivalingam had grown up on the spot there. Like Gupteshwar temple, discussed in the last section, Achaleshwar is said to be a naturally occurring image, but it is a more fabled one. It came up near a pipal tree, we are told, during the time of Maharaja Jayaji Rao, the major Scindia monarch of the mid-nineteenth century. The raja was able to have the tree uprooted to make room for his road, but had no success with the Shivalingam: his workers hit water when they dug and, when they tugged at the Shivalingam with elephants, their chains broke. Finally, the raja had a dream warning him not to disturb the *lingam* but to honor it: thus arose the temple to Shiva Achaleshwar, the Lord *(īśvara)* of the Immovable *(acala)*.

At Kherapati, not even the people in charge could tell me a similar miraculous origin story about it; instead they emphasized the mandir's age. The temple just seems to have begun as an old Hanuman shrine built in a relatively accessible place that was in nobody's neighborhood and that gained a reputation for being practically efficacious (fig. 1.15). Hanuman, however, Ram's powerful helper, doesn't need any special stories to bolster his reputation for granting boons. Regularly serving Ram with his strong monkey body, he is thought to be mightily practiced at getting worldly work done. This is not quite the case with Shiva, the aloof yogi, who is sometimes seen to assign worldly tasks to a more engaged servant such as Bhairava. Of course, Shiva the Lord of the Universe can do anything, but it's better if devotees approach him when he's in the right mood. As Achaleshwar he has shown his willingness to stymie kings.

And people do go to Achaleshwar with requests. College girls come from all over town, we are told, to ask for good husbands, and businessmen from the nearby bazaars ask for help getting their deals done. They swear by Achaleshwar, too, with potentially serious results: when one denied having taken a loan from another who had come to collect it, they say, the latter asked him to take an oath to that effect at Achaleshwar; he did so, and seven days later, we heard, his son died! Yet even though people can be in awe of Achaleshwar's power in the world, not everyone always comes with a worldly request. Some say they just visit regularly on Mondays to offer respect, to keep in touch with a mighty divinity. But I never heard anyone say that they came to Shiva Achaleshwar, the immovable Lord in the busy bazaar, for quiet peace of mind (fig. 1.16).

The two temples are managed differently. As at three of Mehraji's four *dhāms*, Kherapati has a family lineage. It differs from those, however, in that the head priests, dignified as *mahants*, have been celibate, so that the office normally passes to someone in a fraternal line. The present mahant, seventeen years old in 2010, is the great-grandnephew of the last one, having been publicly named to the position by him at the age of two. Counting from the first of a line of unnamed burial sites behind the temple and including known mahants, he is the eleventh. Saying he plans to remain celibate, the teenaged mahant speaks articulately and with

FIGURE 1.16 Shiva's bull, Nandi, at Achaleshwar temple, which juts into the street in a busy bazaar.

authority—sometimes interrupting his father, a modest man who is also chair of the temple committee.

The Kherapati temple committee remains in good part a family affair. Of its eleven members, four belong to the priestly family, five are people with old links to the temple, and two are reserved ex officio for ranking local government administrators; seven members constitute a quorum. The family justifies its relative weight on the committee by saying that it in fact maintains the temple and understands what to do. I heard no complaints about the status quo, and the temple is certainly kept in good condition. The events that the committee puts on, however, are all fairly traditional, with four large public feasts a year at festival days such as Gurupurṇimā—"the full moon of the guru"—and Hanuman Jayanti. Since January 2009, moreover, they have also started providing a daily midday meal to poor people and sadhus. With this daily kitchen, though, they may be playing catch-up to the committee at Achaleshwar, which has been considerably more active and inventive.

The Achaleshwar temple has a lay administration that is elected by its members every two years: there is a board of eighteen and an executive committee of ten. Temple membership, which numbers about a thousand, is for life and is open to anyone for 5,000 rupees (about US$112 in 2010), but this is enough to restrict it largely to those in the economically comfortable classes. With the support of its membership, the executive committee arranges a number of activities and events. Traditional ones continue, of course, although usually on a fairly grand scale: in addition to its daily kitchen, there are large feasts at festivals spaced over the year and the procession of an image of Shiva through the Lashkar bazaars on Rang Panchmi in the spring. But the Achaleshwar committee also undertakes public service projects, some of which are not only impressive in scale but also at least locally innovative. In February 2010, for example, it organized a mass wedding ceremony benefiting 1,250 couples for whom marriage expenses would otherwise be overwhelming.[23]

The Achaleshwar committee also managed to create some more space, in 2008 building a large adjunct on a deep storefront close to the main temple, which protrudes into the street. The sign above the new adjunct identifies it as a Ram Darbar, and it does indeed have images of Ram and his court highlighted against the back wall. In fact, however, it was built to house shrines to all the major North Indian deities: along the side walls are almost equally impressive images of Durga, Krishna with his consort Radha, the elephant-headed deity Ganesh, and Hanuman (Shiva, of course, is honored in the temple outside). The new construction also included a small open area facing the street with fire pits for the performance of *yajñas*, Vedic-style rituals featuring oblations into the flames.

Kherapati temple also saw some major new construction during the years of my research. In 2008 a bereaved widow sponsored "the entire building" of a large new hall housing images of Radha and Krishna in memory of her deceased husband, the name of whose continuing family firm is duly honored on the memorial plaque. In addition, in line with developments at Kaila Devi and Vaishno Devi, a life-sized image of the last mahant has been installed in a sizable room near the temple's entrance, facing the main Hanuman shrine. There was no Ram Darbar there the last time I visited, although as Hanuman's divine masters, Sita and Ram have their names in prominent places on all the new signboards.

For the pious public, all the new construction and large-scale events at these major city temples serve mostly to accentuate the temples' scope and beneficent power. They do not really distinguish them in function, however, from temples found closer to home. As places primarily to offer adoration to a divinity and/or ask for boons, both Kherapati and Achaleshwar resemble most neighborhood temples—and in fact do serve as such for many in their respective locales.

Civic Temples

A few other temples, by contrast, serve the citywide population as civic institutions in ways that are not always easily available in the neighborhood. Of these, the two most named are a place generally called simply the Ram Mandir—the only major temple to Ram in town—and the Sanatan Dharm Mandir, hallowing the eternal (*sanātan*) order (*dharm*) of Hindu tradition. Both are located in Lashkar commercial areas and have taken on civic roles as venues for public religious performances, hosting well-publicized presentations by visiting speakers and devotional singers. Although both are run by people from the same general mercantile background, they differ in their origins, functioning, and styles.

The Ram Mandir has grown up between the prongs of a Y intersection in Lashkar's busy Phalke bazaar, with stalls set up outside by sellers of flowers and other worship offerings—the sign of a temple that steadily draws worthwhile traffic. Over the years, I had had frequent occasion to walk by the Ram Mandir on trips into town and had visited it a few times, once staying a while on noticing a spiritual talk in progress. It wasn't until I actually started researching Gwalior temples, however, that I realized that the place popularly called the Ram Mandir is actually two institutions, a Vishnu temple whose entrance was at the apex of the Y, and the Ram Mandir proper, with an entrance on a street forming one of its prongs. With the two temples sharing a single courtyard and Ram understood as an avatar of Vishnu, many ordinary devotees come and pay respects to each in turn, treating the complex as one. But the temples are administratively separate and managed differently. The managerial style at the Vishnu temple recalls that at Kherapati Mandir, with a family of priests and a committee that doesn't seem to change much: its chairman has been in place for fifteen years and had succeeded his father, who was involved in founding the temple. The Ram Mandir proper is managed in a way that I have seen at smaller places in town but didn't expect to find at a major city temple.

The Ram Mandir is a *pancāyatī* temple, one belonging to a particular caste community, in this case to a group known as the *deśī* ("local") Agrawals. Agrawals are a large and important mercantile community found throughout North India, and many Agrawals with different regional origins have found their way to Gwalior. The *deśī* Agrawals, however, see themselves as indigenous to the area, and those living in Lashkar have formed their own *pancāyat*, a governing body for their community.[24] At the time the temple committee took shape in 1937, the *pancāyat* in fact consisted of just ten extended families, and temple membership remains restricted to descendants of that group, numbering 148 households in 2010. With committee officers changing every two years and potential candidates limited to heads of the member households, most responsible community members are active in the temple at some point in their lives.[25] "We are all one family," said one temple officer in his early thirties, referring to the fact that marriages within the community let most of its members find some extended kinship relationship to one another, "everyone is involved." Active service to the temple, added a recently retired general secretary, "is in our blood."[26]

This collective dedication to the temple derives in good part from a belief in its special power. In a meeting with a group of past and present temple officers I was told that the secret of the temple's power lies in an old image of Ram with his consort Sita, about two feet high, that was the central icon there before the major renovation of the temple in 1953 and the installation then of large new images. Since that time, the image has been kept in an inside cupboard but is taken out for a procession around the bazaar during the festival of Ram's marriage. Faith in the temple is also necessary, I was told, but, given that faith, the temple could be very potent for the devotee: it was a *siddha mandir*. *Siddha* is a term I had at that point never heard in relation to a mandir before. A word meaning "accomplished," it is most often used in religious contexts to refer to a practitioner who has accomplished his or her final goals; "a siddha yogi," for example, can refer to a yogi who won't have to take another birth. I've also heard the term used in popular tantric contexts in relation to a mantra as magic formula: when a mantra is practiced sufficiently, it becomes *siddha*, in this sense "effective," for the practitioner. This was the meaning of the term that seemed to be used by the Ram Mandir officers with whom I spoke. They all recognized that for most people Ram's special place in the Hindu religious world has traditionally been as an ideal of righteousness, but for those active in the Ram Mandir he also has the effective practical power more often associated with Hanuman or the Goddess. For the *deśī* Agrawals, work for the temple is a sort of community dharma, but it can also be of personal benefit to individuals.

Much of the temple work consists in organizing religious events over the year, which is seen at least in part as service to the larger Gwalior Hindu community. Although the *pancāyat* reserves the right to perform personal rituals at the temple for its own members, the annual events, like everyday worship in general, are open in principle to everyone. In this sense, the committee officers said, they see themselves as caretakers of the temple for the public. Broadly advertised events are regularly held in conjunction with four Hindu festivals. Because two of these festivals are not widely celebrated in the city, they provide the pious public with religious excitement when not much else is regularly going on.[27] Performing at the annual events are speakers and musicians invited from large cities and pilgrimage places all over North India. When I asked the Ram Mandir program chair if they ever had *kathās*, presentations of mythic stories, he said no, just religious lectures and song. At the time I was surprised at his definitive answer, but later surmised that it might have been due to the fact that one of the members of the priestly family at the adjoining Vishnu temple is a practiced *kathāvācak*—a teller of traditional tales—who sometimes gives performances in their shared courtyard himself (fig. 1.17).

Although no one with authority at the Ram Mandir or the Vishnu temple would give me a straightforward answer when I asked if they ever formally coordinated events—which I took to mean they didn't—both

FIGURE I.17 Women in the shared courtyard at Ram Mandir. The hoarding adver-
tises the services of a *kathāvācak* connected to the place.

sides insisted (perhaps a little too much) that there is no friction
between them, and they do in fact seem to complement each other.
The Vishnu temple was founded after the Ram Mandir, when people
in the neighborhood decided to consecrate an old image of Vishnu that
was already there next to it. Smaller than the Ram Mandir proper, it
continues to have a warmer, more popular feel, with regular morning singing of prayer songs by local devotees and an avuncular senior
priest looking on and meeting with worshippers while one of his sons
serves as pujari. The pujaris at the Ram Mandir, by contrast, are distinctly "employees"—the word used by one of the committee members
emphatically was *naukar*, also commonly used to refer to servants. The
pujaris are hired to work as ritual officiants only: when I approached
one with questions, he referred me to the telephone numbers of the
current committee members on the entrance wall and told me to
call; discussing temple matters was not his business. More than the
Vishnu temple, the Ram Mandir is a polished institution: its images are
grander than those at the Vishnu temple, its main hall much larger and
with a shinier floor, and its events generally more elaborate. Although
the chair of the Vishnu temple said they sometimes did bring in outside speakers, most of the action there seemed to be in-house. It was
definitely a more modest, less ambitious operation.

With their relatively ample space in a common central location and
varied events held at different times, the Ram Mandir and Vishnu temple

together presented a place seen as a regular venue for public religious performance. But being "in the heart of the city" as one Ram Mandir committee member said in English, even the sizable common courtyard had limits to the numbers it could accommodate. For very large public religious events, the people in charge at both temples affirmed, the place to go was the Sanatan Dharm Mandir.

Gwalior's Sanatan Dharm Mandir—located on a street that bears its name—was started by design as a public community space. As a term for Hinduism, *sanātan dharm* ("the eternal order") was used in the early twentieth century to denote a revivified modern traditionalism in contrast to the more radical reform movements of the era such as the Arya Samaj.[28] The temple, built in 1944, was meant to be a place for the wide-scale propagation of Hindu tradition. It does this first of all by offering a large, highly inclusive place for Vaishnava-inflected Hindu worship, which is open to all. It has a great hall featuring an image of Vishnu holding his discus, with a courtyard in front that is bordered by substantial shrines to other major Hindu deities. The annual festivals of all these deities are celebrated, although special attention is given to the festivals of the Vaishnava deities Ram and Krishna. To help attract devotees to evening worship, prayer songs are performed daily by professional classical musicians. More important, as leaders of the Ram Mandir and Vishnu temple attested, the Sanatan Dharm Mandir is the prime organizer of religious events in the Gwalior area. Located in a less busy commercial area of the city than the Ram Mandir, the Sanatan Dharm temple, I was told at a meeting with some of its officers in 1997, can accommodate 10,000 people on its own grounds, which include an adjoining school with its own large courtyard (fig. 1.18). Events needing even larger capacity are held in different public venues: those attended by 50,000 people were not uncommon—people came from the surrounding areas, where "they can't have these kinds of functions."[29]

As at the Ram Mandir proper, the Sanatan Dharm Mandir is run by people with a mercantile background—but one that is more broadly based, limited to no one particular caste community. The temple was founded by the commercial elite of the day and its main initial benefactor, Lala Ramji Das Vaishya, had a hand in many of the local manufacturing enterprises of the late princely era—including Gwalior potteries and Jayaji Rao Cotton Mills, named after the nineteenth-century Scindia raja. For his efforts, Lala Ramji Das bore a Persian title in the erstwhile Gwalior State: "Faithful Merchant of the Country and Treasure of the Scindias" (*tājirul mulk wafadār / daulat-e*

FIGURE 1.18 Religious murals frame a map of India in the Sanatan Dharm Mandir's adjoining schoolyard, which can accommodate overflow audiences for its programs.

sindhiyā). Another significant early benefactor was Jugal Kishore Birla, of the Bombay-based Birla industrial family that then had a very large mill operation in the city. Membership in the Sanatan Dharm Mandir remains largely within the established Gwalior business community, which continues to come largely from traditional mercantile castes. Members also are (or are at least thought to be) financially quite well off. In the plain-spoken words of one inside temple observer, "They are all *baniyās* [of merchant caste] and they are all rich." This is no doubt an exaggeration, but probably not a great one.

However some people may regard the status of Sanatan Dharm Mandir members, for those in the established business classes (and some others, too), membership can be a mark of distinction—one suggesting not only financial solidity, but also a certain Hindu civic-mindedness. Their number is limited to about five hundred and prospective members are carefully vetted. People need two recommendations from existing members and approval by a committee; only then are they invited to join. (This careful vetting, I was told, emerged from a concern that people might use membership as a platform for personal benefit.) Although members are expected to pay their fees and make contributions as appropriate, they will also ideally perform service. "Anyone can give money," one active member exclaimed to me, "what's important is giving time."[30]

Those active in the Sanatan Dharm Mandir have to cope with the mundane but delicate details demanded by artists, donors, and scheduling that are faced by event planners all over the world. After getting ideas for speakers through the media or through recommendations, board members have to deal with the logistics. These include figuring out the best way to approach a particular speaker, estimating how many people are likely to come, devising a balanced schedule, and considering how to finance a particular event: will one person sponsor it or will they take donations? The everyday finances of the temple, I was told, were not a concern—donations came in—but financing specific events could be challenging. While the members of the Ram Mandir seem to deal with these sorts of recurring practical problems out of a sense of collective caste dharma, members of the Sanatan Dharm Mandir do so sooner out of a sense of individual, religiously oriented, civic responsibility.

The work at both Ram Mandir and the Sanatan Dharm Mandir has been effective. The members of both institutions, sharing a concern for propagating a public, Vaishnava-oriented Hinduism, have helped give that variety of Hindu tradition a greater influence in the city than the number of temples devoted to the great Vaishnava avatars would suggest. Indeed, in part because the Sanatan Dharm Mandir and the Ram Mandir had such large public presences, I expected to see a good-sized number of temples to Krishna and Ram in the neighborhood temples we surveyed. These, however, were relatively few, and their distribution within the neighborhoods was telling. Before launching into the details of our survey of neighborhood temples, though, let us examine more closely what people do at them.

Going to Temples: Large, Medium, and Small

When asked about why they went to temples, people often said simply that they were going for *darśan*, a word deriving from a Sanskrit root meaning "see" that can be used to refer to a very basic interaction between worshipper and deity.[31] This "seeing," importantly, is understood to be reciprocal: when devotees look intently at the image of a deity, the deity—somehow embodied in the image—also sees *them*, and in doing so can bestow its grace (often perceived as emanating from an image's eyes).[32] People thus "take *darśan*" at a temple (*darśan lete haiṃ*): they receive the deity's grace-bestowing gaze.

How best to increase the effectiveness of that gaze? Putting oneself in a receptive frame of mind can certainly help, and one way to do this is by performing familiar acts of respect and affection. People thus approach the image with folded hands, or bow, or make a motion to touch its feet.

Gestures such as these also have the added effect of demonstrating clearly to the divinity the devotee's receptive attitude. Most people in addition at least sometimes make offerings of flowers, sweets, or fruit. Devotees may light incense or sing songs, for, like them, the embodied divinity too appreciates sweet smells and vibrant sounds: larger temples frequently have hanging bells that visitors can ring. Worshippers frequently give monetary offerings as well, usually fairly small, which may help ensure that the deity residing in the temple is well served by its attendants and that its abode is well maintained.

In some larger, well-tended temples, the idea that the place is an embodied deity's home leads to its main image being open for *darśan* only during certain periods of the day, when the deity is assumed to be well disposed to meet visitors—after he is woken from his nap, say, or while partaking in a light refreshment.[33] (In these cases, the deity, like everyone else, is understood to appreciate some time alone and peaceful sleep.) The periods when the deity is available, however, may then become occasions for vibrant congregational worship—sometimes elaborate, with pujaris offering extended ritual worship and trained musicians perform- ing. Most neighborhood mandirs, however, are not so well organized or methodically tended and simply have their images open for *darśan* all day. Many of these, though, still have a regular morning or evening worship (or both), led by a pujari who comes for the occasion. The service normally features an *āratī*—the waving of a lamp in front of the deity as an offering of light—and perhaps a simple hymn chanted by assembled devotees.

Neighborhood temples, then, can be visited in a number of different ways. A visit can mean just going to an unattended mandir according to one's own schedule, silently standing with bowed head in front of an image for a minute or two, and maybe ringing a bell. Alternatively, people can plan to go in groups during the day and wait while each member of their party pays their individual respects to the deity; if the weather is nice, they may then decide to spend a little time together in the courtyard. During evening *āratī* times people often go alone, staying through the event and perhaps appreciating the assembled crowd. With a pujari pres- ent, this visit is likely to include a simple ritual exchange: making a small offering in cash or kind and receiving a small bit of *prasād*—food offered to and subtly tasted by the deity, who then, through the pujari, distributes it to his devotees. Taking and eating the *prasād*, usually a simple sweet or piece of fruit, gives the worshipper's contact with the deity a substantial form that most of them value.

Many people regularly renew this contact by making a habit of worshipping weekly at a particular shrine. While doing our survey, we heard from a number of devotees who traveled long distances across the city to worship at a particular place. Although this was most often to a major city temple such as Achaleshwar or Kherapati, it could also be to a less well-known one. In these latter cases, the person had often lived near the temple in the past, moved across town, but kept returning to the particular image of the divinity to which he or she had grown attached.

Large temples built in scenic locations outside the city, such as Gupteshwar Shiva, often draw people who like the quiet and calm. But that kind of quiet can also be found at many temples within the city, of different sizes, when there are no crowds around—which often means much of the time most days of the week except the one dedicated to the temple's main deity. Someone living in a full and busy joint-family compound might go, pay respects to the divinity, and then stay for a while to find a little peace perhaps not so easy to find at home. When we visited neighborhood temples during off-peak times we sometimes encountered people just sitting there who said, like Gupta of the secluded Gupteshwar temple, that they appreciated the temple's serene atmosphere.

People can go for all these reasons but also sometimes want to make a request of the deity, particularly if they have a problem. This may in fact be the most compelling reason of all for people to visit shrines and temples. We recall Laxman Prasad of Gwalior's Vaishno Devi temple being quite frank about this during his discussion of how his institution grew: people ask for boons, the goddess grants them, and the people come back. In Gwalior, as in much of North India, the goddess is most frequently worshipped in the fierce but benevolent visage that might be called Durga or Amba in Sanskrit texts (and of which most of the main deities at the goddess temples described so far can be considered specialized forms). The mother in this guise is often presented riding on a lion or a tiger, both of which can be denoted by the word śer in Hindi, and she is often referred to informally as śervālī, "the one with the fierce beast." On her threatening mount and with weapons in multiple hands, the goddess nevertheless has a fair, conventionally beautiful face and smiles beneficently (fig. 1.19). She clearly has the means to aid devotees in trouble and is patently ready to do so. "Mother Durga," as one devotee explained, "is quick to help." We heard many comments to this effect as we carried out our 1997 temple survey.

FIGURE 1.19 A small shrine to Durga at Gupteshwar temple.

That survey, I am afraid, may not have been up to the highest standards of quantitative research. My assistant Giriraj and I went out armed with a chart specifying some points to observe about a particular place of worship. These points included, among others, the place of worship's main divinity, its size, age, management arrangements, and the provenance of its attendees. We also thought up some rough-and-ready categories to describe each of these: for example, age—old, new, renovated; size—large temples, medium, or small ones, or a shrine. (To offer an example of our practical method, we categorized a Hindu mandir as a shrine instead of as a small temple if two people couldn't comfortably sit in it.)

In a limited but we hoped representative number of neighborhoods, we tried to make an exhaustive categorization of all the public places of worship of any religious tradition—the vast majority of which, given Gwalior's demographics, were Hindu. Our aim was to get a concrete idea of the kinds of temples most prevalent in the city and their distribution in neighborhoods of different economic class.[34] Although the neighborhoods we visited were primarily residential and thus more or less economically homogeneous, people also lived in commercial districts that were economically diverse: merchants with nice residences above their shops, workers with modest rooms. These commercial neighborhoods, whose temples counted in our overall tallies but which escaped our economic

classifications, sometimes found prominent places for smallish, interesting, and often old places of worship, which were maintained by nearby
business families for their own spiritual (and perhaps material) welfare—
and possibly for a local public relations boost, too.[35]

Back in the United States, I put our separate categorial descriptions of
neighborhoods and temples in a relational database that produced some
results surprising me a bit at first, if not Giriraj when I told him about them,
but which in most cases seemed to be explainable. In particular, some relationships between economic differences and kinds of mandirs were suggestive, as were the relative numbers of a particular deity's mandirs in the city
as a whole. In the sections below—out of consideration for the numerically
disinclined—I have put most of the detailed results in the notes.

The 1997 Survey: Some Results and Analysis

What struck me most forcefully on looking at the figures that emerged from
the survey database were two results about the total numbers of sites devoted
to particular divinities. First, in terms of the sheer quantity of mandirs of all
sizes, the goddess, mostly as Durga, is decidedly the most popular deity in
town.[36] Second, mandirs to the goddess, Hanuman, and Shiva together constituted almost 70 percent of all the places of worship in our sample.[37] Given
that the remaining 30 percent of our sample was split about equally between
Hindu and non-Hindu sites (Jain, Muslim, Christian, and Sikh) this means
that the mandirs dedicated to these three divinities numbered more than
four and a half times more than the combined total of all the other Hindu
deities in our sample.[38] The apparent concentration of popular attention on
only three of the many Hindu deities surprised me, having always thought
about the multiplicity of deities in Hinduism as a bit more balanced within
devotees' affections. Whatever methodological qualms I had harbored about
our survey, this lopsided divergence in absolute numbers of mandirs seemed
like it had to be somehow statistically significant. These results, however,
were tempered and made more understandable by considering the mandirs'
size and distribution within the neighborhoods of our sample as well as the
characters of the particular deities themselves.

Although the goddess had the greatest number of mandirs within
neighborhoods of all income levels, a little over half of them turned out to
be in lower or lower-middle-class areas, and a large majority (72 percent)
were small temples and shrines. The goddess thus appears as someone to
whom people of modest means are likely to turn at modest places of worship: small public mandirs for the many often put up by individuals—by

a devotee fulfilling a vow, say, or as an entrepreneurial endeavor by a priest. The distribution of Hanuman mandirs by class is similar to that of the goddess: high numbers overall, but with just over half in lower- and lower-middle class neighborhoods.[39] What makes these divinities particularly attractive in the poorer areas?

When asked about either of the two deities, devotees often respond with a remark about their practical benevolence: "The goddess works fast" or "Hanuman gets things done." This readiness to offer results is evident in the deities' iconographical representations. If the beautiful, smiling goddess with her many weapons and fierce mount is obviously able and well disposed to help devotees in distress, so is Hanuman. He is very strong, with the body of an ape, and can become very big—but he has Ram in his heart, and all his power is devoted to the good (fig. 1.20).[40] Although people of all classes may ask a deity to help solve practical problems, the poor may more often see that option as the solution most readily available to them. It makes sense, then, to see a particular abundance of efficient, hands-on gods in poorer neighborhoods.

FIGURE I.20 This new small shrine to Hanuman, holding a mace and carrying a mountain, displays his attributes of power.

Shiva is also seen to be very powerful, but not always in a particularly hands-on way. Often depicted as an aloof yogi meditating on the mountain, his ultimate state of yogic consciousness may be cherished as a transcendent goal for some. Gupteshwar Shiva's temple, we recall, was valued by its patron for its peacefulness. Shiva's asceticism, however, also gives him tremendous vital strength, which he can use in the world as he sees fit.[41] Although in parts of rural India, Shiva's earthbound strength is usually channeled into the world through his tough, dog-riding servant Bhairava, the latter is not so important in urban Gwalior.[42] Instead, Shiva is approached through representations fabled to be potent, such as Achaleshwar, and is asked to do the job himself. Shiva's dual role as a high-cultural icon of ultimate consciousness and a potentially vital personal protector may help explain his popularity in the middle-middle-class neighborhoods of our sample, where the bulk of his mandirs (45 percent) are found: although middle-class people may also need some personal help, more may have the time, space, and education to consider transcendent goals, too.[43] Whatever the reason, Shiva was clearly much less evident in the lower- and lower-middle-class neighborhoods of our sample than the goddess and noticeably less than Hanuman.[44]

For their devotees, of course, most divinities are seen to be able both to grant boons and to offer some kind of salvation—the attitude of the Ram Mandir officers is just one of many possible examples. Still, the goddess, Hanuman, and Shiva in some of his personae are understood by many to be particularly ready to deal with pressing problems of life. Some devotees talk frankly about the pragmatic motives of their temple going; others are silent. But the number and distribution of mandirs dedicated to the three divinities best known to effectively respond to requests suggest that a desire for practical results is an important reason that temple deities attract many, especially among the less prosperous classes.

The great Vaishnava avatars Ram and Krishna make a different sort of impact on the cityscape, presenting themselves much more often in larger temples in more prosperous areas. These temples are thus likely to play more important roles than might seem warranted by their relatively small proportion of our total sample (6.5 percent): their generally large size can make each one a more significant social fixture in its locality, while the relative prosperity of their supporters can heighten the Vaishnava deities' civic profile, as seen in the roles of the Ram Mandir and Sanatan Dharm Mandir described above.

Although our sample suggests that people devoted principally to Ram and Krishna are most often fairly prosperous, those devoted to Krishna appear to be more so. We found the most Krishna temples (by a longshot!) in upper-middle-class neighborhoods (64 percent) and exactly half of the Ram temples in middle-middle-class ones.[45] This distribution of the Ram and Krishna temples in our sample is striking, lending credence to some assumptions in the sociology of Indian religions long familiar to scholars. At the beginning of the twentieth century, Max Weber wrote about the attractiveness of Krishna worship, forms of which can get quite elaborate, for the well-to-do mercantile classes.[46] Meanwhile, among the more solidly middle-class bourgeoisie, the sustained popularity of righteous Ram—taken in North India to be the incarnation of traditional Hindu virtues—has taken new nationalistic turns.[47] Certainly, the distribution of the temples of the two together in the totality of our sample indicates that the Vaishnava predilections of the less privileged classes tend to be concentrated on Ram's servant Hanuman rather than on either of the great avatars of Vishnu themselves.

While much of Hindu worship is individual, Vaishnava—and especially Krishnaite—worship has important congregational strands, often entailing musical performance. Musical performance can play roles in the worship of other divinities, too, and many well-to-do people are happy to sponsor visiting lecturers or storytellers.[48] These events, when they are not too big, sometimes occur in the larger neighborhood temples. In thinking about a temple's size, we used its ability to host functions as a criterion for our categories, with small, medium, and large temples able to serve as venues for increasingly elaborate congregational events.[49] Although not all temples are regularly used to their full capacity, many large and medium-sized temples at least occasionally are. Within the more prosperous neighborhoods of our sample, the ratio of these more substantial public mandirs (dedicated to any deity) to smaller ones was much higher than in the poorer areas—no doubt in part because wealthier patrons were ready to support them for events while maintaining shrine rooms in their houses for private worship.[50] With the mandirs housing images of Ram and Krishna in our sample mostly in more prosperous neighborhoods, they ran decidedly to medium and large sizes: those of Ram in all instances and those of Krishna in a majority of them.[51]

The temples to Ram and Krishna also tended to be *old*—that is, according to our criteria, built in noncontemporary styles and apparently dating from the times of Gwalior State or earlier.[52] Because the old temples to Ram and Krishna are for the most part well preserved and sometimes delicately finished, this usually turns out to be old in a good way—offering a cherished atmosphere and a long-revered image usually seen to be particularly sacred. These substantial and mostly old neighborhood temples could thus not only serve fairly large numbers from their communities for everyday worship and religious events, but also often did so with some traditional architectural panache. If the Ram and Krishna temples in Gwalior were relatively few, they often stood out in ways that many middle- and upper-class people appreciated. Even though greatly outnumbered in the more prosperous neighborhoods of our sample, too, by usually smaller temples and shrines to the goddess and Hanuman,[53] they generally outshone them.

Temples serving specific caste, ethnic, or voluntary religious groups also tended to be substantial, if not always so nicely finished. These temples began to appear in our survey as we came across deities that were specific to certain local groups or, more often, to groups that had a provenance from outside the area (we called them *regional*). Of the nineteen such regional temples in our sample, eleven were used primarily by members of the Maharashtrian and Sindhi communities, ethnic groups with a strong presence in the city who will be discussed in chapter 4, but they also included temples maintained by other regional and sectarian associations.[54]

Because all these temples also often serve as social centers for their specific communities, they were all large (nine) or medium (ten) in size. With the Maharashtrians and Sindhis nicely positioned in the city and members of established voluntary religious groups often well educated, fifteen of the nineteen temples were in middle-middle-class neighborhoods or better. Only one large caste temple, for the formerly untouchable Valmiks—whom we will meet in chapter 3—was in a lower-class area. While in all the areas we sampled, the more prosperous neighborhoods tended to have a larger proportion of good-sized mandirs than did the poorer ones, this pattern could take a special form in planned new development.

Temple Growth and Management: Some 2010 Examples

The best example of planned development in our 1997 sample was in an area near Jiwaji University, on the southern side of the city. There we found a group of three small, named, contiguous middle-class residential colonies that we took in our 1997 survey, together with three larger colonies nearby, as a single extended neighborhood. We did this in part because four of the six colonies, including the three small contiguous ones, contained just one public mandir each.[55] (Because all the other neighborhoods we had surveyed had a number of mandirs, it seemed odd to us to count localities having only one as separate neighborhoods.) The public places of worship in the area were five medium-sized temples, each in its own colony, all with regular daily *āratī* and attended almost exclusively by colony members.

These temples were planned during the separate colonies' development to suit some contemporary middle-class worship practices. As is common in such colonies throughout India, the temples were situated in small parks, where community halls were also often found. They offered colony residents a single place for some group worship to supplement the home shrines for which, if the need is felt in middle-class houses, a little space can usually be made. Home shrines are dedicated rooms or corners of a room where an altar is set up with pictures and small-scale clay or metal images of one or more divinities (fig. 1.21). (The small altars are sometimes called pujas, in a special use of the word for ritual worship itself.) Home shrines can be focused on any divinity; the five medium-size temples in

FIGURE I.2I A home shrine in a separate room, Tara Ganj, Gwalior.

the area appealed to what were obviously widespread middle-class religious sentiments: three were dedicated to the goddess, and two to Shiva.

In 2010, I revisited these colonies to see what thirteen years had brought to the mandirs planned for these new middle-class environments. Although a few more mandirs had sprung up in the larger outlying colonies, none had in the three small contiguous ones. All three mandirs there, however, had undergone significant development: each now included more deities, and one had some substantial physical additions.

The greatest amount of physical growth had occurred in Anupam Nagar, the oldest of the three colonies. The original Shiva temple had expanded to include a Hanuman shrine that had previously been outside. In the expanded space, the temple's "Ladies' Circle" *(mahilā maṇḍal)* built first a Ram Darbar and later an altar to Krishna with his consort Radha. (The women meet weekly to sing devotional songs, which often allude to the love between the last two.) From there, it was a short walk into Saraswati Nagar and *its* temple, where a substantial new image had been constructed. Built as a site dedicated to the goddess, it was now also home to a large figure of Hanuman, standing on the same platform that supports the main goddess shrine. With images about equal in size and position, the temple now serves the city's two most popular divinities. In 2010, I was told, the temple saw as much activity on Tuesdays—Hanuman's day—as it did on Fridays, special to the goddess. The expansions at each temple broadened its community appeal by increasing the number of deities it housed and had both obviously required some effort and organization.

The changes seemed more casual in Tagore Nagar, which had never had a full-sized temple, just a Hanuman shrine. The site was still an open shrine when I visited again, but instead of the main figure of Hanuman alone, I now found a rather large number of divinities sharing a very limited public space. On the floor inside the small shrine was, on one side, a Shivalingam just a few inches high, and on the other an aniconic image of the goddess. Above the main image of Hanuman was a lithograph of Ram with his court, and outside, to one side, was a somewhat larger Shivalingam and a small shrine to Bhairava. I didn't see Krishna, but otherwise no major divinity was missing (fig. 1.22).

In 1997, we had listed the Tagore Nagar Hanuman shrine as being *informally* managed, a category that emerged when neighborhood people, when asked, replied that no one in particular had responsibility for some usually small place of worship. Often they added that there were a few people who nevertheless cared about it and kept it up. We then began

FIGURE 1.22 Hanuman shrine at Tagore Nagar with a lithograph of Ram's court above and a very small Shivalingam (covered with rice) and aniconic Goddess on the floor. Close-ups of the latter two are at bottom.

to use "informal" as a residual category that indicated we could find no signs of a place of worship's private ownership or active committee oversight. We assumed these were places that may have been built and actively tended by someone for a while but were no longer or, as in this case, put up by a housing society and then left alone for the community to tend. At Tagore Nagar, this seems to have led to a fruitful sense of collective ownership, with colony devotees having different spiritual predilections making small additions to the existing shrine without really having to seek anyone's approval. The result was a very active place: three people came within fifteen minutes one morning on a Monday, special to Shiva, two of them giving oblations of milk to the small Shivalingam in the main shrine. Because it was primarily a Hanuman shrine, there were likely to be just as many on Tuesday as well—not to mention on Friday for the goddess, whose aniconic image sits not far from the Shivalingam. It was many people's shrine and many people used it.

This middle-class example of an informally managed shrine, however, is not particularly typical: informal arrangements are especially common in lower- and lower-middle-class neighborhoods, where they were apparent at more than half (54 percent) of all sites in our sample. The large majority of these (87 percent) were at small temples and shrines—also, as noted, more common in poorer areas than in more prosperous ones. In some of these cases, sturdy stone images receive occasional offerings of flowers and incense, but remain largely untended. In other cases, the sites are still sometimes well kept up, either by sometimes unspoken arrangements among neighbors or by committed individuals. A devotee at Tagore Nagar explained that in the recent past maintenance of the temple had occurred largely through *gupt dān*, "hidden contributions"—someone would come and clean; another would whitewash.

Matters at Tagore Nagar, however, had recently become more organized. Two months before my last visit a small brick room had been built in the shrine's courtyard to provide shelter for a regular unsalaried pujari; his prepubescent son, who lived at home in a colony not far away, was sitting in it offering *prasād*. Devotees seemed generally satisfied with the new situation, even the one reminiscing about the old ways of "hidden contribution"—after all, having a pujari, in addition to facilitating the happy occasion of *prasād,* is also a sign that a shrine has come of age. Still, with the new arrangements, the shrine had again come to the attention of the housing society, with contributions likely to be less hidden and feelings of multiple personal ownership diluted.

The temples at the other two adjacent colonies functioned on variants of the new model at Tagore Nagar. They were under the general oversight of the colony's housing society, but were not normally very high on its agenda. Both had the traffic to generate enough offerings to support unsalaried pujaris—who were, though, supplied with housing. The pujari at Anupam Nagar was an old sadhu—an ascetic who slept in the temple itself and didn't need much. At Saraswati Nagar the pujari lived with his family in a small dwelling put up just within the grounds of the colony's park; he supplemented his income by performing occasional rituals in the colony and elsewhere. There, improvements came largely through the initiative of individuals. One colony dweller who said he likes the temple's atmosphere provided a large, sturdy, wooden cot on which he and others could sit. Another sponsored the creation of a courtyard in front of the temple with a low wall around it: perhaps he had intended it for summer evening devotional singing, or maybe he liked to sit outside and warm himself in the winter sun. At Anupam Nagar, by contrast—with its new construction, several large new images, and an organized women's group—the housing committee has had a more active hand, a fact that was clearly recognized by the temple's pujari: once he finally understood what I was asking about (my less-than-perfect Hindi together with his diminished hearing caused some initial confusions), he took me to a committee member with an interest in the temple who lived nearby. The committee member treated the sadhu respectfully, responded to my questions helpfully, and served us both tea.

Some neighborhood temples have their own dedicated committees. This sometimes indicates a collective enthusiasm that can transform the temple into an institution that provides more than an opportunity to make contact with one or more divinities and to participate in occasional (or even regular) hymn-singing sessions. At Govindpuri, across the main road from the three colonies just discussed and somewhat more upscale, the medium-sized goddess temple we noted in 1997 now had added another hall that doubled its size and served as a venue for daily talks by a local religious teacher, a retired professor who lived in the colony and had a small following. When I arrived, a full-time temple manager was busy laying out sheets on the floor in preparation for the 10:00 a.m. session, which he referred to as a *satsang*, "a meeting of the good"—a term commonly used in North India for religious get-togethers of different kinds.

The temple manager, a Brahmin named Dubey who also served as pujari during regular worship times, explained about the temple organization. There was an active membership of thirty to thirty-five who each contributed an annual fee of a hundred rupees (then about US$2.25)—it helps pay for the *prasād*, said Dubey smiling. Interested members helped organize special events, including occasional speakers from outside Gwalior (he mentioned a visitor from Kanpur). The retired professor and satsang attendees, happy to have a regular venue, offered support, while others helped out according to their devotion and means. Given the size of the establishment and the prosperity evident in the colony, this must have included one or more substantial donors, although none were mentioned.

As Dubey finished setting up, people started trickling in—mostly women, more old than young—and then started singing devotional songs. I looked around the temple: there was a large Shivalingam at the back of the new hall and a Radha Krishna shrine built into the side of the old one. What I was expecting to see, however, was a Ram Darbar and so went outside to look for it. There I found Dubey again, who showed me what they had in the courtyard: another Shivalingam and a Hanuman shrine containing a picture of Shirdi Sai Baba, the early twentieth-century Maharashtrian saint who was increasingly popular in North India. Then Dubey took me around back and pointed to small shrine to Bhairava (fig. 1.23). I asked if they offered him liquor, which Bhairava was known to like, along with meat. Yes, said Dubey, smiling mischievously, during his festival we give him *everything*.

This temple certainly had plenty of new shrines, but it didn't appear to have the new shrine to the set of divinities that I seemed to be meeting most regularly these days. About to leave, I asked Dubey if there had been any discussion about putting up a Ram Darbar. "Oh," he said, "we put one up four years ago. Didn't you see it?" He pointed to the main Durga shrine, which was about a meter deep. On one of its walls, facing an altar with a simple aniconic orange Hanuman, was one with an iconic Hanuman bowing to images of Ram and Sita—not a grand Ram Darbar, to be sure, but one placed at the spiritual center of the temple. It wasn't missing. More people had arrived for the satsang, but that would last a couple of hours, I was told, and the speaker was likely to come toward the end. I didn't wait.

FIGURE 1.23 Aniconic representation of Bhairava in an outside shrine at Govindpuri.

Although most neighborhood temples are open to anyone, a number are maintained as semiprivate places. Most of these would be classed as what we called a *house* temple—an easily accessible room built into a private home (or occasionally a freestanding structure in a yard) that was at least sometimes open to a broader public.[56] Some house temples, particularly those in mixed commercial neighborhoods, are run by pujari families who operate them as establishments open to the general public. Those in strictly residential neighborhoods usually belong to pious individuals and are intended primarily for their family, friends, and neighbors. In our 1997 survey we had noted a house temple to Shiva in Vivekananda Colony, abutting Anupam Nagar in the university area, and I returned to see what had become of it. I didn't get very far. Alone and on foot in a rather large development, I searched for a while until people finally pointed me to a Shiva temple in a house at the end of a street where, yes, the neighbors sometimes went. It was late in the day when I arrived there, but the evening *āratī* wasn't imminent and the gate to the house was closed. There was a woman in the yard, though, and I asked if there was a Shiva temple there. Yes, she said, there was, looking me in the eye, but she didn't open the gate. The temple, she made clear, was for people she knew, and I wasn't welcome.

Centers and Peripheries in the New Millennium

Not all mandirs are for everyone. People can certainly be made to feel unwelcome at private temples, and members of particular communities are sometimes regularly denied entrance to public ones—despite current laws forbidding the practice.[57] But there is self-exclusion, too—sometimes practiced by castes, classes, and individuals wary of rituals practiced to certain manifestations of a divinity. The many goddess shrines in our sample, particularly in the poorer neighborhoods, represent continuities with religion in the hinterlands, where goddess worship tends to be even more pervasive than in the cities and her shrines particularly abundant. At these shrines she is likely to receive offerings of liquor and the sacrifice of a goat, and sometimes possesses her devotees. In fact, many inhabitants of the poorer areas are fairly recent economic immigrants from regional villages with no particular inclination to abandon these practices. They, and others, regularly make nonvegetarian offerings at goddess shrines, with occasional enterprising devotees establishing small sites where possessions sometimes occur. Certain kinds of goddess shrines can thus turn out to be sites of religious activity that many respectable people disdain.

This fact may help explain one of the more interesting statistical surprises in our sample. As in the city as a whole, in lower- and lower-middle-class areas the most sites were dedicated to Mataji and Hanuman, but the proportion of shrines to the total of Hanuman's *mandirs* in those areas was about half that of Mataji's.[58] Although Hanuman is a powerful deity, he is also a Vaishnavite one. He is not generally pleased by nonvegetarian offerings and doesn't normally possess people. And like his Lord Ram, he seems to prefer an enclosed temple, at least a small one—a place where he can actually offer shelter to pious devotees.[59] Whatever the socioreligious implications of Hanuman mandirs in the hinterlands, in the poorer areas of the city they seem to represent a Vaishnava thrust outward from a respectable middle-class core. The powerful servant of Ram stands firmly in an area of the city where more disruptively powerful forces also hold sway.

As Mehraji's templed city, then, the Scindias' erstwhile capital at the turn of the twenty-first century could be seen as bounded largely by warrior goddesses—many ruling clans' favorites, who might continue to protect their town. These have found some of their less grand counterparts in the many goddesses enshrined in the poorer, often more peripheral areas of the city, offering their protective power to devotees individually in ways they have long done in surrounding rural areas. In middle-class neighborhoods and upscale colonies, where the goddess is also very much present, she is more likely to be worshipped in sedate Sanskritic ways, but she can still offer devotees powerful help in this world. And for many individuals in all parts of urban and rural India, she is also understood as an image of transcendent divine force. Shiva, too—bound together with the goddess in Hindu lore—is found throughout the city, offering power both effective and salvific. But increasingly, standing in a temple not far from a goddess shrine, is the figure of Hanuman, who seems to serve as her unquestionably vegetarian Vaishnava counterpart.

Rama and Krishna, by contrast, are more firmly grounded in the middle- and upper-middle-class areas, with presences considerably greater than the simple number of their images would suggest. They often herald a more refined and expressive tradition, sometimes embedded in architecture, articulated in story and song, and proclaimed in religious talks. In its Ramaite version, that tradition has long been communitarian as well as individual, giving attention to individuals' roles in family and society—and now sometimes to the cohesiveness of the Hindu community in the secular Indian state. As this new significance of Ram has spread along with a newly normalized Hindu assertiveness, images of Ram and his court have found their way into many temples established to other deities. In these places, however, a Ram Darbar sometimes seems to be more a statement acknowledging current socioreligious realities than a site of active worship: during a 2010 visit to the Achaleshwar temple's large multishrined annex that is called a Ram Darbar, I found most people clustering around the images of the goddess and Hanuman. No one seemed to be paying much attention to the Ram Darbar itself—a fact that didn't really surprise me: even people who think it's good for temples to demonstrate Hindu pride are likely to keep worshipping the divinities with whom they have established familiar relationships—especially if those deities are understood to be practically effective. And when Ram Darbars *are* actively worshipped, in their own temples or those of other deities, they may still be taken in more traditional ways. Ram can be admiringly revered as an ideal of individual virtue or asked for help in distress—just as his devoted servant Hanuman regularly is. Fortunately, alongside Hinduism's nationalistic variants, its more pacific forms of personal religion also remain vibrant.

2

Sufi Shrines for Hindu Devotees

IN ADDITION TO practically innumerable Hindu temples of different sorts, Gwalior also has a great many places of worship dedicated to past Sufis, a term that can refer to many varieties of mystical personages in Islam.[1] These sites, which can include large structures as well as small ones, are all usually just called shrines in English and can be found throughout the subcontinent and in many other parts of the Muslim world.[2] The most famous Sufi shrine in Gwalior is undoubtedly that of Muhammad Ghawth, a well-known sixteenth-century figure favored by the great sixteenth-century Mughal emperor Akbar, who built him a monumental resting place. Although sometimes a religious attendant will be there to show visitors the saint's memorial tomb, Ghawth's immediate spiritual lineage has not survived, and the shrine has remained mostly a tourist attraction, maintained by the Archeological Survey of India.[3] That place, just down the road from the college where I worked during my early years in Gwalior, was the only Sufi site I really knew in those days. The city's active Sufi shrines were largely invisible to me, preoccupied with my worlds of college and ashram. In this I was like quite a few other busy city residents who don't regularly pay attention to religious sites outside their immediate purview (even when they are better apprised than I was of those sites' existence). When I returned to Gwalior as a researcher and began to look, though, I was struck by the large number of Sufi shrines in town that were at least sometimes still active as well as by the composition of their worshippers. Although Muslims were visible at many shrines, at most the majority of devotees were Hindu. What was the attractiveness of the Sufi shrines for *them*, particularly in a predominantly Hindu city such as Gwalior? It took me a few return visits to Gwalior to find an answer.

In Gwalior as elsewhere, active Sufi shrines are understood to mediate the effective spiritual power of particular holy personages.[4] These are normally seen as spiritual adepts who have had a vital connection to the spot, perhaps having lived, died, or at least having left a relic there. Some of these personages have also given rise to historically attested lineages of spiritual and/or physical descendants who continue to renew their connection to the place, but in Gwalior, as in the rest of the subcontinent, such shrines are a relatively small proportion of the total—and are usually larger, more established institutions. If most small shrines have no continuing historical lineage, many of them offer the spiritual presence of a saint with a cogent legendary biography together with a devoted shrine attendant. Still others have an attendant who speaks of the personage he mediates as simply a vague but powerful spirit. In all cases, though, the holy personage is seen as Muslim—and so, for most visitors, is the quality of his spiritual power and the place where it is grounded. This sense of the power available at Sufi shrines as somehow qualitatively Muslim can give it a special place within the religious sensibilities of many Hindus who visit them.[5]

All over India, Sufi shrines really do draw many Hindus. In this they differ from mosques, serving purposes different from them even as they draw some overlapping Muslim clientele. Mosques are primarily places for group observance of the regular prayers incumbent on all Muslims. There are plenty of mosques in Gwalior—several large ones, many smaller—but Hindus, as a rule, have no religious reason to visit them. Sufi shrines are places to approach a powerful spiritual benefactor—Muslim to be sure, but one whose grace is available to all. All those ready to seek the help of a spiritual intermediary may have reason to visit: in Gwalior this usually means many Hindus and some Muslims, too (as well as the occasional Sikh, Jain, and Christian). This does not, however, mean everyone: people following more strictly orthodox or reformist versions of any religious persuasion—Indic or Abrahamic—are likely to keep a distance from Sufi shrines, seeing them as a distraction (at least) from a true, perhaps scripturally defined, religious path. This includes many urban Muslims—probably a larger proportion of them than of Hindus: reformist styles of Islam are popular in the cities, while the attitude of religious Hindus toward plural sources of grace is generally relaxed. Sufi shrines in Gwalior, as in much of India, are eminently heterogeneous places.

Although most of Gwalior's Sufi shrines are small, unimpressive structures, sometimes irregularly maintained, all active shrines become highly visible on the celebration of their yearly festival—known to all by the Urdu term 'urs.[6] Preceding these festivals, posters appear in profusion in the neighboring bazaars. Printed in the Devanagari script used to write Hindi and Sanskrit, they invite everyone to come, almost always highlighting a performance of the rhythmic devotional music called qawwali. Popular local singers are featured, and at larger venues often artists from out of town. Yusuf Niyazi, one of the best-known local qawwals, spontaneously enumerated sixteen shrines that sponsored regular musical performances in 1997. Who comes to these performances? Yusuf didn't hesitate: 99 percent of the attendees *and* organizers were Hindu. And a quick scan down to the smaller print at the bottom of the Devanagari posters substantiated Yusuf's only somewhat exaggerated claim: in most cases, the majority of supporters had Hindu names. One of the central facts of life for Sufi shrines in Gwalior, then, is that they are largely frequented—and often managed—by Hindus.

This does not always seem to have been the case. Although Muslims currently constitute only about 6 or 7 percent of Gwalior's current population, in some earlier eras that proportion seems to have been larger and much more influential than it is now.[7] During the early years of the Delhi sultanate (ca. AD 1200–1550) Gwalior knew a series of unstable Islamic regimes before the establishment of a lasting Hindu dynasty culminating in the fabled Mansingh Tomar (r. 1486–1516).[8] Then, with the Mughal emperor Akbar's consolidation of power in the second half of the sixteenth century, the Gwalior region was subsumed into his empire, the city remaining an imperial outpost until the disintegration of Mughal rule in the eighteenth century. Politically astute Indian rulers of all religious persuasions, of course, have sought to conciliate their diverse populations, and under most successful regimes, both largely Hindu and predominantly Muslim constituencies fared well enough. But cities with Muslim rulers often did draw new immigration from their coreligionists—including Sufis, who might look to the active patronage of a local aristocracy largely inclined toward holy persons with Islamic ways. This was the case in Gwalior for much of its late medieval and early modern past. Things changed with the rise of the Maratha Scindias in Gwalior toward the end of the eighteenth century. While continuing to support some local Sufis throughout their reign, the Scindias attracted new holy persons from Maharashtra as part of a wider, largely Hindu, immigration from that region. At the same time, the newly important Scindia capital drew population from the surrounding countryside, which was also mostly Hindu. These demographic patterns, together with the departure of many Gwalior Muslims to Pakistan with the partition of British India in 1947, contribute to the relatively low percentage of Muslims in the city today.

Most of the larger Sufi shrines in town in fact find their origins in pre-Scindia times. When I would ask people in Gwalior to name the city's most important active Sufi shrines, two of the three most frequently mentioned were places dating from the late fifteenth and sixteenth centuries. The best endowed of these is located close to the main Fort Gate in old Gwalior, on what is now the old city's principal thoroughfare. Like many Sufi shrines, it is generally referred to simply by the name of its saint, Baba Kapur (d. 1571). (This way of referring to a shrine is basically just a handy abbreviation, but it is one that suggests that the saint as a spirit is still somehow present there.) The historical Baba Kapur is remembered to have been a former soldier named Abdul Gafur who later became a celibate ascetic, leaving a lineage of spiritual successors that is still vital.[9] Although these successors are not always readily accessible, often staying on the shrine's endowed village lands, the shrine itself is open, with an attendant usually present. It is an interesting old structure that is well maintained and well frequented, with an 'urs attended by many in the mixed neighborhood and beyond. Its local following seems particularly loyal: an enthusiastic nearby sweet seller I spoke with in 1997, proud to identify himself as a Vaishnava, said that he regularly made offerings of sweets at the 'urs, following a family tradition. The other of the two old major shrines is that of Khwaja Khanoon (1434–1519)—a married Sufi whose descendants continue his spiritual lineage.[10] The shrine is located at the site where the saint is said to have settled after arriving in Gwalior in 1481—then no doubt a secluded spot not too far from old Gwalior but now a sizable complex surrounded by middle-class residential development. It has developed into Gwalior's most important continuing Sufi cultural institution, issuing publications and holding an annual festival that features, among other events, a panel promoting interfaith dialogue with academically inclined speakers from different communities (fig. 2.1).

The place that people usually mentioned first, however, when asked about Gwalior shrines—clearly the best known generally at the turn of the twenty-first century—has neither an impressive old structure, a developed shrine complex, nor an attested lineage. Its legendary history, moreover, looks back only as far as the nineteenth-century Scindia maharajas and remains pretty hazy for most devotees. This is the shrine of Mir Badshah, a saint said to have set up camp in Lashkar's main bazaar area in the nineteenth century but who left no historical record. As a simple structure embodying the force of an only vaguely historical personage, Mir Badshah in fact resembles the majority of Gwalior's Sufi shrines (fig. 2.2). It is distinguished from them most obviously by its site

FIGURE 2.1 During the *'urs* at Khwaja Khanoon.

FIGURE 2.2 The Mir Badshah shrine. The adorned tomb inside represents the saint.

abutting the old Scindia bank in Lashkar's main bazaar, which gives it a central, public place and a physical link to remembered royalty. An ordinary shrine in an extraordinary position, it has become extremely popular: visited daily by Sindhi merchants before they open their downtown shops; always crowded during weekly Thursday qawwali performances; and taking over much of the bazaar during a five-day annual festival with invited qawwals of national reputation. These developments at Mir Badshah, moreover—the focus of this chapter—have continued to flourish amid a new tide of Hindu nationalism that has surged and ebbed nationally since the last decades of the twentieth century, impacting Gwalior as it has most places.

Hindu Nationalists and Sufis as Muslims

Largely on the political sidelines since Indian Independence in 1947, Hindu nationalists emerged as a credible force in the 1989 parliamentary elections. In 1998, capitalizing on disarray among its rivals, a Hindu nationalist party, the BJP,[11] emerged as the dominant partner in a coalition government that lasted through the middle of 2004. Although moderated through necessary alliances, it was in power for six years and established itself as one of only two national political parties. In 2014, with an electorate unimpressed by the government in place, it was swept back into power with a majority of its own.

For core BJP politicians, as for other Hindu Nationalists, "Hindu" refers primarily not to the Hindu religion practiced in the temples of the last chapter but to the idea of a broader Hindu culture—the heritage of all Indians who follow Indic traditions, deliberately including Jains, Sikhs, and Indian Buddhists. Even though many religions coexist in India, they assert, the culture of the nation is Hindu.[12] India should thus be governed by a single set of Hindu cultural norms—to which Muslims and Christians, too, need to conform. This claim is offered as a challenge to policies of the Indian secular state, which—looking to ideals of Gandhi and Nehru that were more tolerant of difference—allows minority communities to follow their own customs in personal, intracommunal matters.[13] Although these more tolerant ideals are still enshrined in the Indian constitution and remain axiomatic for many Indians, in the first decades of the twenty-first century Hindu nationalist sentiments have made a renewed political impact and achieved some real cultural respectability.

Certainly, such Hindu sentiments can be quite at home in Gwalior. The city still retains a certain Hindu self-consciousness that was fostered under the old Scindia regime: although the Maratha court had imported a language and regional culture different from the majority of the population, they were nevertheless its coreligionists victorious against Muslim overlords. Gwalior is a city where Hindus have since then dominated both politically and economically. Although a few wealthy and some middle-class Muslims can be found there, Gwalior Muslims are disproportionately working class—a situation that finds parallels in many Indian cities. The story of Mir Badshah's rise, then, concerns the attraction of Hindus to Sufi shrines in a place where Hindus are unquestionably in charge.

Because now, as in the recent past, personal interactions between urban Hindus and Muslims are often limited—with the two communities often concentrated in different residential neighborhoods[14]—for many city-dwelling Hindus, especially those of Hindu nationalist inclination, Muslims as individuals are largely unknown. Their significance is thus largely as an image—usually some kind of image of the other.[15] When Hindu traditions seem under threat, that image of the other has some-times become demonized—represented in particular by the demon-like rākṣasa that the divine Hindu hero Ram must battle to bring righteous-ness to his kingdom. Examples have been cited from as early as the first centuries of the last millennium—during Hindu India's initial encoun-ters with militarily powerful Muslims—and have led to suggestions of deep historical precedents for the modern Hindu nationalist politicized elevation of the figure of Ram.[16] It can thus be difficult to completely sepa-rate the recent heightened construction of Ram temples seen in chapter 1, however piously conceived, from the violent 1992 destruction of a mosque at a site taken by some to be Ram's birthplace. Memorable for the sus-tained communal organization that preceded it and the suddenness with which it actually occurred, that event was a defining moment for commu-nal relations between Hindus and Muslims in modern India.[17]

What, then, of the image of the Muslim holy man in Gwalior, a place where Hindu nationalist sentiment finds a comfortable home but where the large Hindu majority, ruling with assurance, is *not* under threat? In the myth of Ram, as in Hindu mythology generally, rākṣasas do not really appear as demons in the unreflective Western sense of the term—unredeemable forces of darkness. True, they are often portrayed as lusty, sometimes wanton beings with horrific supernatural powers used for per-sonal ends, but they are not all simply evil.[18] They can also have a touch of nobility and can even turn powerfully toward the good: indeed, Vibhishana, the brother of Ram's chief *rākṣasa* enemy, is driven by his conscience to become Ram's trusted ally. In modern Hindi, the term *rākṣasa* is usually reserved for a "fiendishly evil person,"[19] and I have certainly never heard it used in reference to a Sufi. But if something of the image of a *rākṣasa* does remain in a Hindu's sense of a Gwalior Sufi, this is likely to be of the good, at least partially assimilated *rākṣasa* of old religious lore: one turned to the side of righteousness, whose tamed power can be used for ends that are personal but noble too.[20] To Gwalior Hindus, Mir Badshah may thus suggest something of the dark forces that the *rākṣasa*-other commands, but which, subdued in a Hindu realm, are no longer particularly threatening.

For many Indians, especially those from lower urban classes and rural areas, the idea of a somewhat shady—and for that reason particularly powerful—being is a familiar one. Such beings are worshipped in many parts of India at small local shrines of the sort in which Mir Badshah seems to have found its origins. They include guardian spirits attached to particular places, "demon devotees," and the deified dead.[21] Among the last mentioned, Muslim spirits have frequently figured alongside those of deceased Hindu ascetics, as well as those of heroes and Brahmins who have suffered a violent or untimely death; all may be readily resorted to by Hindus and Muslims alike.[22] The effective power of all these beings, moreover, derives in good part from their being seen to reside close to the human world, certainly closer than supreme deities: willing to intervene readily in human affairs, they may remain less than completely pure.

With the boundaries among these effective, close-to-the-ground beings very often blurred,[23] there is already some practical convergence between Muslim spirits and "demon devotees" as providers of practical help. With local Muslim saints thus often seen as less grand than popular Hindu divinities, they may in some cases be treated more personally and affectionately. Thus, when asked why they went to Sufi shrines, people's answers recalled remarks about the quick response of Durga or Hanuman—also seen to be particularly effective—but sometimes had a more endearing tone. Here a Hindu devotee speaks of a Sufi at a small shrine as "Baba," an honorific that also suggests familiarity and can be used for one's father or grandfather: "Whatever our problem is, whatever our pain, if we go to Baba and make an offering, it goes away." The relationship of the devotee to his Baba in this case appears as one to an affectionate, dependably effective elder; Durga, however benevolent, generally presents a more fearsome visage. If renewed communal sensibilities heighten any sense of a past Muslim saint as *rākṣasa*-other who is no longer threatening and might be comfortably approached, they may just make some of his characteristic powers seem stronger and more reliable.

In any event, the resemblance of Mir Badshah to a type of familiar otherworldly being frequented by very common Indians complicates the socioreligious roles he plays. For depressed classes, as we will see, his humble provenance lets him serve as a point of identification against a Hindu elite. At the same time, when ennobled by his grand festival and weekly qawwali performances, Mir Badshah can also appear to more respectable folk as a great Sufi. Indeed, as a figure of low origins who has achieved some status, Mir Badshah the public personage stands in awkward relationships to some other notable figures in his city, both royal and religious.

Two Sufis in the Scindias' City

As the seat of an influential dynasty under the British Raj, Gwalior remembers a heritage of at least official benevolence toward all religions, and local boosters continue to laud the great medieval musician Tansen—who, a devotee of the Sufi Muhammad Ghawth, seems to have at least died a Muslim.[24] This officially tolerant attitude continued in the politics of the late Raja Madhav Rao, who until his death in 2001 was a major player in the Congress party—still the principal secularist force on the Indian national stage.[25] But as a conservative city in the North Indian heartland, Gwalior fosters many who embrace Hindu nationalism, and has provided more than its share of the movement's political leaders. These include both the prime minister at the turn of the twenty-first century, A. B. Vajpayee—who was born and went to college in the city—and the late Rajmata Vijaya Raje Scindia (1919–2001), Madhav Rao's mother, a politician in her own right and cofounder of Vajpayee's BJP.[26]

As the Scindias' city, Gwalior can thus present two faces to its Muslim minority. The seat of a Hindu dynasty that arose with the successful Maratha challenge to Mughal power, it can, as with the late Rajmata, present some vocal Hindu nationalist sentiments that most Muslims understandably find unsettling. But as the former capital of a successful princely state that managed to sustain cooperation among its different populations, Gwalior has long been home to a small Muslim community loyal to a regime that gave it a legitimate place. Like other

Hindu princes, the Scindias contributed to their Muslim subjects' celebrations: people still talk about the rajas' elaborate *tāziyās*, the replicas of Hussain's tomb carried at the predominantly Shiite holiday of Moharram. But outdoing many of their Hindu peers, the Scindias have also paid formal respect to a Muslim saint whom they saw playing a role in their political ascendancy.

This saint, Mansur Ali Shah, locally called simply Mansur, is said to have been the force behind Mahadji Scindia's initial military success in the north. By the mid-eighteenth century Mansur had settled at Beed, Maharashtra, the birthplace of Mahadji's wife, where his main shrine is maintained today. Mahadji, the story goes, visited Mansur after being frustrated for five years by his own continuing lack of success in North Indian campaigns. He had been urged to do so by his wife—who some years before had been convincingly reassured by the saint when worried about Mahadji's delay in return from battle. From Mansur, Mahadji received a talisman with an Arabic verse that read "Victory is from God," and subsequently had a long string of military victories. The Scindias have since given Mansur and his descendents formal respect. Indeed, in the old regime—where each of Gwalior's Maharashtrian noble families had a definite order of precedence—Mansur's descendents were literally ranked first.[27]

In Gwalior, relics of Mansur are stored at a site in the present collectorate, off the main bazaar not far from Mir Badshah's shrine—a site where Mir Badshah himself, it is said, used to spend his days during his lifetime. So both space and legend connect the two saints—one royal, one much more plebeian. The two also have ritual connections, for the beginning of Mir Badshah's annual festival has been marked by the presentation of a sheet—of the sort customarily used to cover Sufis' graves—at the site of Mansur's relics. As might be expected, however, the ritual link between the two saints is not entirely innocent. For the present collectorate was once a Scindia palace, and the site of Mansur's relics is a personal sanctuary of the Scindias. It is, moreover, obviously a Krishna temple, with worship offered regularly and walls adorned with scenes from Hindu mythology. The offering of a Sufi's sheet at a royal Krishna temple at the inauguration of Mir Badshah's festival thus helps integrate the Muslim saint into an openly Hindu civic sphere.

The scene is a memorable one, with qawwals sitting on the temple floor, singing praises of a Muslim saint against a backdrop of vivid Hindu iconography. The affective power of the scene thus seems to lie in its evident contrasts—not in any easy assimilation. And Mir Badshah's main festival features popular display that is manifestly intercommunal. At the annual festival of Mansur himself, however, the assimilation of the Sufi into the royals' Hindu world is much more thorough. If something of the aura of the *rākṣasa* remains in Mansur, here, through the ministrations of the raja's Brahmins, it seems purified away.

Sufis' Rites at a Hindu Temple

The annual festival of Mansur is a stately affair, featuring the worship of his relics by the reigning Scindia monarch. Of these relics, some are unsurprising: a slipper, an overcoat, a hat. One, however, is most curious—a silver box containing a piece of dry chapati, Indian flat bread. I've heard elaborate stories about this piece of bread, but the gist of them all was told by Khusrao Miyan, Mansur's descendant in the ninth generation, who lives in Gwalior: At Mahadji's departure to the North, the saint gave him a piece of chapati, telling him that as long as the chapati remained intact, the Scindias would prosper.[28] During the annual festival, the chapati in the box is the focus of the royal worship. Performed by a Hindu king, the worship is done with Brahmins officiating in their customary way, but not in a common Hindu ceremony. The maharaja first does worship to the bread in its box. The box is then piled over with fronds, and the fronds are piled over with flowers. Finally, Mansur's cap is placed on top. With the cap in place, the whole is said to signify Mansur in "the form of faith" (*śraddhā rūp*). The maharaja then places a shawl underneath this constructed form of Mansur. Once a flower has fallen into the shawl, the ceremony is over; the saint has indicated its end himself (fig. 2.3).

As celebrated at the end of the twentieth century, that worship still had vestiges of a state occasion. The maharaja performed the worship in person. (When I attended in 1997, Madhav Rao had come down from Delhi for the ceremony on the afternoon commercial flight.) During the worship, praise of Mansur was sung by Dholi Buwa, the successor to a family of revered Nath storytellers and performers who came from Maharashtra during the Scindia Raj and whom we will meet again in chapter 4. After the ceremony, the maharaja received his nobles, one after another, but they were preceded by a representative of Mansur's religious lineage at Beed.[29] Khusrao Miyan, Mansur's successor at Gwalior, in discussing Mahadji's initial public recognition of the saint, emphasized its political

FIGURE 2.3 The maharaja in front of Mansur's *sraddhā rūp*, with its final layer of flowers and the Sufi's cap.

dimensions. Mahadji, he said, wanted to demonstrate his inclusiveness to Muslim ruling classes as he pursued his strategies in North India.

The royal worship of Mansur's relics today continues to appeal to a section of the old upper classes, who form its major audience. While the temple is a sizable building open to the public, space is limited, and most people witnessing the worship came from the more privileged sections of Gwalior's Maharashtrian community—not, on the whole, so well off any more, but many still remembering links to the former nobility. The Hindu-style worship of a Maharashtrian Muslim divine thus becomes a celebration of solidarity for the city's old elite. It demonstrates through its style and substance that even though the elite was visibly Hindu, Muslims could have an exalted—if limited—place within it. Like Vibhishana, the *rākṣasa* king's brother, a Muslim could undergo a true transformation and become accepted in a royal Hindu world.

Participants in the festival of Mir Badshah come from much more humble classes. Indeed, Mir Badshah's urban shrine seems emblematic of those classes not only because it is small and unassuming, but also because it is Muslim. For the Gwalior region in the nineteenth century was not a place with a large number of Muslim landlords, and the majority of Gwalior's Muslims are in fact not particularly advantaged. Most are lower middle class at best: shopkeepers, workers in motor trades, weavers, and tailors. And while the majority of Mir Badshah's most ardent devotees are Hindu, they nevertheless come from similar ordinary working urban milieux.

Thus even while rites for both saints acknowledge the sway of Hindu privileged classes, they signal different attitudes toward them. The annual festival of Mansur reveals the power of a Sufi through what looks like an unusual Hindu royal ritual. It presents the saint in a guise that is not only thoroughly elite but also eminently Brahminic. The ritual offering at the temple that begins Mir Badshah's festival, by contrast, is not performed by Brahmins, but is accompanied by qawwals, and might not in fact be all that welcome to the temple's habitués. It is, moreover, preliminary to a multiday event, open to all, which is not particularly refined and highlights intercommunal show. Mansur, it seems, given a preliminary nod, now smiles out from his royally enshrined relics to give license to popular self-assertion in the name of his more plebeian counterpart. For during the days of Mir Badshah's festival, the main bazaar area—with its old Scindia palace, bank, and raja's statue—is claimed by that saint's diverse devotees as their own.

A Modest Sufi Commands Respect

Indeed, the most famous story of Mir Badshah—known to devotees and organizers alike—entails a confrontation between the saint and a raja over space in the bazaar: the saint interfered with the construction of the Scindias' bank. This could be seen as a very grand feat indeed. For the building constructed by the Scindias to house their bank (the former Krishnaram Baldeo Bank, now a branch of the State Bank of India) is without doubt the most imposing edifice in the immediate area. Designed in a modern style reminiscent of civic architecture from the 1930s, it is a massive structure that is meant to make a statement of rooted power with a contemporary face. Mir Badshah's shrine, however, slightly built into the wall, mars the bank's even lines (fig. 2.4). It wasn't originally supposed to be that way, they say.

Nafeez Qureishi, at the time a sociologist at Kamala Raje Girls College in Gwalior, told the story of the shrine in short. At the present site of Mir Badshah, he said, stood an old, poorly maintained *dargāh*, a memorial grave: "maybe once a week somebody put some flowers on

FIGURE 2.4 The small Mir Badshah shrine is recessed into the wall of the grand bank building.

it." They called it the *dargāh* of Balli Badshah—as small shrines in the area are often called. Qureishi thought the name was probably a corruption of Vali, a "friend" of God, a common term for holy persons in Islam. He didn't think anyone really knew for sure when the saint lived. Original plans for the bank construction called for simply building over the shrine, and attempts were made to do so. But the wall kept caving in at that spot. So eventually the shape of the building was altered to accommodate the site of the present shrine. The name Mir Badshah was attached, and a committee was formed to renovate the shrine. Qureishi, citing Durkheim, saw this committee as a product of the "group mind": Hindus and Muslims all participated when they saw the miracle.

B. B. Bhonsle, however, one of the originators of Mir Badshah's festival in 1958 and long its administrator and guiding force, told the story more eloquently. After the construction at the site had collapsed three times, said Bhonsle, the maharaja had a dream that made him fall from his bed—a playfully violent event of a sort that might take place during an encounter with a less refined supernatural being. A fakir then came to him in a vision and announced: "Don't put me in the bank." It was only at this point the maharaja called in his engineers to change the design. Bhonsle also had a clear picture of just who the saint was.

The story told by Bhonsle emphasizes not only the saint's spiritual power, but also his local roots. Moreover, while Bhonsle, a lower-middle-class Maharashtrian Hindu, admitted that Mir Badshah acted as a Muslim fakir, he didn't care to speculate on his communal origins. "People don't know whether he was Hindu or Muslim," Bhonsle commented, "but that doesn't matter with a fakir." He did affirm that the saint was from the immediate environs of Gwalior, and that he worked in Mansur's garden—the area around the Scindias' Krishna temple. "He did service and spiritual practice there," said Bhonsle, using terms normal for speaking of Hindu traditions, *sevā* and *bhajan*. Whoever he was, from Bhonsle's perspective, Mir Badshah was a common person from the area about whom it was appropriate to talk in the ordinary Hindi (and Hindu) way.

Mir Badshah's main claim to fame, according to Bhonsle, came from curing a mad royal elephant during the reign of Jayaji Rao Scindia in the mid-nineteenth century.[30] The fakir then asked for gifts of food and money from the raja, who provided for him nicely: twice a day meals came to the fakir from the palace. At this point Bhonsle gave his story a turn that lends Mir Badshah an attribute crucial to an important class of powerful local spirits. For the elephant, it seems, turned mad again and came another day, and this time the fakir was sitting where his grave is now. People warned him of the elephant's approach and urged him to leave. Yet the fakir demurred, foreseeing his own death. "Today there will be some trouble," he said. "You people go away." The elephant then came and killed the fakir, and at that very spot his memorial was constructed, the site of the present shrine. Like many of the popularly deified dead, then, Mir Badshah met an untimely, violent end.

The hagiography of Mir Badshah related by Bhonsle does not seem to be an important part of current lore among most of those who frequent the shrine. I've never heard it from anyone else, and wouldn't be surprised if Bhonsle had learned it from Mir Badshah himself, who sometimes visits him in spirit and answers questions. Yet it is not hard to see how the story of the powerful local holy man who commanded the raja's respect and told him the virtues of donations—and then finally sanctified a spot through his violent death—can not only make the shrine appear to belong to a familiar type of spirit, but can also carry a personal significance for Bhonsle and the other shrine organizers. Like Mir Badshah when alive, these have been local people of humble origin, and their authority over the powerful spot—and especially over the elaborate festival that the offerings make possible—has added to their stature in their own eyes and the world's.

Ordinary People

Of the old core group, Bhonsle himself remained the most active in 1997, still the chairperson of the festival arrangements committee. By then long retired, he had worked at the main city fire brigade, whose station faces the shrine. Thus, the shrine was easily an object of his immediate attention. "When we went out, we used to take the name of Baba," as Bhonsle referred to the spirit of Mir Badshah, "and were successful." I first met Bhonsle outside the shrine during the days leading up to the 1997 festival, where he was sitting together with two other members of the festival arrangements committee at the time: Amir Bakhsh, the treasurer, and Abdul Hamid Qadri, known as the city *qāzī*,[31] who was a committee *mantrī*, or "minister." They showed me a copy of the poster for the festival, which also listed two others as members of the five-person committee: Ramjilal Sharma, the *mahāmantrī*, "great minister"; and Gyasiram Sharma, the *pracār mantrī*, "minister for publicity." The two members of the committee I didn't meet that day, however, were locatable on their home turf.

Ramjilal Sharma was a retired journalist with some income from village lands who saw himself as central in the shrine's initial revival. He told of a spirit attached to a particular place with whom he came into unexpected contact. Before the bank was built, he said, there was a park at the site; it was a dissolute area—people used to go there and drink; there were prostitutes. The shrine then was just a clay platform. One day he was passing by the platform and saw a rose at the grave. Afraid someone would step on it and defile it, he picked it up. That night, Ramjilal had a dream. A fakir came to him and asked him to do his service.

"I am a Hindu and a Brahmin," thought Ramjilal to himself, and said to the fakir, "I've never seen you before, do I know you?"

"I am that flower you picked up today," replied the fakir. From that day on, Ramjilal said, he was in the service of the site. For twelve years starting in 1957, continued Ramjilal, he would stand there all day long; he let his beard grow. He said he had written stories about the miracles of the shrine and published them in popular magazines.[32]

Gyasiram Sharma, the other member of the committee, presented another visage entirely—impressive for what he was not. A peon at the Municipal Corporation in front of the shrine, his regular humble presence near the shrine could give him a sense of proprietorship invaluable for the shrine's day-to-day maintenance without threatening the authority of the others on the committee. As "publicity minister," I was told, he handed out fliers.

For four members of the committee, then, the shrine—in addition to whatever miraculous help and spiritual benefit it offered—clearly provided a religious identity and heightened sense of importance: the treasurer's integrity was publicly recognized; the peon who handed out fliers was "publicity minister"; everybody talked about Bhonsle's central role. This should come as no surprise: rewards for lay leadership by ordinary people in religious institutions everywhere are often paid in the coin of enhanced self-esteem and public recognition.[33] This may be less the case with the city *qāzī*, who is not so ordinary—the odd person out on the arrangements committee. As a community leader, his interest in the shrine seemed more calculated. A figure to be reckoned with in intracommunal rivalries among Gwalior Muslims, and an actor in local politics, the city *qāzī* no doubt found his stock raised by his identification with a broadly popular festival. It could certainly be in his best political interests to appear as the most visible Muslim in a shrine committee that was both intercommunal and independent.

Local Spirits and Their Transformations

If important motives of the city *qāzī* in joining up with Bhonsle and Ramjilal seem obvious, the reasons for those two joining up with him seem less immediately clear. Although there is no reason to doubt that they recognized him as a fellow devotee of Mir Badshah, their inclusion of the younger man in an organizing role also had significant socioreligious import. The aspiring Muslim-community leader would give the arrangements committee an authentic Muslim presence and keep the shrine oriented toward Islamic styles—which were probably more attractive to Bhonsle and Ramjilal than some popular syncretic alternatives otherwise familiar to them.

In addition to minor *dargāhs* with qawwali, Gwalior also has many small public shrines to Muslim personages often known as Kamaal Khan or Balli Badshah—a name, we recall, that the sociologist Qureishi said was once applied to Mir Badshah's place. Their relative abundance may be due in part simply to the fact that small shrines identified as Muslim tend to find a wider scope as seats of powerful local helpers in predominantly Hindu cities than in predominantly Hindu villages: although villages often boast a number of local gods, Hindu shrines and temples in urban areas are largely to transregional deities. Even though many Gwalior Hindus recognize the practical value of powerful local spirits, they identify few of their own, and turn to Muslim ones when available—even maintaining shrines to them in their houses. [34]

Interviews about temple-going practices with several Gwalior Agrawals—a large and respectable North Indian Hindu mercantile community—revealed two families who kept home shrines to Muslim spirits. One of these, known in the family simply as Baba, was initially described to me as Balli Badshah, a name it was presumed I would know; the other was called by another generic term, Sayyad Baba. In both cases, the families performed simple weekly rituals that recognized the spirits' Muslim provenance. The shrine in each house was a small niche built into a wall—an empty space for a spirit to dwell, but itself properly aniconic. On Thursdays, the usual day for Sufi celebrations, the shrine was adorned with a *sahrā*, five short strings of flowers that were linked together and hung to dangle in front of it; a lamp was lit and incense was burned. The lamp and incense, of course, were also used in serving images of Hindu deities, around the necks of whom a flower garland might be put, but the *sahrā* was reserved for the spirit seated at the niche-shrine. The service was thus a variant of a generic form of popular worship found in most North Indian religious communities—here used by Hindus acknowledging a spirit's Muslim identity.

The service was also short—just a few minutes—but, all affirmed, was performed regularly. Maintaining the service was important because it obliged the resident spirit to pay attention to the family members' requests—and who knows what might happen if the regular service, once started, were stopped? In one family, moreover, a number of members displayed feelings of heartfelt reverence. Even brothers who had moved out of the family home, I was told, came to see the Baba of the niche-shrine when they had special problems. And while all family members visited gods at different temples, Baba was the one some trusted most.

Further questioning on this apparently curious phenomenon revealed that in neither case did the Agrawal families originate the shrines themselves; rather, the shrines were there first, in their houses before the families took up residence in them.[35] Like Ramjilal visited in dream by Mir Badshah, members of the Agrawal families felt bound to honor a Muslim spirit with whom they came into accidental relationship; like Ramjilal, moreover, they could also develop strong feelings of devotion toward him. The socioreligious parallels between the spirits of the home shrines and Mir Badshah are intriguing. Just as the Agrawal families encountered a Muslim spirit in their private spaces, Ramjilal and Bhonsle encountered one in a public space they regularly frequented. Indeed the shrine to Mir Badshah—as a Muslim spirit without much pedigree who is attached to a particular place—seems to have more in common with the Agrawal families' home shrines than with the well-known establishments in attested lineages such as Gwalior's Khwaja Khanoon and others elsewhere that are described by students of historical Indian Sufism.[36] Nevertheless, Bhonsle and Ramjilal had aspirations to make the shrine of Mir Badshah *look* like one of those grander establishments, well aware of another direction— more syncretic and less respectable—in which their shrine might otherwise likely develop.

Alongside local Muslim spiritual personages who respond to devotees' requests directly, Gwalior has others whose power is mediated through religious specialists, usually from the lower strata of Indian society and often Hindu. We learned of one of these, called Sabir Baba, from a third Agrawal family, whose daughter and son-in-law had visited it in order to conceive a child. The shrine had been inherited by a Hindu potter—fairly low in the traditional caste order—named Pyarelal. It is located in a room off a courtyard of Pyarelal's house in a very modest neighborhood on the outskirts of the city. On Thursdays, both courtyard and shrine-room are filled with devotees seeking the saint's grace, which Pyarelal makes available through gifts of ash and brushings with a small broom. Sabir Baba, I was told by different devotees, can relieve financial distress and give mental peace (*man kī śānti*), but the majority of his petitioners—like the Agrawal couple—come for physical problems, serious and less so. One man's paralyzed arm, I was told, was "99 percent cured," while another brought his young son to the shrine for "colds, coughs, and fevers."

The atmosphere in the shrine room is very obviously syncretic, with walls adorned by lithographs of both Hindu deities and famous Sufi shrines. The yearly festival is idiosyncratically so. Called an '*urs*—the celebration that marks the death anniversary of a Sufi—it is timed to end at the Hindu festival celebrating the birth of Ram. Like a typical '*urs* it is a multiday affair, but its nine days' length is longer than most of those, recalling instead the number of days of the festival of the Hindu goddess Durga, with whose worship Sabir Baba's '*urs* begins. With its obvious referents to the Hindu festival calendar, this is an unusual '*urs* indeed.

The '*urs* of Sabir Baba was not attended by the Agrawal couple, even though their petition to him was successful. In fact, after the wife became pregnant, neither husband nor wife went much anymore, contrary to Pyarelal's advice.[37] They respected Sabir Baba's power and were ready

to honor Pyarelal by inviting him to their home for a meal—an act running against the grain of normal caste convention—but their middle-class
upbringing didn't really let them feel comfortable spending time at
Pyarelal's establishment: too many of his clientele were, after all, lower
class and lower caste. For them the shrine was a powerful place whose
resources they wanted to be able to tap when necessary, but it was not
a place with which they wanted to be particularly associated. Even for
Pyarelal himself, Sabir Baba's shrine was a place for cures and practical
help only, at least for non-Muslims: when I asked Pyarelal if he looked to
Baba Sabir for salvation, his immediate response was no, he was a Hindu
and was a devotee of Baba Jai Gurudev, a popular guru who died in 2012
and will be treated at length in chapter 6.

Sabir Baba's shrine suggests an alternative way in which the shrine
to Mir Badshah might have developed—a viable practical possibility
considering Bhonsle's continuing personal relationship with his saint.
Circumstances of social class, however, seem to have helped orient the
shrine to Mir Badshah in a different direction. Although some of the
shrine's early enthusiasts were from *economic* classes wont to visit establishments like Pyarelal's, the first main Hindu organizers were all, like the
Agrawal couple, from respectable communities: Brahmins and Gwalior
Maharashtrians. Familiar with saints' shrines developed in Hindu styles
among the humbler strata of society, they didn't want to identify with
them. What evolved, then, was *not* an attempt to incorporate Mir Badshah
into a sort of popular Hinduism—the first step of a process that South
Asia scholars have long called Sanskritization. Instead, we see a parallel process we might call "Urduization"—an attempt to present a humble
local shrine in the style of the later North Indian Islamic courtly culture
whose vernacular language was Urdu.[38]

North Indian Muslim courtly culture, which endured in its somewhat
faded glory well into the nineteenth century and beyond, retains a romantic aura for many North Indians. Memories of that culture, as they pertain
to our story, include not only images of nawabs in their gardens and poets
reciting verses into the night but also those of illustrious Sufi sheikhs listening to qawwali with their disciples. If those sheikhs and the culture to
which they belonged are far from the experience of most Gwalior Hindus,
their images are nevertheless high class and, in their romantic distance,
exotic. For the members of Mir Badshah's arrangements committee, glorifying the saint thus conceived has meant making him look like a proper
Muslim Sufi, not like the sort of local Muslim spirit whose powers he can

also manifest. Nevertheless, even as a great Sufi Mir Badshah should still be easily accessible to local Hindus, a personage with whom they could feel comfortable.

An Intercommunal Arena: Cooperation, Dispute, and Change

The banner advertising the 1997 festival at Mir Badshah presented it as no syncretic celebration but as an authentic Islamic event—if for a predominantly Hindu audience who might need some help in under-standing it. Thus, for example, the term for the distribution of food that closes both Sufi festivals and many Hindu ceremonies was given in an (incorrect) Urdu form—*tabarruq taqsīm*[39]—followed in parentheses by a more familiar Hindi word for religious feast: *bhaṇḍārā*. The banner also suggested an elaborate display of intercommunal religious coopera-tion. Of the five members of the arrangements committee, three had Hindu names and two Muslim ones. The titles of the members were Hindi—*mantrīs* of different sorts—but the word for arrangements was Urdu: *intizāmiyāṃ* (the "festival" of course was the Urdu *'urs*). In addition to qawwali by visiting artists and customary Islamic rituals—adorning the grave with sheets, and a celebration of the prophet they called *mīlād*[40]—the printed program featured a spiritual talk and Ramayana performance by Dholi Buwa, the popular local Maharashtrian Nath who also regularly performs at the festival of Mansur. If the appear-ance of Dholi Buwa seemed out of place from the perspective of Islamic authenticity, it was appropriate to the Gwalior civic context and added a note of prestige that came with a religious performer associated with the Scindia court.

The communal cooperation seen at the *'urs* has a somewhat different face during the rest of the year: Muslim religious professionals serving an overwhelmingly Hindu clientele. For even though the everyday offi-ciants and qawwals who sing on Thursday are exclusively Muslim, the attendees are non-Muslim even out of proportion to local demographics. A number of people involved in the shrine explained this phenomenon by noting that many of the more observant Muslims in town are in fact of the reformist bent that disdain shrine worship in principle—although now, they say, a few more seem to be coming. "On Thursdays, people of all communities come to get their work done," said Ramjilal, who had plenty of time to observe, "but mostly it's Hindus." Maybe 90 percent Hindu, he suggested, 3 percent Muslim, and 7 percent others—which included Christians and Sikhs.

The success of the shrine has inevitably led to some disputes. Over the year considerable money flows in and is disbursed largely at the festival—Rs. 75,000 in 1997, according to Bhonsle.[41] It is thus not difficult to comprehend why other religious establishments might have wanted to get into the act, and in 1997 the arrangements committee was facing competition from local Islamic institutions over the control of the shrine. Given the predominantly Hindu makeup of the 1997 committee, this might have given the rivalry a communal dimension. But the issues seemed to be less those of communal rights and identity than the more familiar ones of ownership and control that plague religious operations throughout the subcontinent (and beyond) when there is money or property at stake.[42] In 1997, I heard of two Islamic institutions said to have had designs on the shrine: the Madhya Pradesh *waqf* board—the official overseer of Islamic endowments (*waqf*) in the state—and the well-established local Sufi cultural institution Khwaja Khanun.

In addition to having a continuous lineage succession, Khwaja Khanun differs from Mir Badshah in still serving a proportionally significant Muslim constituency—about 50 percent of its total, according to Rashid Khanuni, its current head. Rashid combines a modern legal education with the traditional magical lore valued by the shrine's devotees. Like Pyarelal, Rashid mediates his saint's grace and is popular for his cures, but he does so through methods deriving from Islamic traditions and speaks with the authority of a long family lineage. Although Khwaja Khanun is not a major shrine by South Asian standards, its pedigree is old and well attested.[43]

The establishment at Khwaja Khanun, by all accounts, had played a hand in the current revival at the upstart Mir Badshah. When the revival of the *dargāh* first started, said Bhonsle, "We didn't know what to do. We're Hindu. So we asked Khwaja Sahib," Rashid Khanuni's father. In deciding the date of the festival at Mir Badshah, the Khwaja Sahib set it soon after the end of the one at his own shrine, effectively presenting it as an extension of that one. Bhonsle had apparently done some research and calculations, and determined that Mir Badshah had passed away 114 years earlier, so the first 'urs they celebrated with fanfare—in 1958—was advertised as the 114th. But without knowledge of the month and day of Mir Badshah's death anniversary, Bhonsle deferred to the Khwaja Sahib's advice. Rashid Khanuni, telling his version of events, said his father had invited qawwals from other cities for the festival at their shrine; he was paying them and could tell them to sing at Mir Badshah, too—he was just trying to help. Bhonsle, telling the story, emphasized that now the committee bears all the expense itself.

Although the successors at Khwaja Khanun can legitimately feel a sense of co-ownership in Mir Badshah, and are said to have been unhappy with the way things evolved, they seem to have given up any fight: "We started the shrine," said Rashid. "Why should we have a headache with it now?" Rashid also noted the absence, in the early days, of the initiation of Mir Badshah's festival with a visit to Mansur's shrine. And certainly, in making explicit Mir Badshah's connection to the royals' saint, that pre-liminary visit might have helped to give the shrine an independence from the sway of Khwaja Khanun. Nevertheless, noted Rashid in 1997, Bhonsle still comes to his 'urs every year.

Perhaps in a further attempt to distance Mir Badshah from Khwaja Khanun after his festival had become popular on its own, Bhonsle made an attempt to change the festival's annual date: the one given by Khwaja Sahib was, after all, arbitrary. In any event, during one of Baba's visita-tions to Bhonsle the spirit of the saint told him the real date he passed from the body: November 6, according to the Western calendar. This new date for the festival, however, never really caught on. "The Muslims said there'd be a problem in changing the date from the established time," said Bhonsle, "so I said, OK, let's have both." Thus, in addition to the major festival following Khwaja Khanun, which falls according to the Muslim calendar, Bhonsle and a few others have had a modest annual ceremony in the morning on November 6.

The *waqf* board was a bigger worry to the committee in 1997, and its claims would ultimately be successful: it saw itself responsible for major local Islamic institutions, and Mir Badshah unquestionably put on the most visible Sufi celebration in town. Most of the committee members at the time, however, had been there from the beginning of Mir Badshah's revival and felt proprietary about the shrine, proud of their work, and distrustful of a government-sanctioned institution: "If the *waqf* board took over the shrine," said Ramjilal, "they would take all the offerings and maybe just put in a light bulb. You see how nice it all is now?" There was an ongoing court case. The board maintained that the present committee was not duly following government regulations and wanted to replace it.[44] The board resisted. While the Indian legal system took its ponderous course, the old committee continued to operate, but it could not do so indefinitely.

I didn't pay close attention to the shrine during most later visits to Gwalior, but I did go by there regularly on trips to the main bazaar. In talking to officiants a few times during the first decade of the new century, I learned that the city *qāzī* had assumed major responsibility. This made sense, since he was of a younger generation than the rest of the aging committee and now the most vital. I understood his succession as a natural continuity in leadership and saw no major changes. When I returned to the shrine in late 2010, something clearly new hit my eye: there was a plaque on its outside wall stating that it was run under the authority of the Madhya Pradesh *waqf* board and giving the name and phone number of a committee chair with whom I was not at all familiar: one Salim Abbasi. Curious about what had transpired, I called him up and we made an appointment.

I met Abbasi at his home, which also housed a substantial weaving operation. He told me that he made rugs for export and had the biggest looms in Gwalior: a number of employees were busy at them when I arrived. A prosperous businessman, Abbasi was also a local politician in the BJP—then the dominant party in Gwalior city (and M.P. state) politics, happy there as elsewhere to broaden its tent a bit by including Muslims ready to toe its Hindu nationalist but politically pragmatic line. Reasonably prosperous and politically connected, he does not seem to have been appointed to the committee chairmanship because of his personal piety alone.

Abbasi told me that the *waqf* board had succeeded in removing the old committee four years before (we met early in 2011) and had asked for proposals for a new one: a number were submitted and his was chosen. The committee, he said, now had nine members, all Muslim. Remembering the cozy mixed-religion committee of earlier years, I was a bit startled. Abbasi assured me, however, that the intercommunal ambience of the shrine hadn't changed. It's still mostly Hindus who come, he said, and Dholi Buwa still performs at the 'urs. The 'urs, moreover, had expanded, he continued, to highlight even more religious cooperation between Hindus and Muslims. Following a recent trend seen at Achaleshwar temple in chapter 1 (and which will be seen again within the Sindhi community of chapter 4), the 2009 'urs featured the shrine committee's sponsorship of its first group marriage for members of the poorer classes—in this case, two Hindu couples along with nine Muslim ones. Considerably smaller in scale than the Achaleshwar and Sindhi events, it was touted in local newspapers less as a grand spectacle than as an exceptional example of intercommunal harmony.[45] Hindu and Muslim couples stood on different sides of the stage constructed for the *'urs*, with Brahmin priests and Muslim *qāzīs* performing the marriages simultaneously according to their own customs. The shrine committee presented basic household items to all the couples as wedding gifts, and local politicians and senior community leaders offered their blessings. The festive, popular celebration of Sufi piety of earlier years' *'urs* now gained a new overlay of civic solidity.

Thus, by 2011, a shift in political currents affecting Mir Badshah led to the tenor of intercommunal religious life there becoming substantially different from that seen in 1997. Certainly, the configuration of authority was altered. Instead of a religiously mixed shrine committee including a Muslim once close to a royal Congress politician, the committee was now all Muslim with a chairman active in the Hindu-nationalist, politically dominant BJP. In its *'urs*, the shrine still presented an image of grand interreligious cooperation, but now somewhat more elaborately crafted, reflecting less the spirit of inclusive royal beneficence than of modern political accommodation. Although the shift from a small, clearly devoted if quirky group to a larger one in tune with the political establishment may have improved the regularity of shrine governance, it also seemed to lead to a diminution of guiding religious vision. If Bhonsle and Ramjilal usually ended up talking with me about the baba of the shrine and their experiences with him, Abbasi, talking mostly about the Hindu-Muslim group wedding, showed me how the shrine had, in its own intercommunal way, kept up with the latest trends.

While the control of government-sanctioned Muslim religious authority might seem appropriate for a visible Sufi shrine with considerable resources, it also meant that people without too much personally invested in the baba of the shrine himself were likely to be running the show. They didn't seem particularly enduring, either. Perhaps Abbasi lost his enthusiasm for Mir Badshah, or maybe the powers controlling the *waqf* board lost their enthusiasm for him. In any event, when visiting Mir Badshah again in late 2012, I saw that the signboard had a different Muslim name as committee head. When I asked people in local shrine circles what happened, I was told it was just politics.

Although shifts in political currents invariably entail winners and losers, the rivalries among those with an interest in Mir Badshah's shrine were manifest in snipes against specific groups and institutions, not against whole communities. If Ramjilal had contemptuously (and mistakenly) predicted that all the *waqf* board would do for the shrine was put in a light bulb, Abbasi for his part suggested that his predecessors must have been prone to financial irregularities: he could do so much more with comparable resources. Nobody was complaining about "those Hindus" or "those Muslims." Instead, people concerned with shrine events worked together pragmatically even while dealing with altered local political realities. Thus, for the 2009 group Hindu wedding, the head of an all-Muslim shrine committee could both consult with his predominantly Hindu BJP party cadres and draw on clerics and publics from both communities to make his new event a success.

This kind of cooperation among Hindus and Muslims, long known among individuals brought together by circumstances of everyday activity, continues to be found in the religious activities of Sufi shrines. Discussing the lack of violence in Ajmer through the communal disturbances of the 1990s, Shail Mayaram points to a number of informal institutions through which Hindus and Muslims come into daily contact and develop lasting practical and affective relationships. Regular cooperation, she argues, fosters urban cosmopolitan identities that mitigate communal stress. Significantly, a considerable part of the face-to-face contact cited by Mayaram takes place in the bazaars around the great *dargāh* of Muin-ud-din Chishti, the burial place of the saint who imported the subcontinent's most widespread Sufi order and arguably the foremost pilgrimage site of Muslim South Asia.[46]

Are there parallels to be drawn between the situation in Ajmer and that in Gwalior, which has usually remained quiet during times of widespread communal stress? Perhaps, but let us not conclude too much from any we might find. Not only is the scale of all of Gwalior's shrines together much smaller than that of the Ajmer *dargāh*, but so also is Gwalior's relative Muslim population less than Ajmer's. The communal quiet in Gwalior may stem more from the large Hindu majority's lack of worry about the relatively small numbers of Muslims in their midst than from familiar interaction among potentially rival communities.[47] What seems worth thinking about in this situation is the broad popularity of Sufi shrines among ordinary Hindus. In a city where Hindu population and culture strongly predominates, during an era when a pronounced Hindu identity has often been at least expedient politically, Sufi shrines have still exerted a strong attraction on many Hindus, including some who do not seek a saint's immediate practical blessing. How can we explain their current broad appeal?

The Accessible Exotic

Certainly, the shrines' appeal does not come from their old lineages. The many shrines with popular qawwali festivals are for the most part, like Mir Badshah, newly discovered or revived—not established cultural institutions like Khwaja Khanun. These new shrines tend to be disdained by scholars of historical Sufism like S. A. Ansari, who has written a dissertation on medieval Gwalior Sufis.[48] That they had Hindu administrators was not an issue for him, he said, but he was troubled that they stood for no lineage or teaching. The reason for their popularity, he claimed, is just "a fashion for qawwali"—a consideration, I think, that deserves to be taken seriously. For qawwali music, combining a particularly vital rhythmic strength and the allure of an exotic other, seems peculiarly emblematic of the distinctive appeal for Hindus of special Muslim personages from this world as well as the next.

As a musical genre, the most noticeable way artful qawwali differs from both classical and popular Hindu devotional song is undoubtedly through its more visceral rhythms. No arithmetically intricate classical Indian *tālas* here, but a driving one-two—often maintained by steady handclapping among members of a qawwali troupe. This strong rhythmic framework is called *zarb*, "pulse"—"often compared with the heartbeat (also called *zarb*) by qawwals and Sufis alike."[49] The corresponding Hindi term—even when used in an expression meaning "to beat time" (*tāl bajāna*)—lacks the connotations of both centrality to performance and very physicality implicit in *zarb* as "pulse." Professional qawwali performances thus usually present a whole-body experience more instinctually rooted than their Hindu devotional counterparts, which tend to be more focused on melodic line—certainly more so than classical Indian styles meant to elicit the ethereal appreciation of a raga.

The pulsating rhythm of qawwali is complemented by a repetitive tune—usually fairly simple—framed around particular devotional verses. The driving beat "considered essential if the soul is to be moved" is exciting, potentially arousing listeners to a physically grounded ecstasy.[50] At the same time, the songs' tunes can capture listeners' attention, with their words directing that attention toward the transcendent. Sung in a variety of languages—Persian, Hindi, and Urdu—the songs are for the most part at least somewhat comprehensible to a Hindi-speaking audience, usually familiar with the Perso-Arabic vocabulary used in less elevated registers of Urdu. (Indeed, for some, an incomplete understanding of the songs may even increase the songs' exotic mystique.) To whatever extent the verses of a song are understood, though, their regular repetition in a lengthy performance, like the repetition of sacred utterances in Sufi (and Hindu) religious practice,[51] are likely to draw listeners inward. With their spirits aroused and attention turned within, both Hindus and Muslims may then find themselves in an emotionally heightened, mildly ecstatic state—not articulately theologized nor even particularly religious in any sectarian sense. When qawwali succeeds in producing in its listeners a sense of rapture in the music—the goal of most Indian devotional song—it can do so very powerfully, producing even in the less spiritually refined some ecstatic loss of self.

Exceptional Sufi saints are understood to have experienced a similar loss of self, but in states more complete and more intense. Even a figure usually called on for mundane help, when contemplated during qawwali at his shrine, may well be perceived as someone who has known such states, someone who even while able to manifest effective powers on earth can climb to the heights, too. As a spiritual being who spans high and low,[52] a Sufi saint like Mir Badshah bears comparison with one of contemporary India's most popular Hindu deities: Hanuman, Ram's faithful servant, the very powerful monkey-deity discussed in chapter 1. As Ram's servant, Hanuman can intercede with his Lord for mundane requests, much as the Sufi saint is able to intercede with his. As seen in chapter 1, Hanuman attracts many devotees in Gwalior (as he does in much of India), and for much the same reasons as a powerful Sufi: he is a strong personage who is ready to get practical jobs done.[53] The question then arises: if Hanuman can do the job, why should a Hindu visit the shrine of a Sufi at all?[54] Certainly, accidental reasons are often likely to be the most important: the shrine is close by; or its power has been confidentially attested by a friend; or everyone has been talking about a particular recent miracle. But the qualities of the two intercessors' images differ, too—with the religiocultural distance of the Sufi itself able to intensify his appeal.

Hanuman is a very familiar divinity to most Hindus. In shops and home shrines lithographs of him are ubiquitous, picturing him in different guises: carrying a mountain, opening his chest to reveal an image of Ram and his wife, or trampling a demon to rescue Ram and his brother from the underworld. Even though his strength comes in part from dubious characteristics like his animal traits and his familiarity with the netherworlds, his devotion to Ram keeps him working toward noble ends.[55] At the same time, however, his very devotion to Ram can put limits on the stature he reaches himself. Even though any Hindu deity is liable to be taken as an image of the supreme, Hanuman—always subordinated to Ram—in popular imagination rarely reaches the status of the very top-most gods.[56]

In comparison to Hindus' vivid images of Hanuman, their sense of a figure like Mir Badshah is vague, its diffuseness liable to give it a further reach. As a Muslim but otherwise indistinct persona, a minor Sufi saint is conceived in terms not of familiar icons, but only of common stereotypes. For many this may mean first of all that he is less than Brahminically pure, which, as I have emphasized from the outset, can add to perceptions of his practical strength.[57] For Hanuman, any impurities that may have been acquired through his part-animal nature and agility in the nether-worlds are redeemed through his association with Ram. Not so, however, with the impurities of the Sufi, who is not subordinated to any divinity that the mind can conceive. His ecstatic leaps into unfamiliar worlds may lead him to infinite, unfathomable heights even as his practical grace—like the somewhat alien medicine of the English—can be particularly quick and powerful. For Hindus at a Sufi shrine, the saint's cultural distance can let him seem, in comparison with Hanuman, to roam farther toward the heights and find more tenacious roots in the depths. In spanning the high and the low, the Sufi's otherness can take him to extremes.

At the same time, both the bliss and the boons that a Sufi saint may grant are not the only reasons for shrine attendance—by Hindus or Muslims either. In discussing motivations for shrine attendance in Rajasthan, Ann Gold lists not only the desire for boons and salvation, but also "a diffuse objective of contentment."[58] Hindus may go to Sufi shrines just for the ambience—one that may be somewhat exotic for them but is still distinctly Indian. For casual attendees whose enjoyment of the qawwali in no way leads them to ecstatic states, qawwali can add to the ambience at a shrine by just seeming exotic. For while qawwali is accessible to most ordinary urban Indians, it is not their usual musical fare, which tends toward film music or devotional songs in contemporary popular styles. Easily enjoyed by Hindus, qawwali is not quite their own: it is attractive and approach-able, but also other. The most frequent occasions for large crowds at Sufi shrines are in fact those of enthusiastic qawwali performance, as is usual during a shrine's annual festivals and in many cases weekly on Thursdays, too. On these days, music really does seem to be a big draw. Discussing the musical and religious dimensions of qawwali in the 1990s, Regula Qureshi also notes its increasing incorporation into mainstream Indian popular culture.[59] Having a big annual performance like that at Mir Badshah seems to be one of the ways in which qawwali is going pop.

From this perspective, the organization of big qawwali festivals by Hindu enthusiasts can appear as the co-optation by the mainstream of the traditional heritage of a disadvantaged minority. We might see them pulling out from Sufi tradition its most vividly accessible aspect, popularizing it, and profiting from it—if not financially, then at least in social prestige. The Muslim attendants at the shrines might then be taken as adding a note of genuineness. We think of the appropriation of the rhythms of black America by white entrepreneurs.[60] But this is not, I think, the whole picture. The effective comparison seems to be not with the creation of rock and roll, but with the popularization of gospel music. And many of those involved in the festival organization have been, like Bhonsle and Ramjilal, also religiously involved in the shrine in a deep personal way. It is not just the music that speaks to them, but also something of the religious power behind it. And the organizers, while members of the majority community, are not, on the whole, privileged members, but common ones—often very much so. At a very basic human level they are ordinary Hindu Indians strongly fascinated by the image of a powerful Sufi saint. Thus even as Hindu nationalist ideology minimizes the contribution of Muslims to the Indian cultural mix, vital elements of Islamic cultural heritage still have an allure in popular life.

True, the charisma of the exotic other, however imagined, does not generally reflect directly back on a Hindu's sense of ordinary Muslims. Indeed the image of the exotic Muslim actually depends on unfamiliarity with the mundane one, an ignorance that also, we know, results in ugly prejudices. But just as ignorant prejudice can have real-life intercommunal consequences, often disastrous, so can exotic imagining, but with consequences less easy to predict. Both Bhonsle and Ramjilal, remember, were first attracted not to a living Muslim person, but to the felt presence of a powerful Muslim saint—which for Ramjilal was expressed precisely as awesome unfamiliarity with the vision of a fakir: "I am a Hindu and a Brahmin. . . do I know you?" The exotic imaginings of both organizers then drew them into increased interaction with ordinary Muslims in the course of shrine affairs. And even as their increased mundane interactions made their specifically Islamic imaginings less exotic, their faith in the Muslim saint, once established, still held.

If the pluralism of secular India sometimes seems to be giving way to a polarizing religious communalism, that polarization may also intensify the peculiar attractiveness of the exotic other. And this in turn can have some unexpected social consequences. In fact, Gwalior's Sufi shrines seem to have flourished with the enhanced allure of Islamic difference in Indian popular culture—or at least with an increased "fashion for qawwali." But the shrines' new vitality doesn't appear to have markedly changed their roles in the personal piety and socioreligious life of most of their old devotees. Much as they have done for centuries, they speak to a diverse population from less privileged classes and lead to some practical intercommunal integration around the power of a local saint. They are still very much alive in Hindu Gwalior, and don't seem to be going away.

PART TWO

Community and Identity

3

Living Together in a Working-Class Locale

CASTE, CLASS, AND PERSONAL AFFINITIES

THE DISTINCTIONS HIGHLIGHTED in the last chapter between Hindus and Muslims as separate broad religious communities remain quite real for most people in India these days, but those communities are just the most extensive to which many feel they belong. People in the subcontinent usually have a number of overlapping group identities—religious, social, regional, and economic—which for most people impinge at least to some extent on their interpersonal relationships. This chapter will examine some different ways in which ordinary people negotiate their different collective identities when dealing with others in everyday life. My method here is largely ethnographic—grounded in participant observation within a particular smallish locale and focusing on specific lived human situations. The last of these is centered around a galvanizing and somewhat traumatic event of the recent past, but the preceding situations generally present everyday realities. Most highlight ways in which one or another socioreligious attitude can color ordinary life. Some of these reveal more complicated dimensions of the broad communal identities discussed in the last chapter. Others illustrate ways in which caste sensibilities figure into people's personal piety. Many at the same time suggest ways in which forms of identity that are primarily social (caste) and economic (class) do and don't affect the ways in which people relate to one another.

The word *caste* is a common translation for the Hindi (and Sanskrit) word *jāti*, which means "birth group."[1] There are literally thousands of specific castes and subcastes in India, most of particular regional scope.

As a birth group, a caste is a community into which one is born and within which one normally finds a spouse. It is thus generally seen as a very *essential* aspect of a person's identity—something I learned in respect to provincial India, at least, soon after my Hindi was good enough to eavesdrop on other people's conversations. The answer to the question "Who is that person?" or even "Who are you?" I discovered, most often started with a mention of the person's caste and sometimes ended there. Then and now, caste provides tradition-minded Indians a simple and sometimes sufficient way of at least beginning to understand who someone is.

Although caste understandings in modern India play out in ways substantially different from those in previous eras, they retain traces of their earlier significances (more, of course, for some people than others). Castes have ideally been taken as a hierarchy of occupational types, which were in turn seen—especially by people at the top of the hierarchy—as marked by greater and lesser degrees of religious purity. Brahmin priests (dealing with divinities) were at the top, mercantile castes (dealing with finished goods and money) in the upper middle ranks, craftspeople (getting their hands dirty) in the lower middle, refuse collectors at the bottom. In practice, caste rankings have varied according to local politics, historical circumstance, and demographic change, while birth caste never unconditionally determined anyone's actual occupation—and has increasingly little influence on it today. True, some groups find nice continuities between traditional and modern vocations: leatherworkers by caste, for example, can still find familiar work and, as we will see, often do it, while members of mercantile groups are well represented in present-day business communities. In the contemporary world of computer engineers and heavy industry, however, people of all backgrounds usually just look for the best jobs they can get, as they are legally entitled to do. Yet even as fewer people express their caste identity through their occupation, all can still do so through customary habits of diet, ritual, and association.

If caste in its complexity seems particularly characteristic of Indic civilization, economic class—in the basic sense of obvious divisions between rich and poor—is nearly universal. Although in India there has been and continues to be some congruence between caste hierarchies and economic ones, these have not been understood to be exact even in tradition: folktales tell of both poor Brahmins (high caste) and wealthy goldsmiths (as craftspersons, not so high).[2] In contemporary urban India, moreover, class has also become a matter of educational standards and thus of somewhat Westernized, cosmopolitan ways—a development that heightens the role of class in personal friendships: people with the more sophisticated educations available to prosperous families are likely to find affinities with those of similar educational backgrounds regardless of caste or religion. This is particularly true among wealthy cosmopolitans in metropolitan cities, who have often had experience abroad, but it is also frequent within the middle classes in a city like Gwalior, who usually remain close to their caste networks as well.[3]

Although the extended neighborhood we will be exploring, known as Hippopotamus Street, has some middle-class families, it is mostly working class. People of diverse castes live there—from Brahmins to refuse collectors—and may find themselves living next to one another in closely set housing. In these conditions, as we will see, caste communities can be valuable for some, but don't usually limit their personal ties. People often form bonds of friendship across caste, class, and religious divides. They do not always do so, however, with their choices depending largely on their individual attitudes and the specific circumstances in which they find themselves.

The Hippopotamus Street Hill

As a broad residential area, Hippopotamus Street usually refers to an expanse of small houses spread out over a hill above the longish Lashkar road to which the name properly belongs.[4] In the first half of the twentieth century the hill was mostly devoid of residents, and the street itself was on the northern outskirts of Gwalior, offering local gentry room to build gardened manors. As the city grew out, though, the gentry largely moved on, and the street now marks a boundary between the older princely city and extensive new development beyond it. Many of the outlying new colonies are middle class or better, their residents driving into town through a congested pass between two hills. From Hippopotamus Street itself, however, it is possible to walk to the city's main commercial district in twenty minutes or so, and many of the hill residents do so daily.

I first noticed the Hippopotamus Street area while working with Giriraj on the temple survey presented in chapter 1. The temples there seemed grander and more plentiful than in most places, but the houses were generally more modest and the people seemed poorer. Substantial temples in fact frame the hill above Hippopotamus Street. At its top is a cluster of structures of different size and age that house several old images, including a good-sized Jain temple and a large one to the fierce Hindu deity Bhairava. The most prominent temple, though, is to Satya Narayan, who lends his name to that area of the hill, called Satya Narayan ki Tekri (*tekṛī*, in the local language, means a hillock). Just below the street, opposite the steps leading up to to the Satya Narayan temple area, is another group of temples—including one with an image of a Jain figure of monumental (for Gwalior) proportions and another with a stone Shivalingam about four feet in diameter, credibly said to be the thickest in the area. The hill seems blessed by impressive divine presences.

Indeed, not so long ago, when Satya Narayan ki Tekri was still on the periphery of the city, urban gentlefolk used to go there on family excursions, picnicking at the temple areas (fig. 3.1)—but they don't go much any more. For over the last few decades, as the city has grown, the working poor have started making their homes higher and higher up the hillside. People from the city visiting Satya Narayan temple now walk quickly up the steps to it from the street, eyes ahead. They tend to think of the hill as a tough, somewhat dangerous district (fig. 3.2), one that no longer invites a secluded scenic stroll. For its residents, though, the hill can be a vibrant and lively place. It forms a network of interlocking neighborhoods, mostly mixed, with a few predominantly Muslim areas and some settlements—more and less homogenous—of specific low-caste communities. People visit within neighborhoods and across them, mixing according to factors of caste, class, occupation, and personal affinity. With neighbors facing

FIGURE 3.1 Small shrines near the main temple area at Satya Narayan hill with a view of the city in the background.

FIGURE 3.2 An alleyway in one of the poorer parts of the Hippopotamus Street area.

similar pressures of urban life, even within its diversity the hill displays multiple forms of cohesion.

Before doing the research for this chapter in 2005, I had already made some acquaintances on Satya Narayan hill. Having earlier concentrated largely on issues of middle-class religion, I was intrigued by the area's religious culture and social styles, to both of which I was unaccustomed. So on a two-month visit during the monsoon season I made an effort to expand my networks there. Although I began by asking questions about religious practice, what I found myself more often observing were patterns of social interaction among castes, classes, and communities, the ways in which individuals adhered to apparent norms and sometimes transcended them. What follows is an account of some dynamics of socioreligious and political community that I encountered. I have changed people's names, but the people themselves are real.

Temples for Communities and Individuals

Hippopotamus Street runs for about three kilometers from east to west, with the steps leading up to the Satya Narayan temple beginning roughly at its middle. Walking from the steps toward the West, one comes to the image-makers' district, with its shops displaying figures of Hindu deities in many shapes and sizes. At its eastern end stands a temple to Valmiki, the legendary author of the Ramayana said to be from the refuse-collector caste—usually called *sweepers* in Indian English. A sizable sweeper community lives in a scattered settlement behind the temple; they call themselves Valmiks after the sage.[5] In contrast to most people living on the hill—who did not particularly favor the impressive old temples in their immediate vicinity, many preferring the well-attended places of worship in town—members of two low-caste groups, the Valmiks and the leatherworking Ahirwars, did regularly pay attention to deities enshrined at local sites. These sites, however, were not old ones, but newly built structures providing each community with a religious and social center.

For both the Valmiks and the Ahirwars, the new structures served special functions for them as historically marginalized communities with sizable settlements on the hill. But because the communities present a contrast in their economic condition and cultural priorities, the sites served them in different ways. While both the Valmiks and Ahirwars are Dalits, "oppressed ones," as the former untouchable castes now often prefer to be called, the Valmiks include a number of people with middle-class jobs and the higher aspirations that go with them. With a longer history of politicization in the area, further, they are more ready than the Ahirwars to express their discontent, sometimes in eloquent ways. Their temple has thus played a role in their political as well as sectarian development—neither of which is pronounced among the Ahirwars. Although not all Ahirwars I met were happy living on the hill, many seemed happy to be living in a homogeneous settlement. On the whole less educated and leading more traditional lifestyles than the Valmiks, these valued the close-knit caste community that the settlement provided. For them, the new shrine they built on the main lane in the area (fig. 3.3) had become a point of communal pride.

Ahirwar Community

The Ahirwars' settlement is just to the east of the steps leading up to the Satya Narayan temple. It begins about halfway up the hill and stretches to the top, bordering the steps in its final expanse. About forty families live in small-roomed houses there; many of them are related to one another, some closely. In 2005, the majority of the Ahirwar men remained in

FIGURE 3.3 Outside one of the nicer houses in the main lane above Hippopotamus Street.

leatherworking trades, expanded these days to include working with sandals made from synthetics; visiting in 2013, I was told that many still did, but fewer. When asked about their profession, leatherworkers would usually specify "manufacture" or "repair," with the former more prestigious. Others have worked in small factories or as shop assistants; married women might stay at home and roll *bīḍīs*—coarse, country-style cigarettes—that they would pass on to a distributor. Although some Ahirwars are educated and articulate, many are not, and of these, some don't place much value on educating their children fully either.

Bhupati Ahirwar, although not well educated, is articulate—and expressed obvious satisfaction in living in the settlement. The oldest of three brothers, he lives in a joint family with them, a divorced sister, and a widowed mother. They all share a courtyard, but have separate rooms for their families. Bhupati and his next younger brother are both in leather-working trades. Bhupati is in repair, setting up a sidewalk shop in a bazaar in an older section of the city beyond the main commercial district, where his brother works in a small shoe factory. Bhupati's youngest brother and almost grown son were both unemployed at the time I met them. The youngest brother, with a twelfth-grade education, was prized in the family for his literacy and was looking for an office job where he could use it. Bhupati's son had been working as a cook in a catering business, but there weren't many weddings to cook for during the monsoon. Life has been hard, but together they manage, and community life has its consolations.

Bhupati smiled warmly when asked how he liked living on the hill. "My family is here," he said, "my children and grandchildren." Moreover, the settlement itself served as an extended family in a literal as well as a figurative sense: like most residents, Bhupati had relatives living there, in his case maternal grandparents and uncles. They invited one another to eat, went to one another's weddings, and celebrated the Hindu holidays together: "the forty families keep together in everything they do." Although this idealized picture of village-style community in an urban environment undoubtedly left some internal stresses unstated, it was a vision that Bhupati treasured and was shared to at least some extent by many of the Ahirwars on the hill (fig. 3.4).

It was not, however, shared by all. Savitri Ahirwar is the only member of the community there attending college, her absent father earning a decent government salary as a member of the Indo-Tibet Border Police.

FIGURE 3.4 Relaxing with a dog on a roof above Hippopotamus Street, where simple pleasures remain available.

Unlike most people there, Savitri did not have extended family in the settlement; her father's parents lived in town and he bought the place on the hill because it was an affordable way to have his own home. Savitri kept aloof from the younger generation in the settlement, preferring the company of her middle-class college friends, whom she visited at their homes in town. She too would like to live like them, or better: "in good society, where people have education and understand its meaning. Here education is given no value. They think it's bad if a girl goes out"—even to study. Still, Savitri continued to participate in the community-wide celebrations of festivals and weddings that Bhupati Ahirwar mentioned: they were almost an obligation of local community membership.

A more typical complaint about living in the settlement came from Manik Ram, one of Bhupati's maternal relatives, and like him a leatherworker. Although Manik Ram has studied more than most in his community—through high school, working on the side—he did not express dissatisfaction at carrying on his community's traditional occupation. Having returned from a stint of shoemaking in Delhi, he now, at twenty-eight, lived in the family house and made fancy sandals at a small factory in town. Manik Ram's dissatisfactions were common to people at his stage of life in all castes and classes: he just wanted to be his own person. At his father's house, he said, there is "tension," using the English word. To get some peace, he'd like to live on his own, somewhere in the city close to where he'd be working. Not that he wanted to stay in his present job—he didn't really like working under someone else. His ambitions remained modest: "I just want my own shop where I can work as I like." He was happy to remain "a small craftsman" (*choṭa kārigar*), but for now valued independence over family and community life.

Whatever their feelings about actually living in community, though, most Ahirwars took a collective satisfaction in a newly built shrine to Shiva often referred to as Bhole Nath. Its main donors were two of their own: Phul Chand, a driver, and Raju, who made sandals—their names duly noted on the inaugural plaque. The shrine stood on the main lane running perpendicular to the steps, a mixed area, just opposite an alley leading up to the Ahirwar settlement. It thus at once dignified the portal to the Ahirwar domain and made a respectable Ahirwar mark on the larger neighborhood—whose members did not, however, seem to offer many prayers there. For Ahirwars, though, the shrine was the one place of worship that they all mentioned consistently visiting. In the evenings, young Ahirwar men strolling together on the street pay it reverence as they pass.

On Mondays, Shiva's Day, Bhupati claims that "everyone goes, I mean everyone, the whole neighborhood, they bring garlands and incense." The shrine is uncovered, and not particularly imposing, but it is well maintained and aesthetically pleasing, proudly claimed by the Ahirwar community as its own.

Valmik Discontent

The Valmik temple, by contrast, is a sizable building that has multiple functions—one of four Valmik temples located in disparate areas of the city.[6] Although the term *Valmik* is regularly used as a respectful caste name accepted even by professed atheists in the community, it can also refer more narrowly to adherents of a sectarian tradition (normally from the same caste) who follow the sage Valmiki. The temple serves both groups: the sect through its regularly worshipped images of Valmiki and its large hall, which may be used by visiting sectarian sadhus as a place to stay; the caste community through the same hall when used by its local members as a rest house for wedding guests and general meeting place. Because of the temple's role as a meeting place for Valmiks, I was cautioned about it by a high-caste acquaintance who lives within range of the hill: he thought that it wasn't a safe place to visit. Yet in addition to sadhus and some good-natured youth, the people I met there were retirees from lower-middle-class jobs: a policeman, an office worker, a practitioner of traditional medicine. For the latter—some of them temple officers—the temple seemed to be a bastion of intracaste respectability.

The location of the temple on Hippopotamus Street itself helps contribute to the urban ambiance of the Valmiks' district. In contrast to the Ahirwars' settlement—far from the street, self-contained, and traversed by footpaths, suggesting a village in its layout as well as its community ideals—the Valmiks' is a paved street ascending the gentle eastern slope of Satya Narayan hill, where Valmiks live interspersed with other mostly low castes. This area was settled earlier than the Ahirwars' and is more integrated with the city. Its population, moreover, is also better integrated into the regular urban economy. Although the majority of Valmiks, I was told, remain sweepers by profession, many of these have secure government jobs: working at the railway station, the jail, or city offices. Some, further, have been able to avail themselves of opportunities offered to members of historically disadvantaged castes in education and employment to secure responsible government positions. These local bourgeoisie continue to live in the area in which they were brought up, close to their relatives and having roomier accommodation than they might be able to afford in a classier part of town. Socially and politically aware, however, they often remain discontented with where they are and are quick to express outrage at the way their caste has been treated.

Sundar Lal Shinde (BA, LLB) works as a revenue inspector for the Gwalior municipal corporation. His extended family has had mixed fortunes: two of his brothers had to be satisfied working in "maintenance" in government offices, but another has his own garage in Bombay and is doing fairly well. While Sundar Lal and his Bombay brother have started using the name Shinde, a Maharashtrian name that suggests membership in the old Gwalior aristocracy, the rest of the family uses a more ordinary, not immediately placeable, subcaste name as surname.[7]

Entering Sundar Lal's home after becoming comfortable in the Ahirwars' neighborhood was like entering another world. With its good-sized rooms and plentiful upholstered furniture, it had more than the basic comforts of the Indian middle class. But Sundar Lal wasn't satisfied: the house was "sufficient," he said, using the English word, but he was *compelled* to live there—really he'd rather be living in a nice colony. Economic circumstances contributed to this compulsion, no doubt, but family considerations also entered the picture: many of his brothers and cousins, as well as his aging parents, lived nearby. It was true that he had made some progress personally, he said, but his caste hadn't: its members remained mostly poor, the government didn't help, and Valmiks were still subject to discrimination. "They think we make their temples impure and go shoo! shoo! shoo!" he said with excited gestures. "Do I have a tail or big ears? They're human beings and I'm a human being!" He was vehemently against image-worship and had little use for religion in general. These views were echoed by Sundar Lal's son Suresh, a stylishly dressed young man who was getting a business degree, working in a cell-phone shop, and selling Amway products on the side. I had met Suresh before his father and had been surprised when he told me he was an atheist—not a common confession in provincial India—but now I saw that he was just following a family tradition. Professed atheists but outspoken in voicing the grievances of their caste, Sundar Lal and Suresh have ambivalent feelings about the Valmik temple standing proudly on the street below: although they disdain it religiously, they nevertheless appreciate it as a useful center for their community.

Sundar Lal inherits his strident attitude toward caste prejudice from his late uncle, an old Valmik activist, who had edited a local newspaper for the community in the middle decades of the last century. But that uncle, who lived in the neighborhood—like the majority of Valmiks but more so—also embraced religion. He maintained a shrine to Kali in front of his house, fronting a little square on the main road, which Sundar Lal's wife regularly visits. He recognized Kali's special powers as a supplement to Guru Valmiki's. Powerful Hindu divinities such as Kali can help with things in the world, he told me not long before he died, echoing a refrain uttered by many of the ordinary temple-goers heard from in chapter 1. Guru Valmiki, however, was "a light of God" who offered salvation but did not deign to meddle in mundane affairs. Some years ago, a guru in the Valmik tradition gave Sundar Lal's uncle the *rām* mantra. (A popular mantra throughout North India, *rām* has a special significance for followers of Valmiki, who wrote the classic version of the story of Ram the virtuous king.) "The *rām* mantra is the best mantra in the world," he said. "Everyone who repeats it gets liberation." Clearly, whatever political significance the Valmiki tradition had for him, it also had a vital religious meaning that is comprehended within a broader Hindu worldview. For him, the Valmik temple was a center for political organization and salvation both.

Individual Pilgrimages

Other caste temples around Hippopotamus Street play their own roles in community, often becoming focal points for both conflicts and new alliances. Over in the image-makers' district, for example, leadership at a temple to the divine builder Vishvakarma had for some time been a point of contention in the artisan community that bears his name. There was hope, however, that things would be resolved in a forthcoming intracommunal election. In one of the temples below the street, by contrast, the Malis—traditionally gardeners—had recently seen separate branches of their own community come together. The Mali temple had just hosted a celebration of the formal union of three small historically distinct gardening caste-groups: one with local origins, one from Vraj to the north, and one from Rajasthan to the west. Meeting at the temple, the three groups had voted to unite their separate caste organizations, giving sanction to practices of intermarriage and interdining that they had already begun in practice. For members of communities without local caste temples, however, temple allegiances are largely individual, determined by people's own predilections and personal histories. In these cases, a temple's proximity can be in inverse proportion to its perceived value.

When most Hindus on the hill were asked about their temple-going habits, they named one or other of the better known temples in town—most often one to Hanuman or Durga, the practically effective deities that our 1997 survey suggested were the most popular in town. The cluster of temples on the top of the hill also includes shrines to Hanuman and Durga, but the majority of the people who live on the hill ignore them. When I asked Narendra Mishra, a hill resident and professional religious storyteller, why this was so, he suggested that one reason people go to the temples in town is because of the effort involved in doing so: to get results from a divinity you need to make a sacrifice. At the same time, though, we can imagine that going to the big Gwalior temples reinforces hill residents' identity as ordinary inhabitants of the city. Just because they live in a less than respectable neighborhood that happens to have some nice old temples nearby doesn't mean that they shouldn't go to the popular temples in town like everyone else.

The Satya Narayan temple complex itself is largely visited by middle-class Hindus from outside the neighborhood and maintained by well-to-do patrons in the city. In addition to the Satya Narayan temple and some smaller Hindu shrines, it includes an old Bhairava temple and a newer one housing an old Jain image found on the hill. The attendance as well as the construction and maintenance of the Jain temple, in fact, turned out to be largely a family affair. Not only was it commissioned by the mother of a Jain household in town in order to house a large Jain image found on the hill, but it is visited almost exclusively by members of her family. The temple is locked during the day, although an old Jain caretaker whose son keeps a small shop on the hill has a key to admit appropriate visitors. Every morning, male members of the family walk up from the city in their street clothes, change into traditional dress at the temple, and perform a service for about an hour; women from the family join in for the second part of the service. For this family, as for others from the city who visit temples at the complex, hiking up the hill is treated as an ascetic effort, reinforced by the tough reputation of the neighborhood through which the steps pass. If the hill residents' visit to popular city temples helps normalize their identity, city dwellers' trek up the now disreputable Satya Narayan hill can lend their temple-going practices an air of ascetic exoticism.[8]

The relatively small number of hill residents who do regularly visit the temple complex do so for ordinary and less ordinary reasons. Upendra Joshi, the college-going son of a middle-class Brahmin family, is drawn to the Bhairava temple. The family lives low down on the hill, so the temple is not close by. He visits it weekly like other middle-class devotees, if with a somewhat shorter walk. For Lal Chand Ahirwar, however, who does shoe repair off the main bazaar, a daily morning tour of all the hill temples helped mark him as socioreligiously special in his own eyes and others'. Perceived as a character by many who know him, Lal Chand is an amiable middle-aged man who is given to high-minded talk. A visible aspect of his high-minded persona is his daily ascent to the temple complex to do ritual puja at all the Hindu shrines and temples there. (Not welcome at the Jain temple because of his caste, he avoids it.) The priests all accommodate Lal Chand and he doesn't hurry: his daily routine takes about an hour. Although a lengthy daily morning puja at a nearby temple or home shrine is a traditional Brahminic practice, if not readily kept by Brahmins these days (particularly in urban India), it was not something Ahirwars, or those from most other Hindu castes, normally do. Whatever Lal Chand's personal reasons for his practice—and no one seemed to doubt his piety or sincerity—it also presented him as a sort of Brahmin among Ahirwars, an anomalous status that he obviously relished. As an individual, he practiced temple worship against the grain to his own idiosyncratic ends.

Caste, Class, and Friendship

Upendra Joshi and Lal Chand Ahirwar lived in close proximity to one another near the steps, in an area that included small, unfinished, one-room dwellings, older, multiroomed houses with places for livestock, and a few new homes built to basic middle-class norms. Because this neighborhood is on the path leading straight up to the Satya Narayan temple area, it is itself sometimes referred to as Satya Narayan hill. Most of its three or four thousand residents live off small alleyways branching out from a wider lane running toward the east, perpendicular to the steps; that lane, after a few bends, turns into the wider road passing through the Valmik neighborhood. A few houses line the west side of the steps—older, village-style ones below, with places for animals; and newer construction above. As with many neighborhoods on the hill, the area is mixed in both caste and class, with individuals intermingling according to caste familiarity, class style, and personal affection. In general, caste ties seemed more important for older and more traditional people and class attitudes more important for the more urbanized and young. Among the young in particular, personal friendships could transcend both caste and class—but not for everyone, and less readily for extreme divides.

Jitendra and Jitendra

The Brahmin Upendra Joshi's younger brother, Jitendra, was best friends with a neighbor from a Gujar family, also named Jitendra. The two were usually referred to by their nicknames: Jitendra Joshi as Chikku and Jitendra Gujar as Guddu (his family followed the common practice of using their caste name as a surname); both boys were in their late teens when I met them. The two had grown up near each other in houses on the west side of the steps and remained close.

The Gujars' house is older, in a village style, and lower down on the hill. Although Guddu's grandfather had been in government service, the family had maintained the caste profession of dairying on the side and had kept milch animals there before the hill was well developed. The family had been living in the Hippopotamus Street vicinity for "a hundred years," said Guddu's grandmother, having earlier lived near the big Jain temple across Hippopotamus Street from the hill. They had moved to their present house thirty years ago. The grandparents still kept milch animals and let neighbors come for dairy products, but Guddu's father had prospered in the transport business before his premature death and had built a large house in one of the outlying middle-class colonies; Guddu had access to a family motorcycle.

Chikku's father, by contrast, was the first from his village to take a middle-class job in town: he worked in a bank. With no established city networks and limited means, he built on the hill above Guddu's family because land there was affordable. His sons were serious about their education and two had also managed to find work. Jitendra, the youngest, took both college classes and orders from shops for Cadbury's chocolate; Upendra, the middle brother, was pursuing an MA; the oldest brother had a business degree and did specialized marketing for a big corporation. All were striving toward some recognizable goals of the educated middle class.

The Joshi family also maintained its Brahminic sensibilities about purity, which Chikku seemed to take seriously, politely restricting my access to his home's puja room and kitchen. He would idealize the village, which he visited, for the way in which Brahmins could maintain their separateness and regretted that it was so hard to do so on the hill. Still, Chikku tried to keep aloof. Although he would lounge on the steps like others, he often just sat alone and watched. I never saw him being chummy with any of the Ahirwars who also sometimes mingled there. He tended to speak of them and the Valmiks (both of whom he generally referred to by less dignified names—*camārs* and *bhangīs*) in hushed tones as if even talking about them were improper. Even though he used the same tones to speak of the settlement of poor cowherding Gujars near the top of the hill, he saw his middle-class college-going friend Guddu in an entirely different light. Though certainly among the less elevated castes, Gujars—despite the assumed proclivities of those in the hilltop settlement—are generally not seen to be unclean in the same way as *bhangīs* and *camārs*; in Gwalior, moreover, some claimed to be Kshatriyas—military men and rulers ranked highly in the classical Brahminical world. Guddu's family had some money and his grandmother was an imposing local matriarch; in the evenings, Chikku's mother could sometimes be found visiting her on her stoop. However the Joshis finally perceived Guddu's family's caste status, they included the family in their circle. Chikku treated Guddu as a middle-class friend, not as one of those other Gujars up the hill. Although his caste sensibilities were pronounced, they were not overwhelming. No doubt encompassing stereotypical ideas of low-caste behaviors, they could be transcended when he met someone who conformed to his middle-class norms.

Mohit and the Brahmins

In some cases, though, a tension between low caste and middle class led to unwarranted social pretensions and relationships that could seem strained. Mohit More was one of the most prosperous residents of the neighborhood. An electrical contractor in his mid-thirties, he was born in the neighborhood, and—the only son of an elderly father—had inherited the house in which he grew up. He had done some recent renovations on the house, which stood on the lane running east from the steps: it now had another story on top and a living room with a shiny new floor that looked like marble. Sometimes he came in from town in a spiffy suit and chatted on his cell phone—which at the time was not, as it was in more prosperous parts of the city, an accoutrement many people in the neighborhood had. But Mohit could also frequently be found sitting on his stoop in an undershirt and lungi, chewing pan and shooting the breeze. He was politically active and familiar with local polling figures, thus becoming the source I trusted most for neighborhood population estimates and, because he was in contracting business, for land values.

When I first met Mohit, he was lounging on the steps with Faraaz Khan, a young man in his early twenties who lived in an extended family occupying an old house on the west side of the steps between Guddu's and Chikku's. They introduced each other as good friends, and their relaxed demeanor suggested some genuine affection between them. But, as I was to learn, Mohit was generally garrulous and Faraaz regularly wore a broad smile and seemed friendly with everyone. Faraaz, it turned out, also worked for Mohit, learning the electrical trade, so their good friendship was not without mutual self-interest. Mohit discussed his friendships more pointedly one day at the Sharmas, a Brahmin family who lived in a new house on the west side of the hill and also rented out some nearby rooms. This house, he said, was his "own house"—meaning that he was accepted there like family. Faraaz's house was "his own" as well. "But over there," he said, indicating the other side of the steps, where he lived, "where there are a lot of *camārs*. . . the society's no good. . . . They play dice. They drink." (Mohit himself had invited me to drinking parties more than once.) "I don't have anything to do with them," he continued, and, at my expression of doubt, expanded: "I talk with them all, but don't maintain relations with them. Here," he added, referring to the small group of houses west of the steps, "people are educated."

For Mohit, then, the steps represented a dividing line between a small, demarcated middle-class area on the west and the large, predominantly lower-class area to the east that included the Ahirwar settlement. And as I thought about it, this was a line that others marked, too. People living on the western rim of the steps simply walked down the hill into town; I couldn't remember seeing the young men who lived there standing about in the lane with Ahirwars and others. The steps themselves were neutral territory, where everyone could and did loiter, but there was no real neutral public space to the west of them. It was with this western area that Mohit wanted me to associate him.

Mohit had also alluded (inaccurately) to caste during his excited declaration of this to me: "Here there are only Brahmins and *ṭhākurs*," using a term of respect for people of the Kshatriya warrior class—and it is true that the three Brahmin families in the neighborhood lived to the west of the steps. But what the Brahmin families, the Khans, and Gujars had in common was not caste, but class, in which they were more or less on par with Mohit. Still, after Mohit left, the Sharma patriarch gave me to understand that he didn't feel as close to Mohit as Mohit professed to feel for him: "He's low caste," said Papa Sharma, unasked. When I later inquired among my Ahirwar friends, I was told that Mohit was a Baraar—a caste from which midwives come—and, it seems, the only one in the neighborhood.

Because Mohit used the Maharashtrian surname More, I originally understood him—as I did the Valmik Shindes—to be part of Gwalior's formerly elite Maharashtrian community. Mohit never dissuaded me from this view, even when I asked him if he spoke Marathi—as many from that community still do. In this, he differed from Sundar Lal Shinde's up-and-coming son Suresh, who, when asked the same question, understood my confusion and immediately responded: "I'm not a Maharashtrian. I am a Valmik: do you have a problem with that?" Suresh had an extended caste community to live in and a politicized sense of caste pride. Mohit had neither and sought an uneasy social solidarity with some of the neighborhood economic elite through class. Suresh wore both his caste and class with aplomb: even though most of his Valmik relatives were poor, he mixed with them readily and unashamedly; but because he grew up middle class, he was also able to interact easily with his city friends. Mohit, by contrast, was a lower-class boy made good through shrewdness and energy and had never quite mastered middle-class social graces. If Mohit had actually behaved more like the Sharmas, it might have been easier for them to forget about his caste origins. But they didn't, Mohit knew it, and it made him nervous.

Jains in a Bad Neighborhood

Down the lane from the steps, just past the Ahirwar shrine to Bhole Nath, is a store run by a Jain family. Its wares are most modest: soaps and penny candies and other small goods that might satisfy the immediate needs and desires of people with simple tastes and not much money. The family had earlier lived down in the city, and like most who migrated from there to the hill, came because they would rather own than rent and the hill was affordable. Although they participated in the urban, middle-class Jain culture, they obviously weren't very prosperous.

Suresh's cousin Ramu often came up from the Valmik area, further east, and sat on the curb in front of the shop. Ramu's father was a sweeper in the train station, but Ramu worked for a videographer. Because the wedding season was in hiatus during the monsoon, he didn't have too much to do, so these days, the shop's stoop was his *aḍḍa*, his station. He seemed to enjoy the action that sometimes took place near the Ahirwars' Bholenath temple and was also friends with Ankur Jain, a soft-spoken teenager who lived behind the shallow storefront and often minded it.

I first met Ramu and Ankur together, high on the steps, as I was descending from the temples above. Ramu was older, with a more outgoing personality, and showed interest in my questions about the area. We arranged to meet the next day. Although he would eventually provide me an entry into the Valmik community, at the time, I couldn't place the sub-caste name he used as a surname. Outside any particular context, Ramu and Ankur seemed like any two friends from the area enjoying the evening view. Because Ramu was with Ankur Jain and Jains are treated in the local caste order as a (reasonably high) mercantile group, I presumed Ramu was also from some caste traditionally understood as clean.

When I next saw Ankur, I didn't immediately recognize him. By then Ramu had introduced me to a large circle of his Valmik relatives and friends. We were gathered in the Shindes' living room, the nicest place to meet that the extended family had to offer, and engaged in a rousing conversation on caste, atheism, Hindu nationalism, and patriarchy. Women from the family spoke up and diverse views were aired. It seemed very open and somewhat cosmopolitan, if perhaps sometimes more heated than the usual middle-class parlor discussion. In the midst of it, Ankur Jain came in and sat down. I thought he was another friend from the Valmik community. When he later reintroduced himself, I did a silent double-take but then reproached myself for my jaded presumptions: what was so odd about a lower-middle-class boy imbibing some intellectual culture in a more prosperously middle-class drawing room? I soon got a good glimpse, though, of where my presumptions came from.

Finding Ankur at the shop one day the next week, I asked him about the Jain temple on the hill. This led to an introduction to his grandfather, who kept a set of keys. When I expressed an interest in Jainism, grandfather called his wife and they both spoke to me at length on Jain philosophy. In a cramped little room on the hill, they took turns, lecturing me with fervor and erudition. I was impressed. When talk turned to the temple, they said it was open only for Jains. What about the mercantile communities with whom local Jains sometimes married? Well, they would open it for high-caste Hindus, as they would for an interested foreigner like me, but

they didn't want the riffraff on the hill coming in. (They were likely thinking primarily of the Ahirwars who lived in the temple's immediate vicinity.) What, then, did they think of their grandson's mixing with low-caste
friends? They both looked immediately stricken: they didn't like it at all.
Their faces showed sincere pain. It didn't matter to them that Ankur's
particular low-caste friends were familiar with middle-class ways and even
occasionally helped to widen his intellectual horizons. They may not even
have imagined this was possible. But Ankur knew who he liked and the
worlds in which they lived. So what if the old folks don't like it? In his case,
at least, there didn't seem to be much they could really do.

Hindus and Muslims

For the most part, Hindus and Muslims lived amicably enough on the
hill. Muslims, when asked, regularly reported that there was no "tension" (sometimes using the English word), and genuine intercommunal
friendships were patent. Even an ardent Hindu nationalist organizer who
lived on the hill distinguished between local Muslims—who were "OK"
(*ṭhīk*)—and those from outside. In part this is a factor of Gwalior's demography: because the Muslim population is small and generally poor, the
Hindu majority doesn't feel threatened and so has no real cause to be
intimidating. Muslims recognize the situation and aren't especially asser-
tive about their collective prerogatives. Particularly interesting in these circumstances are some of the variations of religious observance and identity
that emerge—often within the same family—as individual Muslims live
within a Hindu world.

Holidays at the Khans

Faraaz Khan's was the only Muslim family that lived permanently in the
neighborhood of the steps. Some Muslim renters came and went, but
Faraaz's family was a fixture. Their house was an older one, fairly low
down, built before much of the recent development. Their stoop was in a
prominent place—on the west side of the steps opposite the main lane to
the east—and some of the household women who might be found doing
chores there were strong neighborhood personalities.

The women also seemed to have stronger Islamic identities than the
men—stronger, at least, than Faraaz's. Although Faraaz's cousin, who
worked as a mechanic near a large mosque, went to common prayer there

every Friday, Faraaz went "very little. . . a couple of times a year." When asked about his favorite festivals, he mentioned Divali, Holi—both Hindu holidays—and Id, in that order. The daughters-in-law of the household would reverse the order, usually beginning with the "sweet" Id, when they cook vermicelli noodles with sugar, and giving particular attention to Moharram, when they have big feasts. During that time they exchange invitations with Muslim relatives and friends in nearby areas, while distributing food to the Hindu neighbors: "The Ahirwars come and take it as *prasād*," said Faraaz's Aunt Farhana Begum, referring to the Hindu practice discussed in chapter 1 of taking (and then eating) sanctified offerings.

Faraaz's aunts were ambivalent about the Hindu holidays. According to Farhana Begum, they celebrate the autumn festival of Divali "to make the children happy." Naseem Begum added that they, too, like the Hindus, whitewash their houses at Divali and give sweets to the children: "The Hindus do these things, so we have to as well." She was clear, however, that "we don't do *pūjā-pāṭh*" or other specifically religious ceremonies. Naseem Begum (like many respectable Hindus, too) didn't really appreciate Holi, a spring festival that can get a little raucous. "We don't like it," she said twice. Unlike some of her more rigorously observant Muslim acquaintances, however, who would pointedly not participate in Holi at all, Naseem did in order not to offend her neighbors: they "acknowledge you and come; we don't want to refuse those people."

Farhana and Naseem were sisters who came from Sabalgarh, a town in a bordering district that had an intercommunal demographic similar to Gwalior's but was considerably smaller and more provincial. They seem to have been brought up, moreover, in a household that had a more definite notion of Islamic religious identity than the one into which they had married. There, as here, they lived among Hindus but had ties with Muslims in other areas not far away where it was easy to give full expression to Muslim holidays and family celebrations. Now living where they did on the hill, they celebrated in a small Muslim settlement below, just across Hippopotamus Street. This was the way Islamic life went in the neighborhoods they've lived in—they didn't seem to mind.

Muslim Craftsmen and Hindu Images

One of the areas on the hill with a substantial concentration of Muslims was the image-makers district. Although the owners of the five or so image-making establishments in the district—who are also the prime salesmen—are all Hindu, they employ Muslims on the manufacturing end, especially in the less-skilled, labor-intensive finishing work. These image-workers maintain their identities as Muslims and are aware of themselves primarily as craftsmen, not devotees, but they nevertheless sometimes give thought to their relationships to the Hindu images that they produce.

Ehsaan Khan, a lively man in his early thirties who came from a nearby village, had been working in image manufacturing for years, mostly polishing cut images, but sometimes painting them, too. He liked the painting work: demanding higher skills, it paid more, and he hoped to get more assignments in that line. For a while, Ehsaan was renting a room from his (Hindu) employer on Hippopotamus Street itself, but when the employer needed the space for his own family, Ehsaan rented a room by the Satya Narayan steps for a few months, where I first met him. Later he moved in with his wife's family across Hippopotamus Street from the image-maker's district.

Ehsaan was fond of the figures of the Hindu divinities he polished and painted. Although he declined to name a favorite, the one he liked best was clearly Durga: her image "is good to look at," he said, "and to make." But Ehsaan's fondness for goddess figures in general went beyond the mere crafting of an image. He frequently went to a private shrine to Santoshi Ma that was run by an elderly, unmarried Maratha woman; she lived with her natal family on the hill between the Satya Narayan steps and the Valmiks' area. (Not too long ago, Santoshi Ma had been a goddess of very little renown, but her popularity was greatly heightened by a 1975 hit film about her called *Jai Santoshi Ma*).[9] On Fridays, about 8:00 p.m., the Maratha woman would get possessed by the goddess, who answered questions and granted boons. The shrine drew devotees from the city, but people from the hill sometimes came, too. Not all, though, were admitted: some Valmiks reported being turned away, and foreign scholars were not welcome during the time of possession. But Ehsaan and his wife had no trouble going repeatedly: the couple had faith. "I do puja," Ehsaan declared with a touch of defiance. "I am a Muslim, sure, but I accept all." Just as many Gwalior Hindus readily visit Sufi shrines they find powerful, Ehsaan visits Santoshi Ma.

A more complex case is presented by Irfan Khan, who himself sometimes sang at Sufi shrines. His outward identification with Hindu divinities and traditions went further than Ehsaan's, but it was also more ambivalent. I first met Irfan in 2003, when Giriraj took me to a shop owned by a friend of his. Irfan was polishing an image. "This boy not only polishes images," the shop owner remarked, "he also sings." It turned out that Irfan was from a family of qawwals that lived on the hill above the shop. Even in Gwalior, though, they were very small-time performers and none of them seems to have made much of a living out of qawwali. The paterfamilias had kept a day job as a mechanic; other brothers also worked in *nauṭankī*, a popular performance genre, and toured villages.

Irfan's main professional outlet for his music was actually not in qawwali but in Ramayana performances. Small in stature and still then in his late teens, he was well suited to playing women's roles in the Hindu epic. He didn't do these performances in Gwalior, he said, where people knew him and might not accept the fact that he was a Muslim playing a Hindu divinity. As part of a professional troupe, however, he toured medium-sized towns in western Uttar Pradesh. Because devotees gave special reverence to actors in Ram Lila performances even when they were offstage, Irfan took on an overt Brahminic identity while he was on tour: he called himself Sanjay Sharma (the surname a very common Brahmin one) and presented himself as a traditional pious Hindu: he wore a *dhotī*—a long cloth white tied up between the legs—painted a red mark on his forehead, and kept vegetarian. Although Irfan was feeling exuberant during most of his talk, he was reticent at first about his Hindu Ram Lila persona. When asked how he felt about it, Irfan turned reflective: pretending to be a Hindu offstage during the Ram Lila was like pretending to be a woman during the performance. "I am a Muslim," he said, "but my profession... my art: I transform myself—I change. It's also a big thing that even though I'm a man, I change to a woman. . . . Then when I come down from the stage I'm a guy like you." Irfan could play a convincing Sita on stage and a convincing Sanjay on the street. But in both cases he was demonstrating devotion to his craft, not to religious ideals.

Often performing with Irfan in both qawwali and Ram Lila was his younger brother Jamal: "For qawwali, my name is Jamal Khan; for Ram Lila, it's Bunty. . . Bunty Sharma." Jamal was more energetic than Irfan and more ambitious. He had formally accepted a popular qawwal in town as his teacher and had learned some theatrical dance. With his drive and dancing abilities, Jamal was able to find work year-round in theatrical companies that toured villages in the region, usually playing women's roles. He did not, like his brother, have to polish images on the side.

During the course of these village performances Jamal befriended Rajesh Mishra, a young Brahmin a few years older than he who lived on the flat top of the hill above the image-makers' district: "Jamal plays ladies' roles," said Rajesh. "I play gents'," saying *ladies* and *gents* in English. (In the Ram Lila, Rajesh had usually played Lakshman, Ram's loyal younger brother—although after our conversation the sudden resignation of the actor in his troupe playing Ram's wife Sita had landed him that important role.) Rajesh's family maintained their Brahminic traditions—his father doing puja every morning in their very cramped quarters—but Jamal was obviously most welcome in their house. His mother, whom I had previously seen as stiff and dour, ashamed of their current poverty, opened up when she saw Jamal and greeted him with a warm smile. The feeling of genuine intercommunal togetherness at the Mishras' house may have inspired Jamal to comment on how he, as a Muslim, felt about his work in Hindu religious performances. Rajesh and Jamal were discussing their craft when Jamal, talking about the Ram Lila, digressed: "I don't see things as separate. I really *enjoy* working there. Sometimes you find some of our brothers who say: Why are you working in the Ram Lila; it's not in our Islamic tradition (*sarī'ah*). But I don't accept this. Brother, it's all one." He went on to recite a couple of verses from Hindi poets suggesting similarities between Hindu and Muslim mystical paths but concluded on a more tentative, political note, "As far as our city goes, there's unity. . . there hasn't been any strife yet and there won't be. This is what I want." Unlike his brother commenting above, Jamal here took seriously both the spiritual and communal implications of his cross-religious performance. He knew that some people, especially in his own community, could find problems with what he did, and was glad he lived in a place where those problems weren't likely to cause him trouble.

Communal Confrontation Fizzles

The religious extremists in Gwalior were sooner to be found on the Hindu side than on the Muslim, but the local organizer I came across on the hill wasn't having an easy time finding causes to motivate his troops. Arjun Aggarwal was the chairman of one of several Gwalior divisions of the Hindu Mahasabha's Youth Wing. The Hindu Mahasabha is one of the oldest organizations on the Hindu right and—while no longer nationally prominent—has a long history in Gwalior and remains active there. *Youth Wing* is something of a misnomer for Arjun's membership: people could remain in it well into middle age. Arjun was thirty-two and had been a member for twenty years. Born on the hill, he continued to live there with his family in a tall house near the Valmiks' area to the east and a Muslim settlement just up the hill. He had a shop specializing in pulses in a nearby commercial area and said he was happy with his life. I believed him.

Being a leader of the Youth Mahasabha gave Arjun some status—he had a big sign proclaiming his position posted on his door—and an outlet for his energy. But because local issues were hard to come by, he often had to resort to some well-worn national ones. He told me about the function he was planning for later in the week in support of the Hindu nationalist leader L. K. Advani's then recent statements about rebuilding the Ram Mandir at the site of the Babri mosque in Ayodhya. (The mosque was destroyed in 1992, so by 2005 the issue had become pretty stale.) I wondered what kind of audience Arjun would get. Finding local issues took imagination: the Youth Mahasabha was also pressing for guards at Gwalior's major temples. Because terrorists could infiltrate from Pakistan and attack them, said Arjun, there should be armed policemen there from 4:00 to 8:00 p.m., when the temples were most active. But the police demurred, finding no need.

Was it just infiltrators from Pakistan who posed this threat, I asked Arjun, or were local Muslims also involved? No, no, he wasn't worried about local Muslims. "The Muslims that live in Gwalior say that they live in India, that they're Indian." At first he seemed to take this attributed statement as something he believed, distinguishing local Muslims from the Islamic activists he associated with places such as Aligarh. Explaining why he would nevertheless not accept a Muslim as a friend, however, he didn't seem so sure about their Indian bona fides: "How can you trust them? Tomorrow they might go to Pakistan." Arjun lived near Muslims, didn't have much to do with them, and didn't trust them, but their proximity was not a worry. I soon found out why.

We were talking on Arjun's flat roof, and he wanted to show me something. He pointed down to a small, nondescript shrine on the street that went down to the Valmik temple. "Two or three months ago," he told me, "the Muslims took it over (*qabzā kar liyā*)." By this he meant that some nearby Muslims had started offering *sahrās* there. *Sahrās* are short strands of flowers bound together on top and customarily offered at Sufi shrines. But Arjun insisted that this was not a Sufi shrine. Instead it was a fifty-year-old shrine to Shiva. And at a Hindu shrine the custom was to offer not *sahrās*, but *mālās*—flowers strung together as garlands. The Muslims were not honoring the Shiva shrine with flowers—they were, in Arjun's view, desecrating it.[10] The shrine thus had to be "liberated," said

Arjun, employing the language used by those who claimed the Ayodhya site for Hindus by destroying the Babri mosque (*mukta karnā*). In this case, however, Arjun just had to threaten the perpetrating devotees with police action for them to cease and desist. It was difficult for Arjun to find opponents ready to play his game.

Frankly, the site looked to me like a Sufi shrine, although I didn't press the issue with Arjun at the time: it was a platform that held a miniature building with a dome—no familiar Hindu image could be seen. As far as I could make out, it had long been inactive until some local people had started offering reverence to it. Perhaps because they were motivated not by communal assertion but by a surge of customary piety that had not yet led to habit, they decided it wasn't worth a confrontation that would not end nicely for them in any event. Yes, they let themselves be bullied, but this was a battle they saw no point in joining.

I passed by the site several times after my visit with Arjun and noticed neither *sahrās* nor *mālās*: its recent period of activity was clearly over. When I asked people about the shrine and what went on there, nobody had much to say: old inactive shrines are not particularly noteworthy. Certainly, nobody mentioned that an incident had occurred there a few months earlier. Either people wanted to keep neighborhood secrets quiet (Arjun certainly didn't) or, more likely, whatever happened at the site never made much of a public impression. To rally his troops, Arjun would have to try harder.

Ownership and Protest

Violent protest on Satya Narayan hill, however, has in fact occurred, with incidents leading to front-page headlines. The causes were not religious but economic and political—issues of landownership and alleged police brutality. There weren't many renters living on the hill. Most people who moved there did so because they preferred to live in their own house— even if small and inconveniently located—rather than to pay rent in town. The land up the side of the hill was for sale, but the flat top of the hill and some land just below it on the side away from Hippopotamus Street was supposed to be held in public trust. People built there, nevertheless, some- times paying previous squatters for houses and land those had occupied. On August 13 and 14, 2002—just before India's Independence Day of August 15—the municipal authorities decided to crack down. They ended up having to send police reinforcements to clear parts of the hilltop, an area that housed some of the hill's most unfortunate residents.

On the whole, the top of the hill was not a very desirable place to live. It was open to the hot sun and wind, not easily accessible, and had a serious problem with water (fig. 3.5). In general, the further you went up the hill, the worse conditions got. At the bottom of the hill, fronting Hippopotamus Street, a few stately homes, now often subdivided, continue to house the descendants of some old, well-to-do families who first settled there when it offered room for a sizable private compound outside the central city. These families were later joined by middle-class professionals as well as artisans and storekeepers living above their shops. The first layer of houses behind the street had easy access to it, and even more important, to public taps connected to the city water supply. Some of the homes there seemed roomy and well built. Higher up the hill, however, there were no public taps. Although land was cheaper there, the daily hike down the hill for water was more onerous. Poor people built small houses. At the flat top of the hill, where water was pumped up to one spot for an hour or two in the morning, all that many people had in common were their hard-luck stories.

In particular, one hears the story of the closing of the mills. As the former capital of an important princely state, Gwalior had once been a center for large-scale manufacturing. The maharajas were successful in

FIGURE 3.5 A small goddess shrine on the hilltop. The structures on the left and right in the photo are people's houses.

attracting businesses and even starting a few themselves: mopeds were built, pottery made, and biscuits baked and packaged for national distribution. Most important for the local economy, however, was a complex of cloth mills located in a part of town called Birlanagar, named after the prominent Bombay industrial house to which the mills belonged. Founded in the 1930s during princely rule, the mills remained vital in independent India through the mid-1980s. Some of their products, moreover, lent the city some national panache: Gwalior Suiting was long advertised in wide-circulation publications through ads featuring well-turned-out men with haughty gazes.

While the mills were flourishing, they offered thousands of workers steady jobs with union benefits, but when the mills became outmoded, the Birlas decided to close them and build new ones elsewhere. Although some smaller-scale manufacturing had developed during the mills' decline, it was in newer industries that demanded technical skills different from those of the millhands (TV monitors were a going enterprise); the jobs, moreover, were less in quantity and, largely ununionized, in quality, too. People who had spent their working lives in the mills and lived in company housing didn't know what to do or where to go.[11] Several ended up on top of the hill. One of these was the father of Rajesh—Jamal's Brahmin acting friend—Murlidhar Mishra.

Murlidhar had come from a middle-class family in the oldest part of the city—the part near the old fort gate known locally as Gwalior proper. His extended family still had a house there, which Murlidhar's wife continued to refer to as their own. When the mills closed and Murlidhar was left without income, he moved his family to the hilltop near his wife's brother Narendra, who was also suffering from the mills' closing. The two, however, had contrasting responses to the loss of their longtime jobs: one attempting to find a new internal identity, the other pretending to have an old external one.

Narendra had worked at various manufacturing jobs at the mills— weaving cloth and printing it too. Even though he knew his way around machinery, he could not find another job in production in town. Discouraged, he underwent an apparent transformation. A Brahmin who had always had an interest in religious performance, he was now trying to make a living as a professional religious storyteller and musician. He looked the part—wearing beads and keeping a red mark on his forehead—and got some work, but he wasn't very successful at supporting his family from it. Adding to his burden in advancing middle age was a new baby boy, born from a wife they had both presumed was past childbearing age. "It was a mistake," he said sadly. But it was more than that: a new baby for someone his age who dressed as he did and exhorted his listeners to traditional piety wasn't really very seemly, either, and may have contributed to his lack of success in his new career. Narendra's transformation from a longtime factory hand to a householder religious professional seemed incomplete and not particularly fulfilling.

Murlidhar, by contrast, who had worked as an accountant in the mills, managed to keep some continuity in his profession, eventually finding bookkeeping work in town. At his new job, though, Murlidhar felt he had to keep up pretenses. "He's let them think that he lives in the Gwalior house," said his wife, Lakshmi Devi. "At the shop, they call him the Gwaliorwale Pandit, not by the name of this place. . . . We'd be ashamed to invite the shop owner here—we live in this shack." Lakshmi Devi's description of their house was accurate. The couple lived together with their three sons and a daughter-in-law in a single small, roughly built room with a kitchen and a little covered porch. When it rained, the roof leaked. Murlidhar had to live with pretense and poverty, too.

It was difficult for those from the fallen middle and once stably working classes to pretend they were happy on the hilltop, and most didn't even try. In addition to the two Mishra families, these included a high-school-educated son of a policeman supporting his family through day labor, which sometimes made him sick, and an educated Maratha widow who moved there with her children when her husband died. Although she and her now grown son were both working at low-level jobs for the same firm and were managing, they recalled better days. Lakshmi Devi seemed particularly disturbed by her family's current situation. One of the first things she mentioned in our initial conversation was the family house in Gwalior. Even though they didn't live there now themselves, they had some rights to it, and it was a mark of who they really were. She regretted that she had no nice place for visitors to sit. In addition to her current poverty, she commented on the relative isolation of the hilltop, which was not good for her grown sons—one of whom was poorly educated and chronically unemployed. "Coming and going is a problem. When you go down, you don't feel like coming up; and when you're up, you don't feel like leaving." She didn't like not knowing when her sons would come home, but there was no work to be had on the hill. "At least when they're down, they do a little something."

It's finally better, for Lakshmi Devi, if her children are off the hill, even though it's home.

Still, because the hill *was* home, those with less distressing personal histories were able to look at the bright side: the air was good, some would say, and they had nice views—both of which were true. Of course there was a water problem, all admitted, but living on the hilltop was like living in a little village within the city, with a village's peacefulness and community. Some of those who spoke thus had in fact recently come from a village and were happy with a more familiar setting. Others had been there a while but seemed to be doing all right financially, with sturdy, large-roomed houses. One of these was Parsuram Gujar, who talked about the "family relations" (*pārivarik sambandh*) among the people on the hilltop: they were all "loving people" (*premī log*). For Parsuram, the hilltop was indeed his community. He had actually been among the first to settle the hill twenty-two years before and was treated by many as a local elder. Parsuram in fact has had an interest in politics and was sometimes referred to as *netājī*, "respected leader," an epithet for politicians that is sometimes used ironically but not, apparently, here. He thus assumed an important role in the events of August 13 and 14, 2002, when the people on the hilltop did rally as a community against a common foe.

On August 13, following the city magistrate's orders, a joint force from the city and district administrations came to clear the hilltop's illegal settlements. The only way for vehicles to ascend the hill was by a narrow access road up the hill's back side. Once the news of the force's impending arrival reached those on the hill that morning, they organized quickly. Largely women—who were most likely to be home during the day—they offered unexpectedly effective resistance, slowing the advance of the force with their bodies and then protecting the houses. Not until police reinforcements arrived were eleven homes razed. According to news reports these were new, well-made houses, and it wasn't easy to level them.[12] The destruction of those eleven houses, however, was not enough: the full job that the force had come to accomplish was left undone, and the officers in charge said they'd be back. That first day, at least, there were no reports of injuries.

The next day, both sides were better prepared. The civil authorities brought in more police, while the people armed themselves with rocks and a plan of attack, surrounding the intruding party on all sides as they started up the hill. Rocks hit many in that party—including some of its leaders—but no one was hurt too badly. The most seriously injured was a driver named Munnalal Valmik who was bleeding from the head and would require eight stitches.

It was difficult for the police to make the people stop stoning them. The tear gas they first used was ineffective, so they fired in the air (one report says the ranking policeman wanted to fire into the crowd at this point, but the civil magistrate said no). In the melee that followed the shooting, the police started grabbing people to arrest—women, men, young persons—not all, apparently, people who had actually thrown stones. Once those arrested were hauled away, the bulldozers came in. The police, understandably angry and jumpy by now, are said to have forcibly removed people from their homes, sometimes injuring them and damaging their property; there were specific allegations of wanton brutality.[13] Twenty-four houses were razed that day, and forty-two people charged with disturbing the peace and arrested—more women than men.[14] Netaji was among them, and, known as a leader, was a prime defendant in the court case that arose from the day's events. He was held for ten days, he said, although the case against him continued for two years more. But it was finally dropped for political reasons.

The city government in 2002 was dominated by the Congress party, most often championing the cause of the poor but in this case deciding to enforce the law. The member of the national Parliament from the area, however, was from the BJP, a party more oriented toward middle-class business interests in addition to its sometimes aggressive Hindu nationalism. The city government's unfortunate timing of the raid ("it had to take place sometime")[15] together with the overzealous reaction of the police made it easy for the local member of Parliament to make political hay of the situation. "It's a pretty sorry state of affairs," said Jaybhan Singh Pavaiyya, the MP, "when one day before the anniversary of our independence the police do a demonic dance of destruction. The city and police officials on the spot at the time must be held completely responsible." He himself was on the spot right away, listening to victims' stories of horror and offering them sympathy and promising support. Members of his party, he said, were on their way to the state capital to intercede there.[16]

In fact the organized response of the hilltop residents and the consequent reaction of the public took the city government by surprise. Sympathy for the residents was not so difficult to muster even among middle classes prone to favor property law. Not only were the allegations of wanton police brutality too numerous to ignore, but the hilltop settlement also didn't really conflict with any practical middle-class interests: it bordered no nice new colony and did not block any imminent development. It was just a case of poor people staking claims on isolated land nobody else really wanted. Some even had notarized documents to show that had paid previous squatters who claimed ownership: there were rumors of a land mafia with government officials involved. The city magistrate's assertion that he simply wanted to stop further encroachment on government lands did not seem enough of a reason.

In any event, the outcome of the pre–Independence Day raid was messy enough to stall both further threats to the settlement and the case against the residents. Then, in the 2004 elections—despite the Congress victory at Delhi—the Gwalior city government swung toward the BJP, which, fulfilling some electoral promises, managed to get the case closed. The result of the local Congress government's attempt at enforcing the law was both to solidify the de facto ownership rights of the remaining hilltop residents and to lead them to give their political support to the BJP, whose major interests are not typically their own.

The dramatic events on the top of the hill can help give some perspective to life on the slope leading up to it. Although the caste mix of the people on the hilltop is similar to that at other places on the hill, people there seemed less rooted: more were newly arrived, many in the previous eight or ten years. Many, further, had come compelled by very difficult circumstances and with the knowledge that their rights to their homes, while temporarily secure enough, were in fact tenuous. On the hilltop, one doesn't get the feeling of urban density that one finds on the hillside: dispersed on larger plots, the houses sometimes appear as solitary shacks and are often very flimsily built: why invest in construction when your title isn't clear? The (un)built environment conveys a greater sense of individual isolation.

Much of the community that has existed there was stimulated by the ill-fated pre–Independence Day police incursion, which did bring the residents together into intense, active cooperation, and three years later a sense of mutual solidarity remained: many could remember in detail their part in the collective experience, while injured victims recounting their stories of injustice found empathetic listeners. But the community thus born was primarily one of resistance, deriving from the unfortunate circumstances of many of its members and a traumatic, galvanizing event. In this it differed from most of the communities on the hillside, which were older, denser, and generally happier—if not integrated by caste, than by ripened personal relationships. On the hilltop, community seemed more circum-stantial: people found themselves in the same place through different forces of economic adjustment, were brought together by a magistrate's ill-conceived and poorly timed order, and kept together in part by shifting political tides. In the communities closer to the street, by contrast, coher-ence came not through accidental political sparks, but through shared identities and personal affinities that seemed more rooted and enduring.

4

Ethnic Communities and Regional Hinduisms

MAHARASHTRIANS AND SINDHIS

MORE THAN PEOPLE in most countries, Indians living outside their home regions light up when finding out a new acquaintance is from the same local area—particularly if that area is somewhat off the beaten track. Shared local language, customary practices, and religious cultures can bring an immediate sense of affinity between strangers; people may then go on to discover networks of mutual acquaintances. A sense of regional community draws on some larger dimensions of the dynamics of local community seen in the Hippopotamus Street neighborhoods: the rooted interpersonal familiarity of the hillside, for example, or the hilltop's cohesive response to crisis. In regional communities, however, the expanded dimensions of these dynamics can carry more social and political weight. When shared affinities are rooted in a common language and culture, not just in personal dynamics, they become more inclusive and thus a basis for effective political and social action. They can lead not only to regional movements seeking self-government in heterogeneous Indian states, but also to cohesiveness within groups from the same region living elsewhere in India.

People living outside their homeland but still identifying with it are sometimes said to be living in diaspora. A Greek word that was used in the late medieval world to describe the dispersion of the Jews from their Palestinian homeland, *diaspora* has become used in a more general sense. There has been much written about the contemporary Indian diaspora in Africa and Asia as well as the West,[1] but there have also been internal

Indian diasporas: groups of people moving from one region to another, but not forgetting where they came from. These diasporas share many characteristics commonly found in definitions of ethnic groups: they maintain their regional languages, identify with a sometimes romanticized homeland, and are understood by themselves and others as distinct groups.[2] On the ground in India, however, they tend to be treated as broad caste groups—despite any internal diversity their members may know—and the civic associations to which they give rise seem comparable to caste associations, registered societies devoted to the betterment of life within a caste community.[3] This chapter will explore the histories, internal organizations, and contributions to Gwalior's broader religious life of two large ethnic communities who have become rooted in the city: the Maharashtrians and the Sindhis.

Two Ethnic Communities in Gwalior

The Maharashtrians and the Sindhis came to Gwalior at different times and for different reasons: the first the heirs of a former elite that gained power in the area during the late eighteenth century; the second arriving largely as refugees from Pakistan after 1947 to a place where a Sindhi industrialist had already established himself. The two diasporas thus differ as broad types. The Maharashtrians' was an imperial one, an expansion of Maratha adventurers into other parts of the subcontinent in the seventeenth and eighteenth centuries, one that presents a small-scale parallel to what European powers were doing at the same time all over the world. The Sindhi diaspora, by contrast, started in the mid-nineteenth century as one of trade (like that of Chinese in Southeast Asia) but after the partition of British India turned overwhelmingly into a desperate dispersal, as Hindu Sindhis—like Jews in AD 70 and Armenians in 1915—became victims of historical disaster. The internal organization of each of these diasporas in Gwalior is consonant with its corresponding broad type, to be sure, but also reveals the community's own distinctive cultural and political history.

Gwalior Maharashtrians

Although Maratha forces first took the Gwalior fort in 1755,[4] the political situation remained precarious until the final disintegration of the Mughal Empire at the end of the eighteenth century. Large-scale migration of Maharashtrians into Gwalior did not begin until 1810.[5] The new arrivals included soldiers, to be sure, but also administrators, the servants they both brought, and religious officiants who could serve the new population in the style and language to which they were accustomed. For somewhat less than two centuries, Marathi-speakers were, on the whole, privileged inhabitants of the Scindias' city.

In Maharashtra, the new immigrants had known different caste identities. Although some of these identities tended to converge in Gwalior, others remained distinct. At the same time, though, Gwalior Maharashtrians also recognized one another as belonging to a particular broad ethnic group with an origin outside their current North Indian home: alongside caste differences were bonds of language, culture, history, and legend. For both Gwalior Maharashtrians and those among whom they lived, their collective ethnicity as well as their separate castes have provided important group identities.

In diaspora, ethnic similarities among Maharashtrians that were ignored in the homeland became marks of a privileged community, while certain internal caste distinctions counted for less. By the mid-twentieth century at least, only two main Maharashtrian groups were clearly recognized in Gwalior: Brahmins and Marathas. In Maharashtra, Brahmins have been known for traditional occupations of broader scope than those in most of the rest of India. Not just characteristically priests and scholars as elsewhere, Maharashtrian Brahmins were also recognized as men of action: administrators, businessmen, and political leaders. In Gwalior, many of these came to work in the state administration and soon constituted a significant professional class within the city. The Marathas, importantly, included the actual ruling elite: the Scindias themselves together with most of the court and ministers of state. But the Marathas also included people of humbler occupations—soldiers and more. Coming from the land in rural inland Maharashtra, the Marathas had much in common with many industrious farming castes who were also ready to bear arms. As the Marathas' military traditions led to triumphs in the seventeenth and eighteenth centuries, their leading families began to see themselves as Kshatriyas, the elite military class in traditional Hindu society. Their commonalities with peasant castes, however, were never quite forgotten. Thus, in early twentieth-century Maharashtra, Marathas, including some princes, participated in political alliances with peasant castes in opposition to Brahmin political forces.[6] The parallel in Gwalior, however, was a wholesale identification of most non-Brahmin castes from Maharashtra as both Marathas and Kshatriyas. This caste convergence helped at once to consolidate the strength of an elite class with outside origins and to assuage the sensibilities of the ruling Marathas about their predecessors on the land.

Sindhi Hindus

The Sindhis in Gwalior had occupied a place in their homeland different from that of the Maharashtrians. Neither a political elite nor energetic peasants, the Hindus of prepartition Sindh were by and large a prosperous middle class. A minority in the Muslim Northwest of the subcontinent, they were in good part a community of urban traders, but they included a significant class of high government administrators as well. Although a limited number of Hindus were also eventually able to acquire land, the old landed families of Sindh were all Muslim—as were the rulers and nearly all the peasants. This restricted the ways in which Hindus could make a living there, so that alongside the traders and administrators, only a few artisan groups were able to emerge, together with a small caste of Brahmins—the latter treated more as a respected service class than the apex of a socioreligious order.[7]

Although the large population of traders did recognize hereditary groupings among themselves, these were seen sooner as clans of different local origin than hierarchical subcastes. Status among the traders was instead, as might be expected, largely a matter of wealth, while the administrative families—about 10 to 15 percent of the population—were generally well educated and sometime sometimes politically well placed. Tending to look down on the traders, they normally married among themselves.[8] The administrators, called *āmils*, and the traders, known as *bhaibands*, thus in fact did form two caste-like groups: named, professionally differentiated, implicitly ranked, and finding marriage partners among their own. Isolated in Sindh, however, they developed in their own way, without the ethos and rituals of fine-grained caste differentiation still often found in the North Indian plains. The two groups, then—even though caste-like—do not present a neat parallel to the plural ranked castes seen in the last chapter: interdining, importantly, was not an issue between them.[9] Hindu Sindhi communities as wholes, moreover, constituting minorities in Muslim principalities, maintained robust institutions of self-regulation and self-help. These had developed from the established model of village councils and were called, like them, *pancāyats*.

While most Hindu traders of Sindh remained occupied with local markets, others, by the mid-nineteenth century, had ventured far into the wider world. In particular, the handicrafts of Sindh had captured the fancy of European visitors, and crafts from that part of the subcontinent became particularly prized abroad. Trading networks developed throughout the British Empire as Sindhi merchants purveyed "Sindh work" and other fancy goods. Hindu Sindhi businessmen also moved beyond their province to pursue opportunities in other areas of India. In Gwalior, under an industrializing princely regime that encouraged investment from outside, J. B. Mangharam established a biscuit factory that by the 1940s had become a large-scale operation with distribution across North and Central India. After the partition of the subcontinent in 1947, when most Hindu Sindhis found life in Pakistan intolerable, there was a mass emigration to Bombay and, to a lesser extent, Rajasthan. While some of the refugees were eventually able to join relatives settled outside the subcontinent, many others dispersed throughout India. Of these, more than a few found their way to Gwalior, where Mangharam's established presence helped ease their transition. Although not a major center of Sindhi resettlement, Gwalior does have proportionately more Sindhis than most other mid-sized cities outside Maharashtra and Rajasthan—some sources saying as much as 10 percent of the population.

In Gwalior, Sindhi tradespeople eventually prospered. Many started in small goods—underclothing was a specialty—but it wasn't long before Sindhis began running upscale shops and started manufacturing ventures. A refugee community, they worked hard and offered good prices. As in other places, this caused some understandable resentment among the established trading classes, who were now pushed to be more competitive. The increased competition, however, was undeniably good for consumers, who didn't hesitate to patronize Sindhi shops. By the end of the twentieth century, with a new equilibrium in the market, Sindhi businessmen and professionals had been thoroughly integrated into the local economy.

Two Styles of Community Organization

The Sindhis' arrival in Gwalior in the years after Independence coincided with the beginning of the Maharashtrians' decline. By the time of my research for this chapter in 2004 and 2005, the economic arcs of the two communities had crossed: Sindhi businessmen were prospering nicely in increasingly capitalist India—some doing quite well indeed—while the

Maharashtrians, on the whole, had seen better days. At the same time, the different social legacies of the two communities remained evident: the remnants of a settled and stratified elite among the Maharashtrians, with some continuing old political rivalries; a core, relatively homogeneous, trading community among the Sindhis, with inevitable business competition. Both the economic health and the social legacies of the two diasporas were reflected in their community organizations, with Sindhis maintaining vital *pancāyats* and the Maharashtrians having a group of associations, some inherited from a colonial era, that even together seemed less effectual in comparison. The institutions of both diasporas practiced intracommunal charity and promoted ethnic identity, but the Sindhis *did* more.

Two Sindhi Panchayat Organizations

When Sindhis first came to Gwalior in large numbers after 1947, they tended to settle, as in other places in India, within distinct neighborhoods.[10] This facilitated the establishment of local *pancāyats*, community organizations that could help settle disputes among members and provide some useful collective resources. Indeed, it was enthusiastic mention of the latter function that first met my inquiries about the roles of the local *pancāyat*: it maintains large stores of utensils and tableware for common use. Neighborhood Sindhis can borrow from these stores when they need them for weddings and major religious performances—events, of course, to which many in the local community are likely be invited. Sometimes, moreover, officeholders from the local *pancāyat* board will be called on to help settle problems within the local community. Most often, I was told, these are family quarrels, but smaller business disagreements are also heard. Not only a source for banquet supplies, local *pancāyats*, are also a court of first redress.

The local *pancāyat* boards themselves have about fifteen members elected by the Sindhis living in a particular area. As the Sindhi population has grown and dispersed through the city, the number of *pancāyats* has increased, the newer ones often being greater in area but with lesser density of membership. The Venerable Sindh Hindu General Panchayat of Greater Gwalior, a citywide *pancāyat* organization, counted fifty local units in 2005.

The Venerable Panchayat was started not long after partition by J. B. Mangharam, the biscuit manufacturer, and includes representatives from each of the local groups. Taking its initial shape during a time when an increasing refugee population sought to establish itself in a new place and devise an organization for mutual aid, it developed to give Sindhi businessmen prospering in India a vehicle for contributing to expanded community life. By 2005, the Venerable Panchayat maintained eight general committees and sponsored four trusts.

Several of the committees administer charitable projects for less fortunate members of the community. About 250 families receive regular monthly help in the form of cash and supplies from the Welfare Committee. The distribution is boisterous but well organized, with recipients assembling on the second Sunday of the month in a community hall, being called by name, receiving a passbook, and going by a few stations where they collect basic foodstuffs and cash.[11] Members of the Education Committee distribute school supplies to less-well-off Sindhi students at the beginning of the school year. As with the Welfare Committee's distribution, students come personally to collect their supplies from members of the committee themselves, who keep track of the recipients and what they receive. In these cases, work on the committee gives its members an opportunity not only for active community service but also for establishing new contacts and enjoying the company of their peers. Although a chance for personal conviviality is a less obvious benefit for work on the Health and Medical Treatment Committee—which for the most part helps out financially with filling prescriptions and, when necessary, paying for operations—it does give those Sindhi physicians who donate their time a structured opportunity for important personal service. Both vertically among rich and poor and horizontally among the community's more actively involved burghers, these committees are a way in which the *pancāyat* increases community solidarity. Other committees help provide community order.

The Ritual Reform Committee articulates some common norms of social behavior and religious practice: women, for instance, shouldn't dance on the street at weddings (they can do so indoors); the community's Brahmins shouldn't demand more than Rs. 1,100 to perform a wedding (although more can be given freely as donation). This committee also arranges for the collective performance of important life cycle rituals of childhood: the first haircut, done at the *daśahra* holiday in the fall, and the bestowal of the sacred thread, done at Vaisakh in the spring. Although families are not compelled to participate, the majority do: it's much more economical for them than having to pay for separate ceremonies themselves. Many also like participating in a large community event, one in which all the Sindhi Brahmins are there working at once. As with that of the education and welfare committees, the work here, too, brings together practical concerns with an experience of community solidarity.

The force of established community solidarity is what backs up the work of the Justice Committee, which resolves conflicts that the local committees can't manage. These seem to be most of the more serious cases, as well as those involving people from different neighborhoods. In addition to problems among family members (quarrels among brothers are common), these include disagreements over marriage arrangements and business deals. Even for cases within the community involving significant monetary claims, the Panchayat is often more appealing than the civil legal system. In addition to being cheaper (no lawyer required!), it is also much faster. While a case proceeding through the courts often takes years, the committee attempts to come to judgments within a few days: community members should resolve their conflicts quickly and move on. Further, the committee attempts to function more as a mediating body aiming for reasonable compromise than as a court ruling in favor of one side alone. People expect to get at least some satisfaction. But even when parties remain unsatisfied, I was told, they are still likely to abide by the committee's decision because it carries the weight of the area's Sindhi community at large. Defiance would involve significant social consequences. Only very rarely does a case that has been taken to the committee then proceed to the civil authorities. Anand Karara, general secretary of the Venerable Panchayat for two and a half years when I spoke with him, said that during his time 540 cases had come to the Justice Committee and only two had wound up in civil court.

The Venerable Panchayat's standing charitable trusts provide funds earmarked for continuing regular expenses. Two support the work of committees, with one supplying grain and cash to the Welfare Committee and another providing the Health and Medical Treatment Committee with money for drugs and hospital expenses. Two other trusts aid young adults from less prosperous families: one is for college scholarships; another for the considerable expenses associated with a daughter's wedding (including dowry and a reception). In helping young adults get settled comfortably through professional degrees and marriage, the Panchayat promotes the prosperity of the community as a whole.

Certainly, most of the organized Sindhi charity remains within the community, but not all of it does. Soon after witnessing the distribution of school supplies to students from less fortunate Sindhi families,

I was invited to a well-publicized distribution of similar items at a local non-Sindhi orphanage. There was a function with local dignitaries and journalists in attendance; cameras flashed as students came to collect their books, uniforms, and other supplies. Humanitarian motives notwithstanding, the event was also a good public relations gesture for a somewhat insular business community.

Although the Venerable Sindh Hindu Panchayat of Greater Gwalior had existed for more than fifty years before I came to know it, it was only registered with the state government as an official society with bylaws in 1984—the result, it seems, of an internal coup. Younger members of the Panchayat, I was told, resenting the hegemony of an older leadership that wasn't ready to give them the active roles they wanted, applied to register the society with themselves as officers. Able to gain the support of a substantial majority of the local *pancāyats* (twenty of the twenty-two then in existence), they persuaded the state government of their case. At the time, there was too much bad blood for the older leaders, who retained some support, to join the new in subordinate positions, so that group registered their own society. Dropping the honorific "Venerable" (*pūjya*) from their name, they called it simply the Sindh Hindu Panchayat of Greater Gwalior.

Of the two organizations, the revitalized Venerable Panchayat is definitely the more robust, with its fifty local *pancāyats* and a leadership group including men in their thirties and forties who like to get things done. By contrast, the older leaders of the other Panchayat (some remaining since 1984) coordinate only twenty local units and tend to conduct business more slowly and genteelly. The smaller Panchayat also has fewer committees than the Venerable Panchayat—retaining the five important ones from the time of the split[12]—with the programs that duplicate those of the Venerable Panchayat tending to be quieter, scaled-down versions of what the others do. The welfare distribution, for example, draws a considerably smaller crowd, and is conducted largely by a single person with a couple of helpers. At the same time, however, the smaller Panchayat has also started a new initiative to facilitate marriage arrangements among Sindhis in the region. Following the recent lead of other caste associations, some of its active members have begun to arrange large events where prospective brides and bridegrooms and their families can meet one another. Having two *pancāyats* can provide more options.

Leaders from both *pancāyats* say they have tried to reunite them, but blame the other side for intransigence. As long as those in charge of each group at the time of their split remain in authority, as was the case in

2005, it would be hard to see the two *pancāyats* uniting. Nevertheless, the two do sometimes manage to cooperate effectively. This is facilitated by the fact that although the majority of local *pancāyats* send representatives to only one citywide *pancāyat*, some of the larger locals send representatives to both. Thus, institutionalized avenues of communication remain open at ground level and events can be coordinated.

When reflecting on the lasting split in the community, Prakash Chaudhary, a vice chairman of the Venerable Panchayat, became reflective: even though it looks bad that the Sindhis do not present a single united front, he admitted, the competition to which the division gives rise is one of good works, which can benefit the community as a whole.[13] Perhaps, moreover, this competition increases cohesion within each of the two teams: Shrichand Valecha, the Venerable Panchayat's longtime chairman, says that he has no problem letting the others do what they want—it's their choice; nevertheless, among his fifty local *pancāyats*, at least, there's more unity than will be found in any citywide Sindhi Panchayat in India.[14] Even if they have polarized around two centers, the Sindhis of Gwalior are at least enthusiastic and well organized.

Many Maharashtrian Associations

If the Gwalior Sindhis' two organized competitive teams reflect the spirit of an active business community, the much looser organization of the Gwalior Maharashtrians suggests a more segmented group that has lost some of its important internal moorings. Long settled in and with its own internal stratifications, the Gwalior Maharashtrians once knew a center of influence and patronage in the Scindia court and administration. Certainly no basis of quasi-democratic organization like the Sindhi *pancāyat*, the court nevertheless did provide a common reference point and some genuine political and economic advantage. Although loyalty to the still powerful Scindia family continues to exercise a pull on Marathas especially, that alone is not enough to provide a practical nexus for the interests of all Maharashtrians. Different caste and community organizations have developed to serve specific groups, and they operate more or less on their own.

The Marathas have two associations, each focused on a separate education-oriented institution and both led by members of the old Maratha noble families, called Sardars. The Maharashtra Kshatriya Benevolent Society (*mahārāṣṭra kṣatriya hitcintak sabhā*) operates a hostel for Maratha college students who live outside the city. The hostel is located on one of Gwalior's busier commercial streets, next to a similar hostel for Rajput students; on my visits to the hostel in 2004, the head of the trust supporting it, Sardar A. B. Phalke, could often be found sitting at the upscale electrical appliance store he owns across the street. Started by the royal family at the beginning of the twentieth century, the hostel was intended for young men descended from old Maratha fighters and now settled in outlying rural areas: the hostel would make it easier for them to get a modern education. Rent is free or subsidized, depending on family income. When I visited the hostel in 2004, however, I was told that only ten or fifteen of its twenty-five rooms were filled. Yes, there were enough Maratha students to fill it, said one of the clerks, but the hostel has rules that date from an earlier era and today's boys often don't want to abide by them. For many of them, little or no rent just isn't worth having to be in by 10:00 p.m. Another association, the Maratha Welfare Society (*marāṭhā hitkāriṇī sabhā*) maintains a primary school in a compound called Shivaji Bhavan (after the seventeenth-century Maratha warrior Shivaji), where the Society's longtime president, Sardar P. K. Kadam, also held office. Originally built for Maratha children, the school is in a neighborhood that is now mostly Muslim—and so, consequently, are most of its students. Although pictures of Shivaji can be found on display in the office, there's not much market for teaching Maharashtrian culture here—not to mention Marathi language. What *is* Maratha about the school, explained Kadam, is the teaching staff: the school gives employment to Maratha women. Neither the Benevolent Society's hostel nor the Welfare Society's primary school quite fulfill the purposes for which they were intended. In the first decades of the twenty-first century, the societies have been working, with lesser and greater success, at adjusting their principal institutions to new situations.

Although maintaining the primary school is the most ambitious project of the Maratha Welfare Society, Kadam also mentioned a few others. Like the Sindhis' Venerable Panchayat, the Maratha Welfare Society helps poorer families in the community with funds for medical treatment and wedding expenses for their daughters. While these activities, as with similar ones among the Sindhis, help maintain practical social solidarity, the other project Kadam mentioned is more symbolic. The Marathas are Kshatriyas, Kadam explained, a military people, and celebrate *daśahrā*, a Hindu festival held in special regard by Kshatriyas. Because the contemporary embodiment of Kshatriya hood is found in army men "of any caste," Kadam explained, "I help our defense people every year." At *daśahrā* he gives a small cash gift for the local forces, a gesture that seemed personally important to him.[15] Kadam's use of the first person here, while perhaps partly just a manner of speech, is also indicative of his role in the Maratha Welfare Society, which as chair, he seems to manage pretty much single-handedly: he never mentioned a board. My appointments with him were one-on-one affairs—a contrast to those I made with individual leaders of the Venerable Sindhi Panchayat, where one or two others would always show up. While the Panchayat consistently maintained its sense of collectivity, with Sardar Kadam, as well as with Sardar Phalke, one sooner got the sense of individual Sardars' feelings of noblesse oblige: they had taken on the responsibilities of smallish, established organizations out of a sense of honor and obligation—and treated them, at least in part, as personal projects.

The main project of the Maharashtrian Brahmin Society, by contrast, was clearly a collective one: a funerary institution named Vaikunth Dham, "heavenly abode." Coming from another region, the Maharashtrian Brahmins have preserved rites differing substantially from the North Indian rites commonly practiced in Gwalior. The full funerary rites are elaborate, taking place over a number of days that mark different stages in the soul's transition from earthly to heavenly realms. Vaikunth Dham provides a place for these rites to be performed properly and efficiently at relatively low cost. According to Shantaram Moghe, president of the Society in 2004, it was built at a cost of 1,600,000 rupees (then about $40,000)—money raised from the largely middle-class Maharashtrian Brahmin community, for whom reasonable contributions might well be considered money well expended. "Other priests," said Moghe, "are charging more than five thousand, six thousand, eight thousand. They are bargaining."[16] The Society, on the other hand, did everything for thirteen hundred rupees, using its own priests on regular salary. The place was bustling when I visited, with three sets of funeral rites proceeding at different stages of completion. Vaikunth Dham's services are not restricted to local community members, and are also sometimes used by Maharashtrian Brahmins residing elsewhere in Madhya Pradesh and by South Indians resident in Gwalior: the Maharashtrian rites are closer to the South Indian than are the usual North Indian rites. But for the most part, Vaikunth Dham was meant to serve the Maharashtrian Brahmins of the city. "We perform the religious functions of the Maharashtrian people. We want them to join together and jointly. . . perform" the rites. Death, too, can be an impetus to community solidarity.

Beyond the separate institutions for Brahmins and Marathas is the Maharashtra Samaj, which considers itself "the parent body" of Maharashtrians in Gwalior: it is for all Marathi-speakers. The board of the Maharashtra Samaj, when I met it, included some familiar faces. Officials of the Maharashtrian Brahmin Sabha were well represented, as well as a local leader of a religious movement formed around a Maharashtra-based guru with an organized following in the city. Present also, however, were leaders of other, less parochial cultural institutions—founded in better days by good Maharashtrian citizens to serve a broad constituency and maintained in substantial part by their families and others from their community. These include a theater group putting on plays in Marathi and Hindi and an institution for women's welfare. Although a fair share of the people in attendance were Maratha, the Sardar leaders of the two Maratha Kshatriya organizations were missing. The meeting, in fact, seemed to be a chummy, middle-class affair—not really an atmosphere that old aristocrats would find congenial. Indeed, among other benefits, meetings of the Maharashtra Samaj leadership provide a comfortable forum for civic-minded Maharashtrians to get together, share ideas, and, perhaps, coordinate projects.

The explicit goals of the Maharashtra Samaj are social and cultural. It attempts to maintain Maharashtrian culture in Gwalior by supporting activities for children and especially by staging public celebrations at Maharashtrian holidays. In particular, it sponsors a large-scale Ganesh puja, a multiday Hindu religious festival that is performed more elaborately in Maharashtra than in most other parts of India.[17] It also celebrates Makar Sankranti, another Hindu holiday of which Maharashtrians are particularly fond. The Maharashtra Samaj of Gwalior shows off these celebrations publicly in its own Hindi-speaking city.

At the same time, the Maharashtra Samaj makes arrangements for observance of more secular holidays, too, which appeal to different segments of the community. Shivaji's day can be a celebration of general Maharashtrian nationalism but has a special appeal for Marathas, who see Shivaji as their greatest hero. Vir Savarkar was a Maharashtrian Brahmin revered by many Indians as a fighter for Indian independence but who was also one of the first ideologues of right-wing Hindu nationalism: his day can be particularly special for Maharashtrian Brahmins and Hindu nationalists—constituencies that in fact often overlap. Bhimrao Ramji Ambedkar, on the other hand, a leader more active than Savarkar at the actual time of independence, had risen from the lowest of social positions to become a champion of the rights of groups facing the very strongest caste discrimination. In celebrating Ambedkar's day, the Maharashtra Samaj makes clear it is meant to serve all Marathi speakers. Described as rather tame affairs—perhaps featuring a lecture by a local notable—the celebrations of these secular holidays are nevertheless performed regularly. As continuing active appeals to different groups of Maharashtrians, however, they merely help the Maharashtra Samaj to become an inclusive umbrella; the Samaj does not seriously attempt to bring all Marathi-speakers together to interact practically as a community. This suggests, of course, that the majority of Maharashtrians feel no need to participate actively in community-oriented activities. Indeed, Maharashtrians are very nicely integrated into Gwalior's religiocultural landscape, so much so that a few of their characteristic religious institutions even play roles in the religious life of the city as a whole.

Two Regional Hinduisms in the Religious Life of the City

Maharashtrians and Sindhis both practice styles of Hinduism that differ in noticeable ways from that of the generic North Indian variety commonly practiced in Gwalior, but each community, in different degrees, offers religious resources on which other Gwalioris can and do draw. Each does this, however, through its own dynamics of difference. Because Maharashtrian variants of Hinduism do in fact have many similarities to those in the North, ordinary Gwalior Hindus can be readily drawn to those of its traditions that fill religious niches not nicely served by other local resources. This is not the case, though, with a number of frequently performed Hindu Sindhi practices, which many North Indians may not see as their own at all. Still, many Gwalior residents appreciate the annual procession organized by the Sindhi community at its regular annual festival—presented in a generic Hindu style and by all accounts the most elaborate religious display in town.

Sindhi Distinctiveness and Its Public Display: The Jhulelal Procession

Hindu traditions in Sindh developed in an area cut off from the main lines of Indic religious tradition, strongly influenced by those of the Punjabi Sikhs to the immediate east and by mystical strains of the surrounding

Islam. Most Hindus in Sindh were Nanakpanthis: people who revere
Nanak, the first Sikh guru, together with the canonical compilation of
his and his successors' verses, the Guru Granth—but who do not observe
the customs followed by Khalsa Sikhs, the visible Sikh majority since at
least the early twentieth century.[18] This Sikh majority has deliberately kept
itself outwardly distinctive, most visibly among its men, who are enjoined
to keep their hair unshorn, tied up under a turban. Sindhi men, by contrast, are normally short-haired and bare-headed and are not bound by any
Khalsa Sikh customary restrictions. This means, importantly, that Sindhi
Nanakpanthis could thus also be most liberal in their reverence for Hindu
deities, different Sufi saints, and local Hindu holy persons—all of whom
flourished in Sindh. Although Hindu Sindhis in diaspora have begun to
stress the mainstream Hindu elements of their traditions, many remain
quite comfortable with syntheses that diverge greatly from those more
commonly seen in Hindu India.

Some normal Sindhi religious practices, moreover, may strike others
as characteristically non-Hindu. Thus, although Sindhi men don't wear
turbans, following Muslim as well as Sikh practice they cover their heads
in a place of worship—usually with a handkerchief, its corners tucked
behind the ears to keep it in place. Religious practice among Sindhis var-
ies widely, sometimes in ways with which many North Indian Hindus find
it difficult to identify. Alongside small Sindhi ashrams in common Hindu
molds, for example, Gwalior also has semiprivate establishments dedicated to Sindhi saints—where Sindhi religious verse might be chanted in
styles showing obvious Near Eastern influence. Sindhis sometimes sponsor recitations from the Guru Granth by Khalsa Sikhs or chant characteristic Sikh holy phrases, such as *vāhī guru*. At the same time, individual
Sindhis, following styles of holy man-oriented piety particularly popular in
Sindh, adapt nicely to forms of religious practice familiar to many Gwalior
Hindus: many are avid visitors of Gwalior's Sufi shrines and active in
branches of its guru-centered movements. The two main Sindhi temples
attempt to offer most of the varied strands of piety favored by the community under one roof. Together with devotions sung in familiar North
Hindu prayer-tunes, one can hear a Near East–inflected style of chant and
regular readings from the Guru Granth—the latter kept on respectful display alongside images of the major Hindu divinities and of a few Sindhi
Hindu saints. Traditions from different Near Eastern and Indic sources,
however, give pride of place to the worship of a deity that is distinctly
Sindhi: a figure with a white beard named Jhulelal. Although Jhulelal is

depicted according to popular Indian iconographic norms, he is not in fact known to most Hindus: he took birth in Sindh and has come to be a symbol of Sindhi Hindu identity.

Jhulelal came into the world, they say, during dark times: an oppressive Muslim king was pressing Hindu Sindhis to convert to Islam on pain of death. The Hindu leaders (*panchs*) prayed to Varuna, lord of the Indus (and the waters generally), and there was soon born a miraculous child who successfully challenged the oppressive king. As a savior who descends in a time of crisis, Jhulelal is not only a distinctly Sindhi divinity, but also a recognizably Hindu one, taken by many Sindhis as an avatar of Vishnu—a divinity from the highest heavens who comes down to this world when his devotees face disaster. Jhulelal thus gives Sindhi Hindus their own place in the broader Hindu world. In painted images, he is usually depicted as a bearded old man who sits upon a red flower on top of a fish swimming in the Indus. In temples, however, Jhulelal is often set high on a swing suspended from the ceiling (*jhūlā* means "swing"), where he may sway back and forth during celebrations (fig. 4.1). He is the deity above all.

FIGURE 4.1 Jhulelal on a swing in the Sindhi temple at Madho Ganj. To the right is a stand holding covered copies of the Guru Granth. Above that are lithographs of Guru Nanak and Hindu deities.

Jhulelal was originally the patron deity of the Lohanas—an extended clan group including the majority of Hindu Sindhis—and was consciously popularized in Bombay in the 1950s as a special deity for all Sindhis around the world. Spearheaded by a professional singer named Ram Panjwani, the Jhulelal movement found much of its initial appeal through newly written devotional hymns that were circulated widely in India and abroad. The movement was a cultural intervention as well as a religious one, taken up by the less pious in good part because it offered a vivid icon of Sindhi Hindu identity in diaspora.[19] Indeed, it is this new conscious Sindhi identity—sometimes called *sindhayat*, "Sindhiness"— that may be playing the biggest role in diminishing the significance of the Sindhis' old caste-like distinctions, a fact that some Sindhis explicitly recognize: "caste has ceased to be very important after partition—we are all Sindhis after all."[20]

In Gwalior, the most vivid public expression of Sindhiness is the Jhulelal procession, the culmination of his forty-day festival period that takes place annually in the rainy season. Large floats depicting Jhulelal, other Hindu deities, and Sindhi saints are paraded through the streets of the main bazaar area. Bands are booked from as far away as Bombay and Dehra Doon; when night falls, the central plaza is filled with colored neon lights. Probably more impressive to a wide audience than any other regular religiocultural event in town, the Jhulelal procession was often the first thing mentioned when I would ask ordinary Gwalioris about public religious display. The Jhulelal procession offers a great many floats displaying popular Hindu deities such as Shiva and Krishna in various guises. At the same time, it presents images celebrating aspects of Hindu Sindhi distinctiveness, with floats to Jhulelal and to Sindhi holy men largely unknown outside the community. In this it resembles processions by other Hindu regional, caste, or sectarian communities—who frequently display their own particular revered figures among great Hindu gods, thus dignifying them as well as making them better known.

In my initial recollections of the Jhulelal procession, I thought it must have also included floats to Guru Nanak and the Guru Granth, still dear to many in the Sindhi community. When I looked at some videorecordings of the procession taken in 2005, though, I couldn't find them—if some hints of Sindhi Nanakpanthi heritage were evident in the parade, they weren't prominent at all. This is probably because Guru Nanak and the Guru Granth are too closely identified with Khalsa Sikhs, who present Sikhism as a religion separate from Hinduism. And although Sindhi

Hindus in India tend to be proud of their regional identity and traditions, most want to be religiously identified clearly as Hindus first of all.[21]

The Added Resources of Maharashtrian Tradition: Dholi Buwa and Raja Bakshar

In contrast to Sindh, Maharashtra is contiguous with Hindi-speaking North India. Its traditions have developed in continuity with those in the North, and the differences in the religious life of their respective Hindus— compared to Hindu Sindhis, at least—have not been very wide. Thus, most Gwalior religious traditions recognized as distinctly Maharashtrian do not depart much from comfortable North Indian norms. Although Maharashtrian patrons have built temples to Dattatreya, Vitobha, and other Hindu deities popular in Maharashtra but not commonly worshipped in the North, most Gwalioris have at least heard stories about these deities and don't find the everyday forms of worship offered to them especially unusual. What they see is a familiar form of Hinduism, but one oriented to deities toward which most of them are not particularly drawn. And although Maharashtrian Brahmin funeral practices are distinctive enough to warrant a separate caste institution, they still appear as variants of familiar Hindu customs.

Two aspects of Maharashtrian Hinduism, however, have been the source of religious institutions in Gwalior that do not appear to be simple variants of common North Indian traditions. Both concern areas where religious boundaries can more readily be fuzzier in Maharashtra than in the North, including (1) a blurring of sectarian divisions between Vaishnava and Shaiva religious lineages *within* Hinduism; and (2) an extension of this blurring, in the realm of popular mysticism, to the broad Hindu or Islamic identity of extraordinary holy persons.[22] Although Gwalior Hindus, as we have seen in chapter 2, are drawn to the shrines of Muslim saints, they see them as distinctly Muslim, not ambiguously Hindu *and* Muslim. Maharashtra, however, has produced popular holy persons such as Shirdi Sai Baba who have transcended a limited identification with either Hinduism or Islam.[23] As it happens, the two Maharashtrian traditions in Gwalior I have encountered that have significant non-Maharashtrian followings (there may well be more) are both boundary-blurring ones: the Dholi Buwa lineage of gurus, which recognizes dual Shaiva and Vaishnava origins; and a set of three shrines to Raja Bakshar, a figure who presents an ambiguous Hindu and Muslim identity. In the case of Raja Bakshar, the style of worship that developed from his ambivalent Hindu and Muslim identity was obviously crucial to his wider appeal. The mixed sectarian origin of the Dholi Buwa lineage was probably less important for its success, although it may have helped broaden the base of its later gurus as civic religious leaders. More crucial for the popularity of the Dholi Buwa gurus has been the particular Maharashtrian style of musical storytelling they practice, which has no neat local counterpart.

The founder of Gwalior's Dholi Buwa lineage—Mahipati Nath—came, they say, at the request of its Maharaja Daulat Rao (r. 1794–1827), who wanted to learn raja yoga from him.[24] Although Mahipati Nath himself was a celibate yogi, his spiritual lineage was eventually continued by Kashi Nath Purandare, a nephew on his mother's side, who was a family man. Since then, the religious lineage has continued within the Purandare family at a large compound on the western edge of Lashkar. Known as the Dholi Buwa *math*—a term used most often for a strictly monastic establishment—it grew up around Mahipati Nath's memorial tomb. Flourishing as religious performers, members of the Dholi Buwa lineage continue to give presentations at the *math*, other temples, and private religious events. They also perform frequently in public forums: the reigning Dholi Buwa has been a featured performer at the annual celebration of Mir Badshah as well as at the yearly public worship of the Scindia dynasty's patron Sufi saint, Mansur—both discussed in chapter 2 (fig. 4.2). The continuing association of the lineage with the Scindias can give its reigning head, himself usually just called Dholi Buwa, an exalted civic religious position.

The term Nath seen in the names of the gurus of the lineage indicates that they claim a spiritual descent from Nath yogis—who, though generally taken as Shaiva, have often lurked on the margins of sectarian identity and frequently appear when blurred religious identities come to the fore.[25] *Dholi* in the name of the lineage derives from *dhol*, a big drum, and *Buwa* is a Maharashtrian honorific. While still maintaining a Nath lineage and talking privately, at least, about yogic practice, members of the extended Dholi Buwa lineage are known primarily for their performances, which feature a signature introductory drumbeat. Although the stories told at Dholi Buwa performances may feature tales of Nath yogis, they are often given a devotionally didactic turn characteristic—in North India, at any rate—of Vaishnava traditions. Indeed, in Maharashtra, Nath tradition is generally not seen to be strictly Shaiva, as it usually is in the North. Maharashtrian Naths instead are liable to trace a lineage from the legendary Nivritti Nath to the inspired fourteenth-century Marathi poet Sant

FIGURE 4.2 Dholi Buwa in ceremonial garb at public worship of Mansur.

Jnaneshwar and through him also to the broader Maharashtrian tradition of sant-poets—which included a number of figures such as Tukaram who were strongly pulled toward the Vaishnava worship of Vitthala at Pandharpur. Santosh Purandare, the son of the lineage head reigning at the turn of the twenty-first century, affirms the dual allegiance matter-of-factly: "We are Naths and Vaishnavas both."[26]

Pointing to a long and spiritually inclusive pedigree, the Dholi Buwa lineage presents itself as a charismatic family, with links to the old Gwalior court and aristocracy. It offers a decorous Vaishnava-laced Nath performance tradition with a broad appeal that reaches well into the middle and upper classes of the Gwalior public. Although active links with the royal house appear to have become tenuous after Mahipati Nath's passing, they were renewed with Balkrishna Nath, who reigned as guru for twenty-four years around the turn of the twentieth century. Balkrishna seems to have cut a particularly charismatic figure, gifted at religious performance. He impressed the Scindia monarch at the time, Madhav Rao (r. 1886–1925) to such an extent that the maharaja got his first wife, Chinku Raje, initiated by him. A guru-disciple relationship established with the royal house made it easy for Balkrishna to strengthen religious relationships with many of the noble families of the era. Marriage alliances between these families and the Purandares soon followed. By the beginning of the twentieth century, then, the extended family of Dholi Buwa was nicely enmeshed in the local aristocracy. The performance style cultivated in the Dholi Buwa lineage thus developed to suit Gwalior's more refined classes, drawing on Maharashtrian conventions that were greatly influenced by Vaishnava kirtan styles. These featured musical interludes in the storytelling when formulaic dance poses were displayed and stately circumambulations made (fig. 4.3).[27] Dholi Buwa's religious performances continue to be didactically inspiring, musically engaging, and eminently dignified.

While Dholi Buwa's elegant performances, usually presented with a small troupe, draw many from the higher classes, worship at the Raja Bakshar shrines features intense drumbeats that have a more popular

FIGURE 4.3 A senior member of the Dholi Buwa family strikes a stylized pose during an outside performance.

appeal. In Gwalior, Raja Bakshar has a fairly humble public presence, an object of worship at three small to medium-sized temples in town, none especially well known to the general populace or having much obviously well-heeled clientele. Two nevertheless still enjoy patronage from the court: the smallest, which does not see much action as far as I can tell, is actually on the outskirts of the palace grounds; and the most vibrant, off a busy section of a Lashkar commercial district called Daulat Ganj, receives an annual stipend from the court (although inflation has reduced it primarily to a token of continuing patronage). The Suryavanshi family, which manages the Daulat Ganj temple, also tells of a forebear being invited from Maharashtra by a reigning Gwalior Maharaja—as was Dholi Buwa's Mahipati Nath. The Suryavanshis came well after Mahipati, though, at the end of the nineteenth century.

A Maharashtrian figure on the Gwalior scene arriving later than the Dholi Buwa lineage, Raja Bakshar, like Dholi Buwa, finds some roots among the Naths. The priests at the two main Raja Bakshar temples both suggest that the saint worshipped at their Raja Bakshar temples is actually Baba Chaitanya Nath, a Hindu Nath ascetic. What one sees at these temples, however, is an aniconic form of religious observance that is strongly reminiscent of practices at some Sufi shrines. The principal worship is accompanied by a fast, pulsing drumbeat that is more reminiscent of Sufi styles than of anything in the common Hindu liturgical repertoire. And as at Sufi shrines, the main worship takes place on Thursday evenings, around the replica of a tomb, with the drumming, like Sufi qawwali, sometimes inducing a trance-like state in participants. The participants here, however, are mostly Hindu and use the Hindu term *āratī* to refer to the worship, itself presided over by hereditary lineages of Maharashtrian Hindu priests. Although the priests at both shrines admitted aspects of the shrines' Hindu/Muslim provenance, they were not both equally proud of it.

On Thursday evenings, the Raja Bakshar shrine at Daulat Ganj is an exciting place. The drummers here are especially skilled—sometimes professional musicians—and many of the worshippers, packed into the shrine's small area, seem drawn inward, lost in the drumbeat. Inside, there are smells of sweat and incense. From the courtyard outside, the overflow crowd (including all the women) peer in intently. Until the drums reach their climax, the place could easily be mistaken for a straightforward Sufi shrine. But as the service concludes, it winds down with Sanskrit chants, and the shrine priests, with Hindu forehead markings, come to the fore.

One of the Suryavanshi sons, who had looked particularly absorbed during the drumming, performs healing rituals for children brought to him by anxious parents. The healer's father, the head of the family, looks on benignly and greets members of the dispersing crowd—which is mostly non-Maharashtrian and almost exclusively Hindu.

Here, Raja Bakshar, too, is without doubt really a Hindu. In conversations with the Suryavanshi family, I was told that "Baba Chaitanya Nath is a Hindu name," which was later changed to Raja Bakshar. The old Nath, it seems, had the foresight to anticipate the famous temple-plundering of the Mughal emperor Aurangzeb, so asked his disciples to build him not a Hindu-style *samādhi*—as memorial tombs are called—but a Muslim-style *dargāh*, a common Urdu term for Sufi shrine (fig. 4.4). As a Hindu Nath yogi disguised as a Muslim, I was told, his tradition was able to survive.

Raja Bakshar has a decidedly more ambivalent identity at his temple over in Jinsi Nala, about a ten-minute walk away. The signboard over the lane leading into it from the street indicates in parentheses that it is also a *dargāh*, and two names adorn the freshly renovated shrine itself. One, engraved in the new marble, calls it a temple to Chaitanya Nath Raja Bakshar, who is given the title Satguru, "the true guru." Above that is a professionally made plaque in Islamic green calling it a *dargāh* to Shri Pir Saheb Raje Vali. That name contains both Hindu and Islamic elements. *Śri* is an honorific usually used for Hindus, and *Raje* (a Maharashtrian

FIGURE 4.4 Inside the Raja Bakshar Dargah, Daulat Ganj.

form of the Hindi and Sanskrit Raja) normally denotes a Hindu king—Muslim rulers used other titles. Pir Saheb, by contrast, means a respected Sufi master and Vali, meaning *friend*, is a Sufi term for someone close to God. Raja Bakshar is both the guru Chaitanya Nath, and a Sufi who somehow seems partly Hindu.

With its renovations, the Jinsi Nala shrine is larger than the one at Daulat Ganj, and the Thursday night worship seems less packed. It also seems less excited, with people sitting on the floor while the drum plays a fast but less complex rhythm. The priest himself is clearly worked up during the *āratī*, but most of the rest don't seem too absorbed, some looking around to appreciate the obviously mixed Hindu and Muslim crowd. Here, too, the crowd is mostly North Indian—most in Western clothes but with a few Hindus and Muslims sporting religioculturally distinctive dress.

Devotees I talked to were proud of the shrine's dual identity: "At this shrine, Hindus and Muslims pray together, in other places they fight." But still, the togetherness could sometimes be complicated. The shrine's 'urs—its annual festival—is a three-day affair with three separate feasts. On the first day is a special meal for Brahmins, with Maharashtrian food, and on the second, a large event for everyone with the usual vegetarian banquet fare of fried bread (*pūrīs*), pulses, and vegetable curries. The feast on the third day, however—for the Muslim fakirs—is decidedly nonvegetarian, entailing the sacrifice of a goat, followed by qawwali into the night. The shrine thus accommodates everyone—often together, but sometimes separately, especially at an event such as collective dining that strongly impacts orthodox sensibilities. Like the Raja Bakshar temple at Daulat Ganj, this one, too, attracts Hindus drawn to a style of piety normally found at Sufi shrines, but who are more comfortable with a divine presence taken as at least somehow Hindu. Here, though, the ambiguity of that presence is more greatly appreciated.

Regional Traditions in Local Religious Life: Give and Take

The *āratīs* for Raja Bhakshar, the performances of Dholi Bua, and the Sindhis' Jhulelal procession are all visible contributions of diaspora communities to the public religious life of the city. These Maharashtrian and Sindhi traditions differ, however, in the ways and degrees to which they are perceived as somehow foreign—clearly diverging from local culture—and consequently in their roles in integrating their communities into broader Gwalior worlds. Paradoxically, the two Maharashtrian traditions seem at once more foreign and more tightly woven into Gwalior's socioreligious fabric. Although Raja Bakshar's appeal is quite different from that of Dholi Bua, they both offer an experience—intense rhythm with an ambiguous identity at one; a form of stately performance at the other—not regularly found in North Indian Hinduism. Each thus has something special to offer certain kinds of religious aficionados. Ordinary Gwalioris who participate in these traditions recognize their foreignness and appreciate it: no place else in the Northern regions they know has anything quite like them. At the same time, they also see these traditions as nicely enmeshed within the local Gwalior religious world—naturalized in part by the long presence of a large and influential Maharashtrian population. The Sindhis' annual Jhulelal procession, by contrast, is eagerly awaited by many ordinary Gwalioris, but not many of these see it as a distinctly Sindhi tradition. For most it is instead basically a modern, Hindu-style religious festival parade—with some floats featuring a few unfamiliar divine beings, to be sure, but the best regularly occurring procession in town!

Although the Sindhi community has been economically integrated into Gwalior life, its strong internal cohesion means that many of its members don't mix much socially outside it, and its distinctive religious traditions— more different than the Maharashtrians to begin with—have barely been naturalized at all. Most local people who have observed those traditions are likely to see them as something other than their own—maybe not even entirely Hindu. The Sindhis for their part, however—feeling exiled from their homeland because of their religion—in fact have a strong Hindu identity. They want others to see them as they see themselves: Sindhis with a right to their own religious culture and 100 percent Hindu, too. Their annual festival, culminating in a procession that emphasizes the more generically Hindu aspects of their tradition, can be seen as an effort toward that end. Not a niche experience for aficionados, it is meant to appeal to the masses. What might be the effects it produces on them, religious and otherwise?

Against patterns of flashing multicolored lights mounted high on the roofs of buildings in the main bazaar, crowds of ordinary Gwalioris watch as float after float passes by. Images of all the familiar deities are there, Shiva and Krishna, Hanuman and the goddess. Some spectators may wonder a bit when they see the plentiful images of Jhulelal or representations of Sindhi holy men. In most cases it won't matter much, though: almost everyone sometimes comes across images that aren't immediately recognizable, and, displayed as they are, these must be benevolent beings. The atmosphere here is one of a festival, but the images passing by are those of divinities and holy persons, so a religious undercurrent, at least, is also usually experienced. People may not expect to receive the sort of *darśan* one might have from a sanctified image at a temple, but they may get a heightened feeling for their deities' magnificence at least—and perhaps, if they are feeling pious, some blessings. This sort of elaborate event is becoming increasingly prevalent in public Indian religious life, and the Jhulelal procession, by all accounts, presents the biggest and best one that Gwalior has to offer—on an entirely different scale than the public Ganesh puja, say, that the Maharashtra Samaj puts on. Except for some awareness of Jhulelal as a divinity, few in the crowd are going to come away having assimilated much of any distinctive aspects of Sindhi tradition, but most are happy to have seen magnificent images of their own divine beings. The exhilaration ordinary Gwalioris might feel is of the sort they might experience after any good religious procession. And the Sindhis, they have seen, put on a *very* good one.

As the main Sindhi contribution to general Gwalior religious life, the annual procession is offered by the community as a whole in a spirit of community pride, common festivity, and public relations.[28] There are certainly professionals involved in its preparation, but they are mostly technical experts—lighting men and mechanics—not religious specialists. With few exceptions, the religious professionals in the Sindhi community serve its members alone. There are also Maharashtrian religious professionals working in institutions that are meant primarily for Maharashtrians (which often function largely in Marathi): an old *maṭh* to a yogi who arrived in Gwalior before Mahipati Nath, say, or a newer one to the Maharashtrian *sant*-poet Ram Das. But in addition, as we have seen, professionals in a few Maharashtrian religious traditions have successfully developed them to serve sections of the broader Gwalior public. In doing so, they provide the public with something distinctively different from what they had before.

This is not quite the case with the Sindhis. Because Sindhis differ widely in much of their distinctive religious practice from most North Indians, what the Sindhis can realistically offer the broader public is a very exuberant, well-staged version of a broad Hindu worldview they have in common, with its many divinities. Their own regional deities are part of this Hindu world, but processions, conveniently, are not generally expected to display religious *practice*. The Jhulelal procession thus presents the community as it would like, in its present circumstances, to be seen: regular Hindus with some ordinary regional differences. It does this through a grand show organized out of a sense of collective identity. The general public appreciates the procession on its own terms, while the Sindhi community, well organized and fairly prosperous, collectively foots the bill.

No deliberate collective act, however, brought about the exposure of the broader Gwalior public to aspects of Maharashtrian religion, although that exposure may once have been heightened by acts of royal patronage. The Maharashtrian religious traditions patronized by the broader Gwalior community have grown more slowly, and perhaps more naturally, driven by individual religious entrepreneurs' ability to play niche roles. Religious specialists offering something a little different attract followings in the larger community, which helps support them. This more gradual and organic mode of development in tradition may, however, be more characteristic of an earlier era: against it, the Sindhis' impressive Jhulelal procession appears more *modern*. Even while showcasing selected aspects of distinctively Sindhi tradition, it contributes to the vision of a more homogeneous Hinduism that is currently taking shape in India and the diaspora—thriving in contemporary, technologically new forms. If the Vaishno Devi temple described in chapter 1, with its attempt to replicate the experience of the Himalayan goddess through low-tech artifice, is a small, enduring materialization of this vision in Gwalior, the parade culminating the city's annual Jhulelal festival may be another, grander, recurring one. Great big broadly conceived Hindu processions seem to be part of the new religious wave.[29]

PART THREE

Institutions and Personalities

5

Hindu Ways of Organized Service

LEGACIES OF SWAMI VIVEKANANDA

WHILE ORGANIZED ETHNIC and caste communities of the sort seen in the last chapter often provide social services to their own members, citywide religiously oriented service organizations regularly work with members of their own broad-based communities, Christian, Muslim, and Hindu. But with the boundaries of these communities in principal more expansive than those grounded in caste or regional ethnicity, many religiously oriented organizations are happy to serve anyone ready to be acculturated to their particular religion-inflected ways. Although for a few Hindu groups in some parts of India, this attitude can lead to wholesale conversion efforts,[1] there is not much scope for conversion by Hindu organizations in Gwalior. Given the city's demographics, most Hindu-oriented service organizations there are run primarily for Hindus, with many offering a vision of national reconstruction according to their own ideal visions of India. Those visions can shape, in different degrees, their members' personal spiritual goals—which are usually achieved through educational work and charitable service that is sometimes performed in innovative ways.

Some of Gwalior's Hindu service groups are branches of organizations with a pan-Indian or even global purview; others are of local or regional scope. Several, both national and local, consciously draw on the legacy of Swami Vivekananda, a late nineteenth-century Hindu reformer who some people treat as a national icon. One of these, the Vivekananda Needam, underwent a crisis during the years of my research, leading to high drama that can be instructive for understanding the tensions faced by modern Indian religion-oriented organizations everywhere.

The Vivekananda Needam lies on the southern outskirts of Gwalior, on a site that has been developed into a lush green area in what is mostly a rather dry and dusty part of the subcontinent. I paid quite a few visits to the Needam over the years of my research—in part, I confess, because I was attracted to the ambience of the place: the shaded, tenderly cared-for site was always most welcome during Gwalior's many hot months, and the ecological enthusiasm of its founders, a married couple named Anil and Alpna Sarode, could be invigorating. I first visited the Needam in 1997, just two years after construction on its site had started. It wasn't as lushly green then as it would later be, but it was still impressive. Alpna and Anil greeted me cordially and told me that the Needam was meant to be a regional center for the Vivekananda Kendra—a national organization based in Kanyakumari, at the southern tip of India. With the Needam's extended space and facilities, it would be a place where camps would be held for new Kendra enthusiasts in central India and where seasoned Kendra workers could come for further training. Alpna sold me some of the Kendra's publications and carefully issued receipts. At the time her actions seemed unusually fastidious to me—these were very inexpensive pamphlets—but I later learned that close attention to financial regularity was part of the larger Kendra culture. Alpna was just following Kendra norms.

Those norms, however, proved too constricting. On a visit ten years later, the Sarodes told me that things had changed. They were no longer affiliated with the Vivekananda Kendra, having decided to go their own way. I knew the story couldn't be that simple—the Needam occupied a very nice piece of property that no national organization would happily give up—but it wasn't until a visit to Gwalior the next year that I was able to gain any detailed understanding of the events that had actually occurred. These tell a story of unresolvable conflict between national concerns and global visions, ideological agendas and personal fulfill-ment. In doing so, moreover, they highlight some inherent tensions that can appear in service organizations that first developed under the influence of colonial models but also have to contend with Indic sen-sibilities about religious authority. To understand the fraught Gwalior story of the Needam and the Kendra, it will help to review the devel-opment of modern religious organizations in colonial India and the place within that of Swami Vivekananda and the type of organization he founded.

Swami Vivekananda and the Emergence of Hindu Religious Organizations

Although Swami Vivekananda himself founded the first lasting Hindu service organization, he was not primarily an organization man. He was sooner a passionate religious reformer, the last great representative of what has come to be called the nineteenth-century Hindu Renaissance—or sometimes the Bengali Renaissance because it was centered in the province of Bengal, the seat of British power at the time and Vivekananda's home region. Like the European Renaissance, the Hindu one was a cultural movement heralded by a widening enthusiasm for ancient texts that had previously been given little serious attention outside narrow erudite circles. It was sparked by the interest European scholars began to take in the early phases of Indian religion when they came to see its genuine historical place in their own broad language and civilizational stream—now dubbed Indo-European. The new European enthusiasm soon spread among wider circles of English-educated Hindus, who found that the ancient texts might help them grapple with their current cultural dilemmas.

The texts that now came to the fore were the Vedas and the Upanishads—which, valued by Europeans as closest to their own civilizational roots, had also been long revered by Hindus as constituting *śruti*, revealed scripture whose authority was of a higher order than that of later religious texts. The Vedas, in their earliest stratum, consisted of hymns recited at what may originally have been a rather simple fire sacrifice; later Vedic collections augmented these with lengthy directions for carrying out rites that had developed into complex ritual events. The Upanishads were visionary reflections that often started from attempts to understand the meaning of Vedic ritual. They offer some early versions of the metaphysical thought and yogic insights that remain central to much Hindu philosophy. Although people argue about the dating of these texts, no one claims that they were later than the first millennium B.C.E.[2]

By the early nineteenth century, however, Hindu worship traditions in urban areas weren't so distant from those of early twenty-first-century Gwalior described in chapter 1—adoration of deities in mandirs of different sorts. This was nothing many British could relate to as their own and was growing distant to some influential English-educated Indians, too. For the pioneers of the Hindu Renaissance, the Vedic period with its glorious rituals and Upanishadic brilliance became seen as Hinduism's golden age, of which its present form was just a pale shadow, if not a degenerate corruption. For European Orientalists, the idea of a golden age was a prejudice, to be sure, but it also resonated with some traditional Indic ideas about spiritual decline through successive world-epochs. It could thus play powerfully upon the religious sensibilities of the growing number of Hindus exposed to Western letters—sensitive to European critiques but still acculturated to their own lore.

Throughout urban India in the nineteenth century this class was expanding, mediating between the British commercial and political elite and the broader Indian public. Its members, sometimes themselves uncomfortably negotiating Western ideas of progress and social conventions felt as confining, could now look to the traditions of their golden age for some personal religious resolutions. Starting around 1830, a rather upper-crust Hindu group came together as the Brahmo Samaj to explore the philosophical reflections of the Upanishads as the basis of a reoriented religion and society: Brahmo Samaj means "the Society of Brahma"— *brahma* taken here to refer to the ultimate consciousness of Upanishadic discourse. In various incarnations, the Brahmo Samaj continued to be vital among the colonial Bengali intelligentsia through the end of the nineteenth century, but it had little to offer in the way of everyday religion for the many. The unalloyed monism it found in the Upanishads did not speak vividly to prevalent devotional sensibilities, while the social reforms put forward by the Brahmo Samaj—such as discouraging child marriage—were too far ahead of their time. The Brahmos were, however, the first of the modern organized Hindu religious movements and were able to stand as an example for others.

In particular, the vitality of the Brahmo Samaj in the early 1870s seems to have made an impression on the Gujarati Swami Dayananda, who had contact with some notable Brahmos while on a visit to Calcutta in 1872–73 and came away seeing the practical possibility, at least, of a new-style religious organization that invoked the ideal of a golden age. He took that possibility, however, in a direction radically different from theirs. In 1875, Dayananda founded the Arya Samaj, which looked primarily to the early ritually oriented Vedas, not to the later, philosophically tinged Upanishads.[3] A man of extremes, Dayananda was a Hindu nationalist who located his religious culture's superiority in its origins, seeing in Vedic ritual lore the precursors to the triumphs of his contemporary science. He thus became emphatic in acknowledging the *śruti* alone as valid—a radical claim that denied the truth of the cumulative lore that most Hindus took seriously

and the value of the worship traditions they followed. Vital local leaders in a number of North Indian areas sustained Dayananda's dynamic
impetus through the first decades of the twentieth century, when the Arya
Samaj flourished as an early movement of Hindu communal advancement and social reform—arranging some interesting, if ultimately unsuc-
cessful, experiments with the mass "purification" of untouchable castes.
The religious appeal of the Arya Samaj, though—despite its institution
of simple rituals of its own on Vedic models—was severely limited by its
wholesale denial of the prevalent everyday Hinduism. It was left to Swami
Vivekananda to find a balance between the Hindu heritage he knew and a
sense of the present that would continue to resonate widely among India's
growing middle classes. His Hinduism was full-bodied, preserving the
best of the traditions most people already practiced and of the texts they
had come to revere. He presented traditional ideas, however, in ways that
many who had acquired some Western habits of thought could find sen-
sible and offered new avenues of religious practice nicely suited to the
current social conditions.

Vivekananda's respect for the continuing Hindu tradition must have
come in part from his guru, Sri Ramakrishna, who was immersed in it.
Somewhat unconventionally, however, Sri Ramakrishna was immersed
in many different aspects of Hindu tradition—seriatim if not simultaneously. A temple priest at a Kali temple outside Calcutta who regularly
slipped in and out of deep spiritual states, Ramakrishna is famously
portrayed as finding ecstatic bliss in Krishna and the peace of the yogi
in Shiva; he is said to have participated in tantric practice and regularly
performed the ceremonial worship of Mother Kali.[4] Vivekananda could
not but value the many religious paths traversed by his guru, but when
he met him he was a middle-class Calcutta college boy who had already
acquired a clear sense of the new, modern world. Even while honoring
the traditional devotion that most Hindus still in some way cherish, he
revived aspects of Hindu thought and practice that he thought would be
valuable for middle-class Indians of his time. Going beyond the Vedas
and Upanishads into classical Hindu philosophy, Vivekananda offered
popular, long-lived presentations of vital ideas and texts: *Raja Yoga*, for
example, his commentary on the *yoga sūtras* of Patanjali—written in simple, clear English and invoking some scientific ideas of the day—is still
in print in a number of editions. In 1893, Vivekananda made a celebrated
trip to the United States to speak at the World Congress of Religions
in Chicago, not returning to India until 1897. He came back from the

West impressed by the value of active social service as a religious path for men and women in the modern world of his day. If the social service work of Christian missionaries in India could be suspected of a colonial proselytizing intent, such work by Christians on their home grounds could appear benevolent without seeming similarly pernicious. Why not attempt something like that for Hindus in India? Soon after his return, Swami Vivekananda founded the Ramakrishna Mission—the only Hindu religious organization from the nineteenth century to flourish widely in the twenty-first.

As a broad-based Hindu institution featuring social service, the Ramakrishna Mission differs from its Brahmo Samaj and Arya Samaj predecessors. Both those groups brought together a particular religious vision (brahma-consciousness for one, Vedic ritual power for the other) with some attempts at active social intervention (such as the abolition of child marriage and of untouchability); these social interventions, though—however laudable—were too extreme for their age. The Ramakrishna Mission, by contrast, brings together a catholic, if not entirely traditional, version of Hinduism with social service initiatives—through schools, orphanages, hospitals, eldercare, and the like. The mission's first large project, during the year of its founding, was in the area of famine relief. Not active social interventions, these are charitable projects that can be carried out with some success and be religiously rewarding. Over time, the mission's projects might indeed ameliorate the overall social situation, but one of Vivekananda's principal aims, in addition to providing immediate help to the needy, was to give the many volunteers who participate in these projects a new way to be a good Hindu in their contemporary world. Less than a way to change society, this was a religious practice for individuals—a form of karma yoga, the yoga of works.[5] In the century or so since the time of its founding, the Ramakrishna Mission, based outside Calcutta, has spread all over India, with branches in many Indian cities. There is no branch of the mission, however, in Gwalior, although there is an institution that can be easily mistaken for one. It is called the Ramakrishna Ashram (not Mission), has long had an active Bengali sadhu at its head, and houses a wide range of educational and social service institutions. Usually the first place mentioned when Gwalioris are asked about social service institutions in the city, its influential leader made his voice heard early in the open conflict between the Vivekananda Kendra and the Vivekananda Needam. For that story the Ramakrishna Ashram presents a local backdrop.

The Ramakrishna Ashram, Gwalior

Founded in 1959, Gwalior's Ramakrishna Ashram has taken shape over half a century and is very much the creation of its founder, Swami Swaroopananda, still going strong in his eightieth year when I last saw him. Born in 1929 as Amulya Roy in Dhaka—now the capital of Bangladesh— he emigrated to Calcutta with his family during the partition of the sub-continent in 1947.[6] In the late 1950s, Swaroopananda arrived in Gwalior as a young, orange-robed ascetic with a flair for musical performance, acquiring a circle of admirers and devotees. Having spent much of his spiritual adolescence in Calcutta, Swaroopananda was familiar with the workings of the Ramakrishna Mission, and it was clearly the model on which he built his new institution.

The first incarnation of the ashram was located within part of a pilgrim's rest house in Shinde ki Chawni, then one of the higher-class Lashkar bazaars. By 1964, the government had allotted the ashram four acres of land in Thatipur, at the time an underpopulated area triangulated by greater Gwalior's three historical urban hubs. In the same year, Sarvepalli Radhakrishnan—a noted scholar of Indian philosophy and then president of India—laid the new ashram's foundation stone. These auspicious beginnings have been recalled to give the ashram both Sanskritic blessings and national import.[7]

The principal elements of the ashram then took shape quickly. The main building was finished the next year and in short order there followed a school, a library with a reading room, and a homeopathic dispensary. An altar in the main building was a focus for regular devotional worship. Over the decades, with new construction on the campus, these facilities expanded and new ones were added. The schools increased from one to two, with one teaching in English and following the curriculum of the national Central School Board, and the other teaching in Hindi and following the Madhya Pradesh State Board. The library regularized membership arrangements for access to its growing collection of books (about nine thousand in 2005) and got its own building. So did the dispensary, which currently offers treatment through Ayurveda and Western medicine as well as homeopathy. An exhibition hall was built and an old folks home was established, and in the early 1980s a grand new temple to Ramakrishna was built. Swaroopananda's affinity for music has also led to a school of classical Indian music on the campus.

All these projects testify to Swami Swaroopananda's energy and skills at institution building. Still, similar institutions with schools, dispensaries, and libraries can be found in many urban areas, although the Swami's seem to be better run than many. Two of the ashram projects, however, are striking because of their ambitious scope and the widespread support they have drawn.

In 1989, the Madhya Pradesh government allotted fifty-two acres of land to the ashram to build a place for homeless children in the area to live.[8] Sitting on a bluff at the outskirts of the city on the same side of town as the ashram campus, it is called Sarada Balgram, "Sarada's children's village," in honor of Sri Sarada Devi, Ramakrishna's wife. The place has nice views and some of its facilities are exemplary, with children living in small groups in separate, neat residences. They go to schools in the Sarada Balgram itself and participate in the daily worship services normal in religiously oriented boarding institutions. Swami Swaroopananda visits the place frequently, often stopping at a popular Hanuman temple there before making his rounds. Sarada Balgram received initial support from the Scindias—long prominent sponsors of reputable local institutions—and has also managed to secure some continuing per-student support from the Madhya Pradesh government. The recipient of aristocratic patronage and state aid, the Ramakrishna Ashram has managed to situate itself within the generous gaze of the established elite.

This gaze has clearly benefited a separate project—on the ashram campus itself—for mentally and physically disabled children, one that has drawn also on resources from abroad. It is called ROSHNI and began in 1998. An acronym that spells *light* in Hindi, ROSHNI stands for the full English name "Rehabilitation, Opportunities, Services and Health for the Neurologically Impaired." ROSHNI'S longtime director, Manjula Patankar, is from an aristocratic Maratha family and has been able to acquire advanced training in the education of neurologically and physically handicapped children in Britain as well as in India. With a small professional staff and a wealth of local and international volunteers, Manjula runs a sophisticated program that provides education and treatment in the facilities at the ashram and, importantly, moves out to train parents in regional villages to care effectively for their handicapped offspring. To support her work, she has drawn in members of other aristocratic families[9] and tapped her British connections, developing an active fundraising network in the United Kingdom: "Friends of ROSHNI UK." ROSHNI's airy new building on the ashram campus, which opened in 2008, was constructed with help from a British government aid agency.

However crucial the ashram may have been in helping get ROSHNI started, it no longer seems crucial for its material existence; nevertheless, Manjula still appreciates being there. ROSHNI's location in the ashram provides not only benefits from the ashram's general local prestige but also regular opportunities for cooperation with other ashram institutions. Most important practically for ROSHNI are the ashram's cultural events—such as Vivekananda's birthday and Indian Independence Day celebrations—in which Manjula's disabled students can participate alongside able-bodied ones from the ashram schools. The ashram as a popular socioreligious institution, moreover, can help draw her students' parents—attracted to the ashram's annual festivals and everyday worship service—into fuller participation in their children's treatment. But there are also valuable intangibles for all who work at the ashram's different organizations: "we really love community," notes Manjula, and "Swamiji's guidance and support are always there." In ways both concrete and subtle, ROSHNI's place in Swami Swaroopananda's Ramakrishna Ashram is a real asset to it: the Swami graces all the institutions on the campus.

Although the support that Swami Swaroopananda gives to ROSHNI these days may be mostly of the moral variety, he has been an indefatigable fundraiser for many of the other ashram organizations. In doing so, he has had to negotiate worlds of money and power, of which renunciates in India are traditionally supposed to be very wary. Ethical ambiguities may thus easily arise—if not for Swamiji himself, than in the minds of others. Thus, while generally revered, Swami Swaroopananda has not been without his critics. Although I have never heard charges of serious wrongdoing against Swamiji, his position does give him influence over admission to the ashram's highly esteemed schools. Seats in the schools are often sought by middle-class families—many of whom may be able to afford the school's tuition fees, but not much beyond that. Is it right then, some ask—perhaps with a reference to Swamiji's rise from very ordinary beginnings—that admission may be granted to children from families that make sizable donations to the ashram, even if these haven't been on waiting lists as long or aren't quite as qualified as some others? There is room for debate here. If Swamiji has indeed influenced admission decisions in this way, need we fault him too harshly for acting like many school administrators all over the world? True, he is a renunciate, but like other administrators, he needs to look out for the practical needs of his establishment. After all, Swami Swaroopananda's institution is an independent one, drawing no financial support from any larger religious organization.

Even while independent, however, Swami Swaroopananda maintains a visible relationship with the pan-Indian Ramakrishna Mission and Math complex. Although his Ramakrishna Ashram is not formally a part of the Ramakrishna Mission, it is affiliated with the Ramakrishna Math, a related monastic order based—like the mission—at Belur, outside Calcutta. This affiliation means that monks from the Ramakrishna order can live and work at the ashram, which some have been content to do for years. Their presence is readily evident, some serving in vital administrative capacities—as, say, the ashram accountant—and some seeming just to provide an ascetic's holy presence. The Ramakrishna Mission and Math have strong administrative ties to one another and tend to be seen as a conglomerate, which Swami Swaroopananda deftly approaches from its monastic side. In doing so, he adds legitimacy to his presentation of Vivekananda's modernist Hindu piety without subordinating the ashram's educational and social service operations to the mission's organizational strictures. The Ramakrishna Ashram, Gwalior, thus appears as part of a broad and well-respected national religious movement while remaining an independent institution with local roots.

The Swami, moreover, maintains some important freedoms of his own—prerogatives of traditional Hindu holy persons, generically referred to as *sadhus*. One of these is the ability to stay put. In renouncing worldly ties, sadhus gain freedom of movement: they may travel from place to place frequently or can retreat to hermitages for the rest of their lives. But the movement of responsible dedicated workers in a modern religious service organization is often not so free. They may work on a project in one place for a while and then be delegated somewhere else. This periodic movement no doubt derives from the exigencies of the organization's work, but it can also be salutary for the organization as a whole: as we will soon see, it is not always in the best interests of religious organizations with specific agendas to be too strongly identified with any particular local representatives. At the same time, for religious workers in the world, staying in one place and then leaving can also be understood to have spiritual value: although it is good to devote one's self wholeheartedly to a task and stay where one is needed until it is done, it is also good to be able to walk away from a cherished endeavor, to not be attached to one's work as one's own. Whatever Swami Swaroopananda's sense of attachment to the ashram in Gwalior may be, he in fact stayed there for fifty years and never stopped developing it, suffusing the place with his own generally respected version of Vivekananda's religious stamp. All the organizations located on the campus have then become subtly branded by that stamp, which adds to their perceived quality. Most local people see Gwalior's Ramakrishna Ashram, with its temple to Ramakrishna, its imposing statue of Vivekananda, and its monks from the Belur math, as hardly different from a regular branch of the Ramakrishna Mission. But they also see it as very much Swami Swaroopananda's place, too—a particular Gwalior institution.

The Vivekananda Kendra and the Vivekananda Needam

The Vivekananda Needam is also a place strongly identified with its highly charismatic founders, even though some say that it was not supposed to be that way. For while built up with great personal zeal by the Sarodes, the Needam in its conception was intended as the principal regional base in North-Central India for the organization to which they once belonged—whose pan-Indian headquarters at Kanyakumari is about as far south in India as anyone can go. A fabled destination of Vivekananda when he traversed the subcontinent as a sadhu, it attracted the founders of the Vivekananda Kendra through its symbolic association with the revered nineteenth-century Swami.

The Vivekananda Kendra was started in 1972 with the twin objectives of "Man-Making and Nation-Building."[10] As explained on the organization's website, these objectives entail awakening the inherent spirituality in individuals, orienting it toward serving the divine in humankind, and channeling that service toward building the nation.[11] To this end it organizes practical educational programs of several different sorts, including discussion groups in cities and towns, environmental efforts in rural areas,[12] and spiritual retreats and yoga camps at its own regional centers. Although these projects can definitely be seen as religious service, they differ in kind from those seen at Gwalior's Ramakrishna Ashram and the Ramakrishna Mission generally. Indeed, they are not meant to duplicate them. Those were charitable projects such as schools, orphanages, and healthcare programs; the Kendra's main programs instead focus on moral education through discussion and example. This service may well be religiously motivated, but it is also infused with an ample dose of intervention toward nationalist reform. Not as radical (and immediately ineffectual) as the early reform attempts of the Brahmo and Arya Samajes, the Kendra's programs are aimed at molding the character of their participants into good citizens of the Indian nation as envisioned by the organization's activists.

In this interventionist turn to its social service, the Vivekananda Kendra is true to its origins, which are in the broad Hindu nationalist network of organizations known as the Sangh Parivar. The Kendra's founder, Eknath Ranade (1914–82), was a dedicated member of the RSS, the network's core institution, in which he occupied a number of high offices, including general secretary (1955–62).[13] The Kendra's institutional structure also echoes that of the RSS (and many Sangh Parivar groups) in being effectively run by a cadre of dedicated workers.[14] Although the Vivekananda Kendra in no way abjures its Hindu nationalist roots, I have not (yet) seen it demonstrate the most extreme of Hindu nationalism's ideological excesses. Under the banner of Swami Vivekananda, it emphasizes the universalizing spiritual ideals of the Upanishads and presents an inclusive tone: no militaristic rituals like those of the RSS itself here, or strident calls for Hindu assertiveness as found among leaders of the World Hindu Council. Although ideas of nation building figure prominently in Kendra publicity, the word *Hindu* does not; its idiom is that of (nonsectarian) "spirituality" and "the divine."

This public ideal of spiritual inclusiveness does seem to distinguish the Kendra from some of the other Sangh Parivar organizations. One of the younger local leaders I met, for example, when asked about the difference between his group and the RSS expressed his reverence for that group's founders but stressed that, in contrast to the RSS, the Kendra treated everyone the same and tried to make interested Muslims feel welcome, too—and I did indeed notice at least one Muslim youth participating in group activities as a peer. At a more exalted level, the international division of the Kendra, based in Delhi, presents itself as "an initiative for inter-civilisational harmony through dialogue and understanding."[15] When I visited there in 2008, I was told about an upcoming planned dialogue with Muslims. The organizers wanted to start with representatives from Southeast Asian communities, who were expected to be more open than many others. At least, I remember thinking, they were looking for people they could actually talk to. Whatever the motives of some of the Kendra's senior leaders may be, the culture of discussion and yoga that they propagate, together with some of the Kendra's earth-friendly programs of nation building, can appear salutary. The organization, moreover, has found support for some of its initiatives from a wide section of the Indian political spectrum.[16]

Indeed, I was immediately taken with Gwalior's Vivekananda Needam, which can appear as an environmentally friendly New Age oasis in a dusty, rather conventional city. Construction was started on the Needam in 1995 by the charismatic Sarodes, with Anil presenting a quietly wise and empathetic persona and Alpna a vibrant and more forceful one. They had been very successful, they said, in raising funds for the Needam locally. It hadn't hurt, of course, that Anil, like many core members of the Kendra, including its founder Ranade, was Maharashtrian and could appeal directly to the Gwalior Maharashtrian community— largely middle class or better—while Alpna was a North Indian from Allahabad, culturally closer to the rest of the population. A couple cooperating together as more or less equal partners in active religious work is not such a common sight in Hindu India, and for some of the more forward-looking Gwalior adherents this must have been inspiring. The two had obviously attracted many in the area with a modernist bent, who joined them in their work.

Although the Sarodes did indeed develop the Needam as a place for Kendra training sessions, yoga camps, and retreats—there is a large amphitheater space and plenty of housing—Anil, especially, had a larger sociospiritual and environmental vision. The Needam, a Sanskrit word for "nest" (*nīḍam*), would give a contemporary communitarian turn to traditional Hindu joint-family ideals. The site, said Anil, would be a place where different generations could live together as a harmonious family. There was a building meant for active retirees called Vanprasth Niwas: *nivās* means "residence" and *vānaprastha* is the Sanskrit term for an older person who retreats to the forest (*vana*) for spiritual pursuits. Below the building's Sanskritic name, however, stands a modern English motto: "Retired but not tired." The spiritual pursuits for retirees here are contemporary activist ones. There was also plenty of room for more well-to-do supporters only beginning to think about retirement to build small houses; these could be used for visitors until they were needed by the original builders. Retirees were active in supervising the housekeeping, visitors' schedules, and extensive groundskeeping operations. Children were in the Needam from the very beginning, when the hostel for the already ongoing Utkarsh project shifted there.

Utkarsh ("rising toward excellence") was started in 1992 by the Kendra in Gwalior to offer a standard Indian educational experience to children from outlying areas that did not have easy access to one. It was aimed particularly at villages inhabited by people of Sahariya culture, an indigenous group found in Gwalior District that does not have a strong tradition of literacy. Utkarsh offers Sahariya boys board and lodging and an environment for some disciplined study. In doing so the Utkarsh project develops two broader activities of the national Vivekananda Kendra: fostering worthy students; and national integration (which here seems to entail a sort of Hinduization). Although the Kendra doesn't engage in regular K–12 education projects in most places, it does sometimes offer simple boarding at local centers to (usually male) children who seem promising for the Kendra, in hard circumstances, or both.

The areas where the Kendra does operate schools in a major way are in the Northeastern states of India, which have distinctive cultures that can seem rather different from mainline Hindu tradition, as well as large Christian populations. The aims of national integration behind this educational push in the northeast are stated explicitly. Along with high goals of "man-making"—that is, general moral uplift—the Vivekananda cultural institute in Gawahati was "established with the purpose of discovering the cultural continuity of the North Eastern states with each other and also with the rest of India."[17] Similarly, Utkarsh at the Gwalior Needam is primarily for students described in Hindi as *vanvāsī* ("forest dwellers"), or as the English-language sign bluntly states, "tribal"—terms used to describe indigenous communities not well integrated into Brahminically Hindu traditions. The children go out to school during the day, study, and do some chores, all within a program that includes morning yoga and prayers and evening worship. Thus, along with getting what by local standards is a reasonably good education, the boys are becoming accustomed to a version of mainstream Hindu culture.

Whatever critique may be leveled at some of the cultural aspects of this program, the fact that the children are becoming more like mainstream Hindus than their parents does not seem to bother the parents too much. Although there was some resistance by parents at first to sending their children away, I was told, there is none any more. The Sahariya are generally quite poor, and parents have come to recognize the value of educating their children in this way. A waiting list has become necessary, and only one child is taken from any household.[18] Families are periodically reunited when children go home during school vacations, and the children seem generally happy while they are at the Needam. They eat well and have time to run around the grounds; there is a large grassy play area with swings and slides. While the children are expected to abide by the Needam's schedule, I saw no strongly regimented discipline: Anil's affectionate demeanor instead balanced Alpna's occasional stern looks. However much the students may become distanced from their non-Brahminic roots, it's clear to everyone that they are better prepared than otherwise to get ahead in contemporary India.

Some broader ideals and practices of the Vivekananda Kendra also inform Anil's environmental vision. In particular, he has paid close attention to two items that have figured prominently in other Kendra programs featuring sustainable development: cost-effective housing and water management.[19] In the Needam, these items have been taken very seriously indeed.

In building the Needam's cottages, Anil used rat-trap construction, which bonds the bricks on edge in a way that leaves gaps of air between them (so creating "rat traps"). This construction uses fewer bricks and less mortar than a conventional English bond of similar thickness, thus making the houses cheaper to build; the air trapped in the wall, moreover, gives good insulation—important in Gwalior, which is known for both summer and winter extremes. The rat-trap bond also produces interesting, aesthetically pleasing brickwork that requires no plastering or painting (and hence no repainting after the annual monsoon). Although this type of construction has its limitations—the walls cannot support buildings of more than two stories—it is effective here and in much small-scale construction in India. It is, though, still something of an innovation and not widely used. The Needam showcases it.

Water is managed at the Needam in two ways. Tube wells provide the Needam's main supply for drinking, cooking and bathing, with waste water then recycled through a pond and returned to the aquifer. Because the tube wells' storage tanks are not of high capacity and are refilled regularly, water stays in them for no more than a few hours and all that flows through the taps is drinkable. No other purification is used. For irrigation, water comes in good part from a complex system for harvesting rainwater, which, says Anil, never leaves the Needam. Because the Needam is on a hill, the water can be blocked and harvested at seven levels. All the water used at the Needam, Anil affirms, is drawn from the Needam itself. Even if it were not, the efficient use of water there is exemplary.

For someone coming out to the Needam from the city, it is difficult not to be somewhat in awe of the rustic greenery and well-maintained gardens there: about ten thousand trees and shrubs altogether, says Anil.

There are paths for quiet meditation, and a wooded area with benches for silent retreat. Alpna, with a degree in naturopathy, started a center where people can come for cures with mudpacks and baths. Since these natural treatments are slow—often taking a few weeks—people from out of town can stay in the residences. There are also some thoughtful innovations aimed at the boys who live there. Near the outdoor Hanuman shrine where the children do evening worship, Anil has installed a bell at a child's height. "Little children like to ring bells," he said, "it's good for them to be able to do it by themselves." Children should be able to observe religious ritual and be independent at the same time. For visitors, the whole place is meant to stand as an environmental model: informative sign boards draw visitors' attention to the virtues of rat-trap walls and the ways of some public bio-toilets, among other practical exhibits (fig. 5.1). To many in Gwalior and beyond, the Needam has appeared as an interesting experiment in group living and an extremely impressive example of ecological bloom in the dust, tapping into a global environmental ethic that the larger Kendra fosters in certain Indian rural milieux. That was not, however, quite what the Kendra expected from the city-oriented Needam.

FIGURE 5.1 The numbered points written in Hindi describe the specifics of rat-trap bond construction and elaborate its benefits. Vivekananda Needam, Gwalior.

The Kendra versus the Needam

When Anil first told me that the Needam had separated from the center, I was surprised and asked him why. He explained that they wanted to move in some directions that reached beyond the programs of teaching and retreats on which the Kendra focused; for example, they also thought that the Naturopathy Center was a valuable addition. To my query about how it was possible for the Needam to become independent from the Kendra, Anil gave an indirect answer, responding simply that the land for the Needam came from the state and that they had raised money for its construction locally themselves. It was better that they continue to be guided by their own lights. I doubted, though, that things could have been as easy as he was trying to make them sound.

As I later found out, there had in fact been a very painful rupture that had left the local Kendra community in utter disarray for many months and that by the end of my active research still did not seem totally resolved. I had gotten intimations of this from acquaintances in town when I mentioned the Needam to people working with local religious organizations. The first thing most people said was something like, "Of course you realize that the Vivekananda Needam is no longer a part of the Vivekananda Kendra," and many looked at me very gravely when they said it. I didn't really get a better sense of what happened until after I met Mukul Kantikar, a well-placed worker in the Kendra organization at the time responsible for its activities in Gwalior, who introduced me to the Kendra's current activities there.

Mukul is charismatic in his own way, outgoing, seemingly open, and charming. Of a younger generation than Anil, he is very articulate in English and Hindi—neither his native language: like many in the Kendra organization he is a Marathi-speaker from Maharashtra. He was also, when I met him, evidently one of the organization's rising stars. He was responsible then not only for renewing the Kendra in Gwalior but also for supervising its activities in all of Madhya Pradesh. He did all this, moreover, very frequently from Delhi, where he had another job helping to oversee the beginnings of the new Vivekananda Kendra international center there. A very busy man, Mukul was obviously someone trusted by the Kendra's top leaders.

I first met Mukul during the 2008 monsoon season in Swami Swaroopananda's drawing room at the Ramakrishna Ashram. It wasn't clear if he was there on important business or whether it was mostly a courtesy call—probably a little of both—but there was an obvious show of solidarity between these representatives of the two apparently kindred streams of Vivekananda's legacy. As Mukul explained then, with the Swami's assent, in addition to Vivekananda's order of monastic workers, begun during the latter's lifetime, there now was also a parallel order of lay workers in the Vivekananda Kendra. I was supposed to understand a kind of equivalence between the Swami and the busy Kendra man as active workers dedicated to Vivekananda's modernizing Hindu ideals.

I had tracked down the new local headquarters of the Vivekananda Kendra at the Datta temple in Jiwaji Ganj on a visit in the fall of the previous year, as I became more interested in the question of the Needam's independence. It was mid-morning when I visited and nothing much was going on: a teenage boy who lived with his family nearby was tending a bookshop that had been set up, but there was nobody who seemed particularly informed or eager to talk about the Kendra; I didn't feel compelled to return. When I met Mukul at the Ramakrishna Ashram the next year, he was accompanied by Jagdish Thadani, the young man who had taken day-to-day charge of the local headquarters and much of the practical Gwalior organization. Like Mukul, Jagdish was one of those who was dedicating his life to Kendra work, called lifeworkers when English is spoken. Mukul told Jagdish to welcome me and invited me to come some evening when the local members gathered. I soon did, and found a very different atmosphere from that of my first visit. The bookstall was gone (there was now a library in a side room) and the place was bustling—mostly with young people, but with some older folks, too. On my subsequent visits I more often than not found the Kendra's discursive "man-making" agenda in full swing, with lively discussions in groups of mixed gender and often mixed age. In these discussions, an occasional visiting senior lifeworker might join Jagdish in doing a good bit of the talking, but people of both genders and all ages spoke and were listened to; many of these were local leaders who would go out and run programs in their neighborhoods. Hindu worship and festivals were also celebrated in distinctive ways at the Kendra headquarters, and young boys there proudly demonstrated yoga postures they had learned. The yoga, prayer, and presence of some resident students suggested continuities with the Needam, but the atmosphere felt different indeed: this was no peaceful retreat but active life in the city.

At the time of my visit the year before, I learned, the temple had just been acquired and activities there hadn't got up to speed. The local Kendra loyalists had actually gotten used to managing well enough without a head-quarters, so it had taken them some time to put it to full use. For some years, Kendra stalwarts—with no place of their own in Gwalior—had been meeting in members' houses around town. Eventually this temple—like many in India, not really a public building but essentially the front room in the large private house of a priestly family—came up for sale with the rest of the house. Local Kendra members, the young lifeworker Jagdish told me, then raised money to buy it. Even with their new headquarters, though, much of the action still took place at different neighborhood venues around the city.

Whatever the vagaries of the local real estate market, it does not seem to be a simple coincidence that the new headquarters was a Datta temple. Datta is short for Dattatreya, recognized as a divinity throughout Hindu India but not a common object of popular worship in the North. He is widely worshipped in Maharashtra, however, and the few temples to him in Gwalior were built by Maharashtrian devotees, sometimes serving as centers for their community. Jiwaji Ganj, where the temple is located, is a middle-class neighborhood in old Lashkar with a substantial Maharashtrian population. For the Kendra loyalists living there, and Maharashtrian members throughout the city, the temple may have seemed a particularly attractive place, one worth preserving as a temple of sorts (the shrine is still in daily use) and able to evoke their charitable largesse. Maharashtra, further—the home of the first longtime leaders of the RSS as well as of the Kendra—has long been at the forefront of the Hindu nationalist stream of which the Kendra is a part. That stream has also affected many Gwalior Maharashtrians, particularly among the Brahmins, on whose sympathies the Kendra can draw.[20] It is true that the Kendra usually vaunts its national scope, with its main headquarters in the south at Kanyakumari, its international center in the northern capital at Delhi, and much of its educational work focused in the far northeast. But the Kendra's new Gwalior headquarters—a well-worn seat of Maharashtrian-inflected Hinduism inside the Scindias' Lashkar—may project an image closer to its collective heart. That image is in any event very different from the pastoral atmosphere and ecological exuberance of the former headquarters at the Needam.

When I inquired about the Needam from Jagdish—who was himself from Rajasthan, not Maharashtra—he just said that there was some "problem" with "authority," using the English words in his Hindi answer. He said he didn't know anything more, although I only half believed him.

I didn't get a full Kendra perspective on the problem of authority in the Needam until I met up with Mukul in Delhi at the Kendra's new international center. Although some activities had started there, construction was still incomplete, and there were a number of people sitting around with Mukul in one of the few relatively finished rooms, which he was using for an office. Mukul did some business with the people there—one or two of whom were from Gwalior—answered my questions about the center, and showed me around the site. Before leaving, I went back with Mukul to his office and told him I had one last question to ask, about the Needam in Gwalior. I had been there, I said, and spoken with the Sarodes. A hush immediately descended onto the room, but Mukul broke the silence: he decided it would be best to give me an answer.

Mukul began by talking about the anomalous position the Sarodes had occupied in the Kendra as professional workers married to each other. Lifeworkers were in fact permitted to marry, but they were not supposed to marry one another. Mukul said that this was because male and female lifeworkers were like brothers and sisters and so marriage between them would be improper. But in a widespread service organization with a relatively small, ideally mobile, professional core, marriages between lifeworkers could also be administratively difficult and potentially disruptive. Lifeworkers married outside the organization could manage as government servants in India do at their all-too-frequent transfers—sometimes taking their families along, sometimes leaving them in a paternal home—but it would be hard to move lifeworker couples together on a regular basis. Moreover, who knows what kinds of particularized loyalties and new sorts of inbred cliques might emerge? Still, Anil was seen as a gifted and experienced worker and Alpna as a strong and promising one, so as sometimes happens on the rare occasion of a valued lifeworker marrying someone active in the Kendra, arrangements were made for them to remain part of the organization, but outside the inner cadre of lifeworkers, where Anil already had a measure of authority. The Sarodes, said Mukul, had become honorary workers, off the lifeworker track.[21] Anil could see that his advancement in the organization was not progressing, Mukul offered—perhaps projecting how he himself might respond in similar circumstances—and must have been feeling insecure.

Whatever the Sarodes' status in the wider Vivekananda Kendra organization, in Gwalior they were objects of great respect, indeed often of veneration. They had a broad following who supported their work and thought very highly of them. Mukul, talking in English, said they were "worshipped." He used the word scornfully, with the implication, clearly, that lifeworkers in the Vivekananda Kendra should *not* be worshipped. Loyalty should be to the organization, not to the individual.[22] For many brought up as Hindus, however, loyalty to an organization is more recommended than practiced. Although it is obviously viable for dedicated Kendra workers taken with its modernist style, those with more traditional sensibilities whom the Kendra is trying to influence may be more comfortable with versions of the venerable Hindu guru-disciple model. Although the Kendra offers its dedicated members a version of this model through its hierarchical structures and idealized image of its founder, to the multitudes it is trying to reach, it can still remain rather faceless. Many potential members may find it easier to offer their loyalties to an inspiring teacher, as Anil, especially, proved to be.

Perhaps it was the devoted attention of their followers to which Mukul attests that gave the Sarodes the confidence that they could successfully break from the institution with which they no longer felt they resonated. Certainly, it would be more satisfying to be a local leader following one's own path than to be stuck in the mid-levels of an organization that was feeling increasingly restrictive. As Anil once put it to me, it's good to have specific goals and programs (referring to the Kendra), but it's also good to have a wider vision (referring, implicitly to people like himself). I suspect that he thought of himself then less as a worship-worthy guru of the sort we'll meet in the next chapter than as a social and ecological visionary. The institutional problem was that this was not the role the Kendra wanted him to play. The Kendra was an institution dedicated more to "national reconstruction" than to broad-based service, and the ecologically oriented interventionist turn Anil was emphasizing—even though it was consonant with the Kendra's larger program—wasn't the culturally oriented one on which its leaders wanted him to focus. Their paths really had parted, and both Anil and the Kendra leaders knew that their cadre-based organization, where decisions are ideally made by a consensus of the elders, had no room for individual workers who were perceived as gurus liable to take initiatives on their own. The Sarodes seemed the first to realize the direction events inevitably had to take.

As Mukul tells it, Anil and Alpna began making preparations to separate the Needam from the Kendra within a few years after construction of the Needam began. The land on which the project was developed was granted by the Madhya Pradesh state government to the Vivekananda Kendra, not to any entity called the Vivekananda Needam, which was just the name for the Kendra's center at the site. So in 1998 (as Mukul recalled the year) the Sarodes quietly registered their own separate organization called Vivekananda Kendra in Gwalior. In fact there could have been some legitimate reasons of convenience for them to do this, and they must have had something fairly convincing to say to the national Kendra leaders, who eventually found out and did not approve. The Sarodes were told to rectify the situation, said Mukul, and agreed to do so but never did. Meanwhile, the Sarodes continued to raise money for the Needam, some-times in ways that did not conform to the Kendra's agenda for them. In particular there was mention of an elaborate narration of the story of Lord Ram in a major city park. "We don't *do* that!" Mukul exclaimed, referring to this type of event, known as a Ram Katha, which is common in popular Hindu tradition. While a Ram Katha may be fine in its place, he implied, Kendra workers should focus on their specific "man-making" programs. Mukul saw the Sarodes' grand affair primarily as a lucrative fundraising event for the Needam itself and viewed it suspiciously. The Vivekananda Kendra was very strict about financial record-keeping, he emphasized. Where did all the money that must have come in then go? Mukul also had disdain for the Naturopathy Center, which was dear to the heart of Alpna as a trained naturopath. Although the Kendra does sponsor projects that feature natural and Ayurvedic cures, this was not what the Needam was supposed to be for.

Sometime in 2002, said Mukul, the Sarodes told a group of Needam well-wishers that they were becoming independent from the Kendra, giv-ing a press conference to that effect a few months later. Between those two events the Kendra went into action, sending Mukul, who was working in the South Indian state of Kerala, to Gwalior. Charged with re-establishing the national Kendra's authority there, Mukul reports being hounded by some of the Sarodes' followers, sometimes receiving threatening anony-mous phone calls. On one occasion, he said, he was able to identify a cer-tain anonymous caller by his voice and addressed him by name, saying, "So what if you manage to kill me; the organization will just send some-one else." Mukul liked to present himself less as an individual hero than as a fierce and dedicated organization man.

Mukul remembers this period as a terrible time for everyone involved in the Kendra in Gwalior. For about six months, he said, people were in shock and didn't know what to think. Anil and Alpna had been revered so highly. If the great Anil could fall so low, what faith could you have in anyone in the Kendra? What kind of people did the organization produce?

Mukul added that his job was particularly hard for him personally because Anil was his first trainer and he had always looked up to him. When talking to either man about the other, I could see that the wounds were still open: guru-disciple bonds of a sort do form in the Kendra, but Mukul knew where his true loyalties lay.

The essential response of the national Kendra, said Mukul, had been to start its work in Gwalior anew and with more vigor. The Sarodes, focused on the Needam, had not been giving a great deal of attention to the Kendra's basic programs of education and small-group discussion. Mukul threw himself into these programs energetically, organizing local Kendra stalwarts to begin teaching programs in their neighborhoods and finding new recruits. He said he wanted to show people what the Kendra really was. It took some time, he continued, but eventually many who didn't know what to make of the Sarodes' actions now liked what they saw of the *real* Kendra. He added, however, that the Ramakrishna Ashram's Swami Swaroopananda was with him from the start: the Swami had seen immediately that the Sarodes' actions were not correct. Swaroopananda, it would seem, takes the authority structures of large-scale religious organizations seriously, which may help to explain why he has largely avoided becoming entangled in one of them himself.

By the time of my active research on the Needam in 2008, only one of the several court cases concerning its ownership was settled. There had been a ruling that there could not be two Vivekananda Kendras in Gwalior and that the national Kendra had rights to the name. The Vivekananda Needam is now the site of an organization called the Ananda Kendra. *Ānanda* means "bliss" in Sanskrit and *viveka* means "intellectual discrimination." Although publicly, Kendra leaders have refrained from speaking against the Sarodes, privately stalwarts sometimes joked that the Sarodes had lost their *viveka* and now had only their *ānanda*. For the Sarodes, however, this was no joke and those in charge at the national Kendra had no intention of leaving them to their bliss.

Spiritual Personalities and Institutional Place

For a cadre-based religiously oriented institution such as the Vivekananda Kendra, the Sarodes' actions could only be seen as treacherous betrayal. Dedicated people working together closely over the years tend to assume a basic trust in one another—a trust that simplifies procedures within the group. When senior lifeworkers visited Gwalior during the years before the break, Mukul had told me heatedly, the Sarodes took them around and told them what was happening—and the visitors had *believed* them! His indignation was palpable. Individuals violating the trust of the group could not be left alone to enjoy the fruits of their shameful actions; an example must be made.

From the Sarodes' perspective, of course, the conflict between individual expression and collective identity here looked different, but it was also more complex. The Sarodes were each recognized as exceptional individuals—both within the Kendra organization and within the Gwalior community. They had found each other in the Kendra and cherished its values, and were valued enough in the organization to be allowed to start a family within it (they had two daughters). They proceeded to extend their family with the Needam—the "nest" with its children and old folks. The Needam itself then became their extended family home—within the Kendra at first, to be sure, but also theirs to guide and nurture. They developed the Needam imaginatively and in some cases exquisitely, and in doing so came to feel it was in a vital sense theirs. No one disputed that they were indeed its senior members: after the regular morning worship, where they sat on the floor with everyone else, everyone rose and most went to touch the Sarodes' feet—as they might traditionally do to their parents, or to a guru. In this setting, even while remaining a Kendra establishment, the Needam could only appear to be also very much the Sarodes' place.

Kendra leaders seemed to have appreciated the Sarodes' experiment for a while: the Needam was the only "nest" among their regional centers, but all the regional centers were a little different from one another and the place certainly looked impressive. But then the Sarodes started making the place too much their own in ways that interfered with the national Kendra's agenda for it: Alpna's Naturopathy Center was a sticking point that kept coming up in conversations (the Kendra had demanded that it be closed). And now that the Needam had become nicely established, shouldn't the Sarodes be getting more actively involved in promoting the basic discussion programs of the Kendra? The Sarodes had begun to see the Needam, and their mission there, as more their own than most Kendra higher-ups did and many locals would. To those people, what was crucial was that the Sarodes were members of a broad-based organization and as such were *not* supposed to be independent actors like Swami Swaroopananda. They shouldn't be able just to settle down into their own place and make it theirs.

Indeed, the Sarodes' situation was in fact different from that of Swami Swaroopananda. Although Swaroopananda's Ramakrishna Ashram sometimes seemed to pose as a branch of the pan-Indian Ramakrishna Mission, it was never legally a part of it and the mission had no hand in getting it started. In fact, in one of our early conversations the Swami told me that he had initially approached the mission about starting a Gwalior branch, but they demurred and told him to start something himself. Whatever the mission authorities eventually thought about the Swami building a separate local institution on the mission model, with his success they found it best to co-opt the Gwalior Ashram as best they could. If the Swami seemed to encroach on their brand, he nevertheless respected it and gave it local credence. Perhaps there was a bit of indignation on the part of the mission for a while, but there was never any sense of betrayal. He was, in his style of piety, visibly their man, but they acknowledged that the ashram was his own place. Devotees didn't have to make a choice between seeing the ashram as a respected institution in the Ramakrishna Mission style and as Swami Swaroopananda's own place; it was, in fact, both. When the Sarodes' declared their independence from the Kendra, however, members of the Kendra community in Gwalior would have to choose.

Anil must have known this, but he seems to have miscalculated the results of his actions. Broadly revered within the Gwalior Kendra—many of whose members he and Alpna had personally attracted—he probably thought most Kendra members would stick with him. Indeed they might have, had Anil been left in peace by the national Kendra—but he was out of touch enough with it to underestimate the force of its reaction. The old Gwalior Kendra community split into two camps, with each camp also gaining new members of its own: the Kendra expanding its middle-class Hindu base and the Needam drawing on local New Agers interested in yoga classes and outside people coming to the Naturopathy Center.

During my 2008 visits to the Needam, Anil often looked tired, but he carried on. He had supporters who made donations, and ran the Needam as a retreat center for organizations of all types: that year I saw a group of Osho/Rajneesh devotees, fashionably dressed in the sunset colors they favor, who had come to look the place over and discuss terms; one of them had been to a retreat there before and had recommended it to the others. There was also some income from the Naturopathy Center—particularly in the hot season, when people really take to the cold bath treatment. Anil said that of course he appreciated the Kendra's teaching and discussion programs, which embrace social and ecological as well as cultural goals. What

FIGURE 5.2 Listening to a lecture at the yoga conference, Vivekananda Needam, 2011.

he wanted to do with the Needam, though, was to demonstrate how social and environmental principles could actually be put into living practice. Yet Anil wasn't having an easy time keeping his nicely maintained establishment financially afloat as an independent entity. Meanwhile, the national Kendra was still trying to take it away from him—even though Mukul had told me that the Needam isn't really so important to them as a training site. During his final emotion-laden remarks in Delhi he said that the Ramakrishna Ashram's children's home in the hills could offer a site that readily met their needs: "We don't need the Needam's land or facilities—we can always run our own retreats at Sarada Balgram. What's important for us," he emphasized, "is the principle!" When I left the scene in 2008, my sense was that the Kendra, impelled by its principles, would prevail.

When I visited Gwalior in February 2011, however, I was happily surprised to see the Needam was still flourishing with Anil in charge. There had been further experiments with ecological housing: new accommodations in adobe and thatch. There was also a small memorial shrine (*samādhi*) to Alpna, who had died suddenly of a brain hemorrhage the previous August. Before her death, though, Alpna had expanded the naturopathy operation, starting a degree program in yoga and naturopathy with diplomas granted through an institute in Delhi. People I talked to at the Needam then were excited about a three-day yoga conference to be held at the site later in the month. When the time came, I went to the conference and learned from the naturopathy students managing registration that 350 people had signed up. Although the fee was Rs. 500—enough to make middle-class Gwalioris think twice before attending—delegates included visitors from Bulgaria and Singapore (one from each country). Colorful canvas shelters were erected to provide shade at speakers' venues (fig. 5.2) and there was a large exhibition of Ayurvedic products. The place was buzzing. The last vision of I had of Anil was of him happy and smiling in the midst of the crowd, together with his two grown daughters and adopted young special-needs son. When I returned to Gwalior on a short visit in late 2012, I asked about the Needam and was told that it was still there, and that, yes, a court case had gone in Anil's favor. I still had no confidence, though, that matters were finally settled.

6

Gurus, Disciples, and Ashrams

BEYOND RADHASOAMI

I CAME TO Gwalior in 1968 from Berkeley, California, where many of us then envisioned India as the land of gurus. And even though gurus turned out to be not so easy to find in my immediate provincial environs, I still kept my eyes open for one. My Peace Corps job was steady, but not particularly onerous, so I had plenty of time to scout around. The spiritual teachers I first encountered, however, were not quite what I was looking for. There was, for example, the itinerant *haṭha* yogi who found me not long after I arrived. For a couple of weeks he lived in an empty room at my temporary quarters at the education college, got me up in the morning for a regular routine of yoga postures, and made us great herbal tea from scratch. But I had done yoga postures and drunk herbal tea in Berkeley. We eventually had enough of each other and I sent him on to another member of our Peace Corps group in a different Madhya Pradesh city.

There wasn't much in the way of new religious movements either. The broad-based groups with idealized leaders that would later be conspicuous in town were still at their beginnings. To be sure, Swami Swaroopananda had started the Ramakrishna Ashram, described in the last chapter, and it was gaining popularity among the educated classes. One of the English teachers I worked with was eager to take me there to show me "the real India." Zealous devotees could also be found at the establishment opened by the Prajapati Brahma Kumaris—a place that, as common with this group, was referred to by the English word *museum* because it featured vivid pictorial displays illustrating the group's unorthodox cosmology. Enthusiastic young disciples kept visitors moving through the posters in sequence, explaining them, extolling the greatness of the group's founder, and emphasizing the importance of adopting the meditation techniques he taught. With a founding guru, zealous devotees, and a specific meditation practice, the Brahma Kumaris displayed the marks of an important type of new urban Hindu movement, but it was the only one that hit the casual seeker's eye at the time.[1]

Gurus and their movements were much more visible when I returned to do research in Gwalior in the late 1990s. The mix of guru-centered movements taking root there, however, was somewhat different from the ones found in Delhi, Bombay, and other metropolitan cities. The big cities had seen a surge of movements that felt more cosmopolitan, often catering to an English-speaking elite and easily finding receptive audiences on foreign shores. When guru-centered movements came to Gwalior, by contrast, they were directed toward Hindi-speakers less caught up in global flux. Even when the gurus were the same, the presentations of them diverged. Maharishi Mahesh now had a presence in town, but his principal outpost seemed to be an Ayurvedic school, not a meditation center. The loudest spiritual buzz I encountered in the late 1990s and early 2000s concerned Asaram Bapu, based in Gujarat, who gave dynamic Hindi presentations of traditional lore and who would become a fixture on religious TV. There were also posters advertising the Delhi-based Nirmala Devi, who taught a version of Kundalini yoga that appealed more to ordinary North Indians than to Western devotees. And on public walls throughout the city, enthusiastic devotees of Swami Tulsi Das—whose following extended deep into the lower castes and classes—scrawled the common words of praise with which he would become identified: Jai Gurudev, "Victory to the guru-god."

By the end of the first decade of the twenty-first century, a number of these movements had become well established locally, with new ashrams coming up on the outskirts of the city. Although Asaram's ashram on the southern outskirts of town was already well developed when I visited it in the middle of the decade, the construction at these ashrams often began very modestly and remained minimal for a while. The sites of all of them, however, were quite large: devotees were thinking big. Baba Jai Gurudev's ashram, begun in 2008, was still largely unbuilt at the end of the decade, consisting mostly of a sheltered space where devotees could assemble. It was on a new highway, though, and would be very visible to people passing by. And the Beas group of Radhasoamis—the largest branch of an old North Indian movement that will provide us with an exemplar of the guru—for a long time held meetings in a similar shelter on a very expansive piece of land well beyond the northwestern borders of the city.

FIGURE 6.1 Getting off the bus outside Baba Jai Gurudev ashram, on a highway near Gwalior then still under construction, 2010.

On Sundays, buses would ferry devotees out to a number of large outlying ashrams for regular group worship (fig. 6.1), some of it usually oriented toward the movements' leaders themselves.

Gurus in Indian Tradition

The leaders of the broad-based movements that have now become established in Gwalior and elsewhere throughout India vary not only in the specifics of their teachings but also in the ways they present themselves as gurus. The term *guru* has a very wide valence. In common Hindi usage, it can refer to any inspiring teacher. In this sense, it could be invoked by convocation speakers I heard during my time at the education college to refer to their visions of the ideal graduate. In much the same sense, the term could also be used to describe the Vivekananda Needam's Anil Sarode, seen in the last chapter, with his infectious ecological ideals. The *haṭha* yogi of my first Gwalior days, too, might serve as this sort of inspiring teacher for some of his students, even if that was not the case for me. He was, though—however, I felt about him personally—a guru for me in another sense, that of a living embodiment of a type of traditional knowledge I wanted to assimilate. This meaning of the term *guru* becomes particularly important in teaching-lineages of different sorts. An accomplished Indian musician, for example, having thoroughly assimilated the performance techniques of a specific extended musical family (*gharāṇa*) through long study with his own master can pass them on to his disciples. More than just an inspiring teacher, the guru here is rather a living link to a valued stream of traditional knowledge.

A similar sense of the term extends to gurus in religious lineages.[2] Here the valued knowledge often leads, through various paths, to salvation—which may be conceived in any number of ways, but which usually includes freedom from the cycle of birth and death. Although we hear of legendary gurus of the past putting disciples through lengthy courses of learning or strenuous trials,[3] contemporary ways of initiation are usually simpler and less stressful. In some traditions the guru passes on a mantra that the founder of the lineage received from a deity. In others, the spiritual force that is passed on seems to come directly from the guru himself or herself—through a touch, a gaze, or simply a subtle psychic connection readily recognized by ripe aspirants. Especially in these last cases, the term *guru*, which literally means "heavy," suggests someone who is a weighty embodiment of spiritual power.

Although the idea that a contemporary guru's weight is backed up by a long lineage of predecessors can convey a sense of his or her spiritual authority, not all gurus draw attention to their lineages or even have them. Some extraordinary individuals have acquired religious authority primarily through the force of their own spiritual personality without much extended contact with a particular religious teacher. Vivekananda's guru, Sri Ramakrishna, was one such figure, a nineteenth-century saint who has continued to have a lasting influence. He learned from many, but outshone them all—a retiring personage who attracted devotees largely through his own compelling psychic presence. Many of today's popular gurus also do not forefront a unique spiritual lineage—although they are usually more proactive than Ramakrishna in their approaches to the public. These include many media gurus, who—however compelling their psychic presence to those close to them—tend to be inspiring presenters of familiar lore, wise and gifted orators sometimes also adept at devotional music. Through their presentations, they offer their distant followers modernized means to salvation that carry the authority of Hindu tradition as a whole. Many of their devotees thus see them largely as vibrant and highly revered representatives of tradition. At the same time, other devotees—particularly if they have attended a live gathering where the guru offered a mantra—may also revere them as images of the divine.

Indeed, there is an important strand in Indic religious tradition that gives the figure of the living guru an extremely high place, in some ways even more important for the disciple than the divine itself. Frequently quoted maxims to this effect are evident in both Sanskrit and vernacular traditions and are frequently quoted. A Shaivite yogi may thus be reminded (in simple Sanskrit) that "If Shiva gets angry, the guru can save; if the guru is angry, there's no one at all."[4] Many North Indians of all religious persuasions, moreover, have heard a Hindi couplet that asks: "The Guru and Govind both stand there, whose feet should you touch?" Govind, an epithet of Krishna, is a Vaishnava name for the Lord, and touching the feet is a common sign of respect. The answer? "Sacrifice to your guru, who's brought Govind to you."[5] The guru as the immediate medium can be more important for the disciple than the more distant spiritual goal.

This chapter will focus on two gurus who are given comparable elevated roles by devotees: in both cases the guru becomes a figure crucial to their own salvation, sometimes even taken as a living embodiment of the divine. One, the aforementioned Baba Jai Gurudev, was, until his death in 2012, the leader of a broad North Indian movement with an active branch in Gwalior; I met him only once, very briefly, before his passing. I have had a much longer acquaintance with the other, Sant Kripal, whose following, though certainly more modest, is still substantial: he is a local guru based in Gwalior who has also attracted large groups of devotees in a number of North Indian areas. Although my initial contact with both these gurus was fortuitous, I found the contrast between them worth thinking about. I stumbled upon Sant Kripal's father at Adhyatma Niketan in Gwalior during my first stay there and have since maintained a connection with the place (yes, my own guru search came to a successful end).

Through his father, Sant Kripal has a mixed spiritual lineage, one branch of which can be traced to Shiv Dayal Singh of Agra (1818–1878), known as Radhasoami Maharaj—or sometimes, when the context is unambiguous, simply Soamiji. Soamiji was the first guru of the multi-branched Radhasoami lineage, which has an old and established presence in many North Indian cities and beyond. My links to Adhyatma Niketan gave me some familiarity with the Radhasoami tradition, but from an unorthodox angle that prompted some earlier analytic work on it.[6] Baba Jai Gurudev—whose devotees I know from small-town Rajasthan as well as from Gwalior—also traced a lineage to Soamiji but took Radhasoami tradition in a different unorthodox direction. Looking at the two gurus together thus illustrates not only the diversity of spiritually related teachers and their followings but also some different dynamics through which a single lineage of gurus can change.

Radhasoamis in *Sant* Tradition

The Radhasoami lineage emerged in a nineteenth-century middle-class social milieu similar to the one that gave rise to the Bengal Renaissance crucial to the formation of the religious service organizations discussed in the last chapter. The Radhasoamis' birthplace, however, was the North Indian city of Agra—a seat of old Indo-Muslim culture distant from the Bengali cosmopolitanism in Calcutta. To some comparable socioreligious pressures, then, it offers an alternative response. Instead of the intellectualized neo-Vedanta of the Calcutta Brahmos or the simplified Vedic ritual (and nationalism) of the Arya Samaj active in the Punjab, the Radhasoamis turned inward, cultivating a fairly straightforward meditation practice that looked to non-Vedic (or at least post-Vedic) authority. Their tradition brings together some practical elements of Sufi devotion with aspects of the love mysticism flourishing in the Krishna worship in Vrindavan, about fifty kilometers to the north of their original Agra home. It grounds them both in the aniconic sayings of the Hindi sants, saint-poets who appear in North India from about the fifteenth century and are still found today.

Appearing as a highly diverse tradition, the Hindi sants have lent themselves to different interpretations. Emerging in an Indic world that was learning to live with Islamic traditions, they sang of a lord transcending both Hinduism and Islam. In contrast to those Hindi devotional poets enraptured by the images of Ram or Krishna, the object of the sants' devotion is characterized as "without qualities" *(nir-guna)*, not to be imagined with the human-looking qualities *(guna)* of a traditional Hindu deity. The first Hindi sants were largely from the lower strata of society, with some important ones, including the great Kabir, from castes newly converted to Islam. Some of the verse attributed to Kabir himself, moreover, had a particularly iconoclastic tenor, with nothing good to say about the established traditions in any religion. Most sants, however, were more accommodating (or at least less strident) than Kabir, and their styles of piety could more easily also appeal to people in middle and higher castes—from which, by the eighteenth and nineteenth centuries, notable sants increasingly emerged.[7]

Academic writers on sant verse often draw attention to its popular nature: sants' songs, expressed in a language comprehensible to ordinary folk, frequently employed metaphors from everyday life.[8] Some writers also stress the political dimensions of its non-Brahminical origins and iconoclastic elements,[9] and it is true that some contemporary low-caste groups have rallied around sants with caste origins similar to their own.[10] But there is also an esoteric strain that can at least be read into some texts of many early sants and that begins to come clearly into view with a number of eighteenth- and nineteenth-century figures, many of whom were literate and came from the middle-ranking castes.[11] This is the strain that comes to the fore in the Radhasoamis through Tulsi Sahib (d. 1843)—recognized as Soamiji's *parents'* guru, at least, in most later lineages.

Settled in Hathras, about twenty-five miles north of Agra, Tulsi Sahib wrote long Hindi verse treatises with obvious esoteric references in which he sometimes used the term *sant mat*, "the teachings of the sants"—probably the first time anyone coined a term explicitly affirming a common sant doctrine. While just to what extent gurus in diverse North Indian sant lineages taught similar esoteric doctrine may never be determined, elements of some common *practice* can certainly be identified across a wide range of early and late sant verse. Listeners to (and, later, readers of) sant verse have frequently been exhorted to direct their attention to the *śabda*, a term that can mean "word" and that can be exoterically understood to refer to the utterances of a living guru or to those of a past sant as preserved in his verse. The term, however, can also mean "sound" and is frequently read esoterically to refer to a subtle internal sound akin to what the yogis call *nāda*: experiential sant verse often refers poetically to the sound of thundering, or of a drum or flute. Together with these sounds are references to aniconic visions: lights, for example, sometimes described as flames or lotuses. By the eighteenth century, some sants are not only writing about lights and sounds in similar ways but also seem to have been influenced by a similar esoteric theology, one that posits a loving lord saving souls entrapped in the snares of a demiurge ruling the lower worlds. It was this sort of esoteric "teachings of the sants" that Soamiji seems to have assimilated from Tulsi Sahib and later codified, emphasizing its devotional aspects and offering it to disciples through a personal presence that must have been most compelling. Soamiji gave instruction in the repetition of specific names (*simran*), visual meditation on particular internal lights and the guru's image (*dhyān*), and, most important, absorptive listening to specific internal sounds (*bhajan*—in a somewhat different sense of the term than its more common meaning of devotional hymn). The method was called *surat śabd* yoga, where *surat* refers to the attentive conscious being and *śabd* (the Hindi pronunciation of the Sanskrit *śabda*) to the divine sound current into which the *surat* merges.[12] The method wasn't especially easy—it required good concentration—but it was clearly expounded and practically accessible to interested householders.

The Radhasoamis' *surat shabd* yoga emerged as an internal religious path that was well suited to the new middle classes that first adopted it. Practitioners performed a regular quiet practice in the morning and attended an evening satsang, as the group assemblies are called. During the day they could go about their official or commercial business without having to worry about keeping up rituals that might seem superfluous in the new cultural context. To be sure, it could take new devotees some time to assimilate the cosmology—which gave familiar religious ideas about multiple divinities a gnostic turn unusual in Indic traditions—but the doctrines could be understood in terms of some quasi-scientific concepts of the day and did manage to make sense of the states experienced in meditation.[13]

It was just as well that the tradition didn't try to pose as a version of orthodox Hinduism. Although the early Radhasoami adherents tended to be socially and financially respectable, many of the most prominent ones had ambivalent identities as Brahminical Hindus. A number, including Soamiji's family, were Khatris—in those days often Nanakpanthis like the Sindhis of chapter 4. More were Kayasthas, a scribal caste that had flourished in the Mughal courts and had been open to some Islamic ways.[14] Although often well educated and affluent, they were not seen as particularly pure by Brahminic standards. The Radhasoamis offered people ready to assimilate into the middle ranks of colonial bureaucracies a satisfying practice they could unobtrusively pursue, one free of most of the external religious ritual disdained by the British masters and often not taken so seriously by their native officials either. In developing a coherent internal practice shorn of most ritual and accessible to many, the Radhasoamis hit upon a formula that could quietly thrive in growing colonial cities and could later travel easily to the West. That formula set a general pattern for many religious movements that came later: Swami Yogananda in the 1920s, Maharishi Mahesh in the 1960s, and more—all with their own sets of practices, but all making them coherent and accessible, prioritizing internal effort over external ritual. In this respect, the Radhasoamis were pioneers.

Radhasoami Lineages

When Soamiji passed on in 1878 at least four disciples carried on with initiations.[15] The two main ones were Rai Saligram, known as Huzoor Sahib, in Agra and Jaimal Singh in Beas, Punjab. Huzoor Sahib had been an important government official—the first Indian postmaster general of the Northwestern Provinces. He also had some authorization from Soamiji, who told disciples that after he was gone they should go to Saligram with questions. The Radhasoami lineages continuing in Agra stem directly from him. Jaimal Singh was a Sikh military man who settled in Beas and acquired a following including many of his fellow Sikhs and developing into what is now the largest Radhasoami group by far, with branches in many Indian cities (including Gwalior) and international devotees as early as the 1930s. Although the main Agra and Beas lineages all continue the same basic practices taught by Soamiji, the two groups differ on some fine points of cosmology, the divine names to be repeated, and the status of Soamiji as a sant.[16]

Because the question of who a guru's successor should be is often unresolvable, both the Agra and Beas lineages, over the years, have split into several sublineages. The Beas lineage remained largely unified through Jaimal Singh's first successor, but then split, with a substantial sublineage based in Delhi whose original guru stressed a more active ecumenicism and gave greater attention to organization.[17] The considerably larger main Beas satsang is sociologically more diverse than its Delhi-based alternative: although largely middle class in the cities, it also has a substantial rural following in Punjab. The Agra groups are generally smaller and more homogenous than the Beas (and Delhi) ones. The two main divisions, Soami Bagh and Dayal Bagh, have their own middle-class residential settlements near a site once on the outskirts of Agra where Soamiji used to retreat for religious practice and sometimes held satsang. Each of these communities maintains its own socioreligious ethos: Soami Bagh a more quietistic purity; Dayal Bagh a more communitarian spirit.

The two Radhasoami groups on which I will focus derive from two other initiating successors to Soamiji with lineages that have quietly survived over the years and have only recently gained some larger prominence. One of these successors was a sadhu named Garib Das, who after Soamiji's passing went to live at Sarai Rohilla in Delhi; the other was Soamiji's younger brother Pratap, called Chachaji Maharaj (cācā is Hindi for "father's younger brother"). Garib Das's lineage became visible in a big way in the later decades of the twentieth century with the enthusiastic disciples of Baba Jai Gurudev, who have happily proclaimed their allegiance to him for all to see. The lineage of Chachaji Maharaji, although established in Gwalior since the beginning of the twentieth century, has only recently gained significant recognition in some other North Indian areas with the emergence of Sant Kripal at Adhyatma Niketan. Because Sant Kripal's father (and also guru) introduced some important new dimensions to the practice offered to disciples, I'll begin with Baba Jai Gurudev, who in his teachings and practice (but not his style) is closer to the mainline Radhasoami groups.

"*Jai Gurudev Is the Name of the Lord*"

When arriving in Gwalior on a visit in the late 1990s, I was somewhat taken aback as I looked out at the wall of a main overpass near the railway station. There, painted very boldly, were the words *Jai Gurudev*, "Victory to the Guru-god." This was a phrase I knew well: one sometimes used as greeting among circles of disciples—including those at Adhyatma Niketan, where I stayed when I was in town. What was it doing here and the other walls around the city on which I saw it written? I thought it must have been the work of some lone overly expressive disciple of a guru who would later reprimand him for his misplaced enthusiasm. As I was to find out, this was not the case at all. In contrast to most mainline Radhasoami devotees I had met earlier, who were open about their practice if asked but didn't normally publicize their affiliation, devotees of Baba Jai Gurudev were encouraged to be demonstrative about their allegiance to him—often having oversize pictures of the guru in their shops and sometimes small flags proclaiming Jai Gurudev attached to their motorcycles (fig. 6.2). The difference in style was not limited to disciples

FIGURE 6.2 A sign above a vegetable wholesaler's shop in Jahazpur, Rajasthan. Baba Jai Gurudev is pictured, with his monumental temple in Mathura superimposed in the foreground. The large letters read: Jai Gurudev Vegetable—the last word remaining in English but spelled out in Hindi.

alone. Baba Jai Gurudev's own manner of self-presentation diverged sharply from that of most other gurus in Radhasoami lineages, too. These—usually town-bred, married, and with experience of desk jobs—most often cultivated humble devotional personas. Baba Jai Gurudev, by contrast, was a sadhu with a country upbringing who liked to do things on a grand scale.

Thus, on my first encounter with Jai Gurudev devotees in Gwalior, I had no reason to suspect their Radhasoami connection at all. While working with Giriraj again during a 2003 visit, word came that the guru would be passing through town on a Madhya Pradesh tour. There would be a caravan of fifty cars! This definitely seemed worth a look. We waited with the crowd at one of the planned greeting places, and as the cars passed by the growing anticipation was palpable. When the guru's vehicle, in the middle of the line, approached, the crowd surged toward it, leaving me behind. Although I never saw the guru myself that day, the organized spectacle made an impact on me, as did the demonstration of guru-devotion it inspired. Although Radhasoami and other gurus might travel by road with an entourage that needed a number of vehicles, the very long line of cars was like nothing I had ever before seen.

I didn't apprehend the historical connection of Baba Jai Gurudev to the Radhasoami tradition until I visited the house of a devotee family of his a few years later. There I saw a framed poster on the wall containing a series of four portraits beginning with Radhasoami Maharaj and ending with Baba Jai Gurudev himself (fig. 6.3). Although I didn't recognize the two intervening figures (and the family members I first asked were not so clear about them either) I could see that this was the representation of a spiritual lineage. Finally realizing that Baba Jai Gurudev offered an unusual development of a tradition with which I was already familiar, I decided to make it a focus of my research, visiting some Gwalior satsangs and talking to devotees. I got to know the movement better in 2010 when I was based in Jahazpur, a small town in south-central Rajasthan, where my wife Ann was doing anthropological research. There I saw more clearly the extent to which Baba Jai Gurudev had a broad rural following as well as an urban one—and became part of a small satsang myself.

Jahazpur is a *qasba*, as long-established places sharing qualities of both villages and cities are called, a market town and subdistrict headquarters serving the local rural area. With an old walled settlement rising partway up a hill on top of which is a deserted fort, and with substantial

FIGURE 6.3 A framed picture on the wall of a devotee's house, Gwalior. At the top left is the founder of the Radhasoami lineage; at the bottom right is Baba Jai Gurudev in his younger years. To the latter's left is his own guru, Ghurelal Mishra; at the top right is Ghurelal's older brother and guru. (There are no pictures extant of Garib Das, the link between the Radhasoami founder and Ghurelal's older brother.)

populations of both Hindus and Muslims, it was a surprisingly pleasant and interesting place to live. One day not long after arriving I was walking in a lane in an old part of town when I noticed an impressive new house with a large plaque reading *Jai Gurudev Nām Prabhu kā*, "Jai Gurudev is the name of the Lord." The house belonged to Vishnu Soni, a goldsmith with a shop in the main market who was the movement's principal point-person in the area. He was the chairman of the Jai Gurudev organization, as I was later to find out, for all of Bhilwara district, one of the thirty-three main administrative districts in the state. Bhilwara city, the main district headquarters, is a good-sized textile town—touted by boosters as "the polyester capital of Asia"—and has become a booming urban area. The fact that the Jai Gurudev district chair comes from a far-flung rural subdistrict testifies not only to Vishnu's own energy and enthusiasm but also to the rural penetration of the Jai Gurudev movement in the region. (The Jahazpur subdistrict chairman is another goldsmith from a village down the road.)

Vishnu had met Baba Jai Gurudev five years earlier, when the guru had stopped in Jahazpur overnight during a Rajasthan tour in December 2005. On that occasion, Vishnu, along with many others, received *nām*, the term used in the group for initiation into meditation practices that include the repetition of certain divine names (*nām*). By the time of our meeting Vishnu had become an ardent movement organizer and hosted a satsang at his house every Sunday evening. I attended the next meeting and returned the following week, telling people that although I hadn't received *nām*, I had heard about Jai Gurudev in Gwalior and had attended some satsangs there. The local group of frequent attendees was fairly small—on a good night maybe twenty people would show up—and I was welcomed.

I continued to attend the satsang because I was interested in the movement and was happy to make some new Jahazpur acquaintances—but also because the satsang was in many ways something religiously familiar. The *satsangīs* chanted in the *nirgun* style with which I was long conversant and there were comfortably edifying readings in a simple standard Hindi that I could easily understand. (In Jahazpur many people's Hindi was often strongly inflected by Rajasthani.) When time for *dhyān* and then *bhajan* came, I did my own meditation, but the energies in the room seemed benevolent and helpful.

Although I felt at ease at the Jahazpur satsangs, some aspects of them seemed initially jarring, different from those in which I had participated in mainline Radhasoami institutions. When I arrived I saw that most of the men had already put on headcoverings of some sort. I was familiar with headcoverings from my work with Sindhis, but had forgotten from my earlier satsang attendance in Gwalior that Jai Gurudev devotees wore them, too. (When Vishnu saw I hadn't brought anything, he kindly lent me a handkerchief.) As with the Sindhis, the customary headcovering during worship made the Jai Gurudev devotees seem different from most Hindus: the assembled group didn't look like ordinary Jahazpuris. A more striking difference from my experience at mainline satsangs was this one's vital participatory mode. At the mainline institutions, the satsang was generally a reserved affair, with most of the performance done by a reader and someone practiced in chanting the verse (at a large function at Agra's developed Dayalbagh community, I once heard a school choir); a guru or elder if present might comment. In any event, the people in attendance mostly just sat quietly, listening to what was said, sometimes in a half-meditative state. The Jahazpur satsangs were more interactive, with the attendees repeating, verse by verse, hymns read out loud by members of the group in turn. With everyone more involved in the reading, it was begun and usually concluded with a rousing "Jai Gurudev!" I was reminded of Indian village performances where some sort of vocal audience response is customary, although when the evening's program was punctuated at crucial moments with a reader's formulaic questions, it could seem like a cross between a catechism and a school cheer:

"Jai Gurudev is whose name?"
"The Lord's!"
"What is the Lord's Beloved Name?"
"Jai Gurudev!"
"What is the Lord's Pure Name?"
"Jai Gurudev!"
"Is Jai Gurudev the name of a man (*insān kā*)?"
"It's the name of God (*Bhagvān kā*)."[18]

Vishnu had told me at the first satsang I attended that their guru's name was Tulsi Das and that Jai Gurudev was a name for the divine, a distinction I heard repeated several times during my talks with disciples. Emphasizing the difference between the name itself and the guru who was known by it was obviously a major point on the teaching agenda. Later, speaking with a senior devotee at the main Jai Gurudev ashram in Mathura, I was told that divine names tend to get stale after four generations of gurus, and this had happened to the Radhasoami name dear to the hearts of many mainline *satsangīs*. Baba Jai Gurudev had revealed a new divine name—the term sometimes used for the process was *jagāyā*, he "awakened" it, arousing from latency something that already existed. With the newly awakened name, I was told, Baba Jai Gurudev could now ply a very big boat to ferry people across the ocean of existence: anyone who wanted could get on. This was no longer simply another lineage descended from Soami Shiv Dayal; theologically and institutionally, it was something new.

The Big Boat

After I had attended satsang for several weeks, Vishnu announced that their guru, on tour in Rajasthan, would shortly be coming to Jaipur, the state capital about four hours' drive away. I had to visit Jaipur anyway to take care of some business and arranged to go when Baba Jai Gurudev would be coming. There would be a satsang the evening before, and the guru himself would appear in the morning at a 6:00 a.m. session. At that time he would also give *nām*. I set out without knowing quite what to expect or whether I really wanted to get *nām*—which, given my previous connections to Adhyatma Niketan, I feared might be somewhat disorienting: although they were still reading plenty of sant verse at Adhyatma Niketan by the time I found it, the guru was no longer regularly giving formal *sant mat* initiations. In my earlier work on the Radhasoamis, though, I had read about how Beas gurus often gave initiations after public satsangs to a group of newcomers, and imagined the coming situation in Jaipur would be something like that. If things felt right, I thought, maybe I would join that group if I could.

The Jaipur program was held in a vast open field at a school on the northwestern outskirts of town. The evening satsang had already begun when I arrived and there were large crowds. The atmosphere here was altogether different from that I experienced at the few large, mainline Radhasoami functions I had attended. Those were attended largely by established devotees who were predominantly middle class. Certainly, there were plenty of middle-class people here, too—government workers with whom I spoke—and a few people who looked quite well off. But many more looked not so well off: members of the lower and lower middle urban classes, and visiting country folk without much cash. Long rows of vendors sat camped out on mats on the dirt, with their wares set out in front of them: lithographs of Baba Jai Gurudev and his lineage, and many pamphlets and books (including some by Kabir and Tulsi Sahib). These inexpensive, simply displayed goods, together with the numbers of people with rural dress and manners, could give the function the air of an outsize village fair.

There also seemed to be more new people than I had noticed at any mainline Radhasoami functions—people like me who didn't quite know where to go and were in need of direction. This was no doubt an effect of the movement's unabashed advertising and active proselytization efforts, which in mainline lineages usually had a much lower profile. Even in the backwater Jahazpur area these efforts could be organized and extensive. For a number of weeks before the major annual function at the Jai Gurudev headquarters in Mathura, Vishnu had been absent from the satsangs still held at his house. He had instead been going around with a group of Jahazpur devotees to incipient satsangs in villages and towns in the region, encouraging people to attend the function and organizing some chartered buses to take them at minimal cost. In contrast to some Radhasoami lineages, which had arrangements for initiation by proxy, in the Jai Gurudev movement devotees had to receive *nām* from the guru himself. Attendance at a large function at least once was crucial. Repeated attendance was highly recommended: just as a father gives blessings to his children when he sees them, so does the guru to his disciples.[19] With new proselytes and old devotees, the crowd at the Jaipur gathering I attended was extremely large—many intently listening to speakers priming them for the next morning's events. Most people were planning to spend the night and many had already marked out choice spots to sleep under the expansive open tent.

Outside the tent, people with big white sacks circulated through the flocks of devotees, asking if they had made their contribution yet. The approach was not subtle, but remained within its limits. After I had contributed once, I said so to the next person who approached me, who then left me alone. The idea, also reinforced in satsang talks and practice, was that whenever devotees come to a meeting they should give at least something, according to their means. When dealing with a following that is often not very prosperous, instead of waiting for the spontaneous generous gift, organizers reinforce the habit of regular small donations.

The crowd had expanded even further when I returned the next morning sometime before 6:00 a.m. I soon happened upon Vishnu and a couple of other Jahazpur devotees, who had come in on a hired bus with some others from the area at midnight. (They were apparently more interested in the main event than in the evening session—which they had however recommended to me as a newcomer.) Busy with morning ablutions, they suggested I hurry to find a place to sit on the ground near the front of the assembly, where I could get a good view of the guru. Others had given me similar advice: proximity to the guru was important, especially for newcomers—the initiation consisted of more than just instructions; there were energies to be assimilated, too. Treading carefully around some yawning children and still sleeping grownups, I found a spot on the ground not far back from the stage and kept it occupied as people who had spent the night there milled about. At about 6:00 some preliminary speakers began to appear on stage, and at 6:30 attendants of Baba Jai Gurudev carried out a plank bed on which he was sitting.

The guru was an old man, dressed in white robes, his head covered with a white cloth in a distinctive broad style. Although he had some obvious physical infirmities, he wasn't frail: big boned and heavy set, he could speak with authority, if in a throaty voice. While at first glance Baba Jai Gurudev could then pass for someone in his eighties, people said he was 114 years old at the time—not so easy to believe, but not readily disprovable either.[20] Public biographical details about the guru are spare. He was born in Khitaura, a small village in Etawah district, Western U.P. His caste is never officially mentioned, but it's no great secret that he was born a Yadav—a member of a traditionally pastoral and farming community that is numerous in that area and has been politically powerful in the state.[21] The son of a landowner, we are told, the future guru lost his parents early and soon began the path of a religious wanderer. He eventually found his guru in a village in Aligarh district, a Brahmin householder named Ghurelal Mishra who had succeeded his brother in a Radhasoami succession from Garib Das.[22] After Ghurelal passed on,[23] Baba Jai Gurudev performed ascetic practice by himself for several years and gave his first public teaching in 1953. This would make him fifty-seven at the time if we accept the age claimed for him. In any event, his persona as a guru was always that of an older man, but one who for a long time retained his vital, activist energies.

Baba Jai Gurudev's personal style, reflecting his village background, was more folksy and populist than most mainline Radhasoami gurus, who have most often grown up with town or city ways and worked as professionals or government servants. His homegrown manners had been particularly attractive to lower-caste rural folk in the Hindi-speaking areas, with whom he worked intensively in the 1960s and 1970s. In addition to offering a path to salvation, he would help people troubled by spirits—which he continued to do even at big urban gatherings. From 1984 to 1997 he became active in electoral politics by starting the Doordarshi ("far-seeing") party, which eventually fielded candidates in many North Indian states but achieved scant electoral success. He had also begun to give prophecies, mostly of terrible misfortunes in the future that his devotees could escape, as affirmed in another line of catechism/cheer that is sometimes repeated:

> "Who will save you from the coming troubles?"
> "Jai Gurudev!"[24]

Baba Jai Gurudev was a popular, activist, millennialist who also offered a version of *surat śabd* yoga.

Soon the guru started his discourse. He began with themes familiar to me from listening to previous *sant mat* (and other Indic religious) discourses—an individual's great good fortune in having a human body and the crucial necessity of doing spiritual practice. Not hearing anything particularly new, my mind began to wander. When I turned my attention back to the discourse, I realized the guru had segued into actually giving *nām*—disclosing the five names that are given at initiation, each understood to emanate from a distinct heavenly sphere. I had enough background in Radhasoami tradition to know that these were the same five names revealed in Beas initiations and recognized as potent in others. Baba Jai Gurudev led the crowd in chanting them, first one name repeated a few times, then another, then both together, then three, and so on, helping new initiates learn them. Wedged fairly tightly into the middle of the crowd, my shoes under a mat someone else was now sitting on, I couldn't easily get up and didn't really want to. The die was cast: I was getting *nām* from Baba Jai Gurudev. He later went on to describe particular lights seen in each of the heavens and sounds associated with them. This was the secret, revealed over microphones to thousands of people.

The secret was actually a lot to remember, but lithographs containing icons indicating the particular lights and sounds in sequence—cryptic enough to be mystifying to the uninitiated—were inexpensively available from most of the vendors camped out at the site. And if you paid five rupees to register (then about the price of two cups of tea), you could get a half-page photocopy with more detailed instructions that you were told to memorize, destroy, and by no means divulge! After the session was over, registrars posted at a number of places filled out (and kept duplicates of) five-rupee receipts for jostling groups of people squatting around them—many of whom, as they looked on curiously, didn't seem very literate. Here, truly, was an esoteric teaching for the masses.

A Secret Tradition for Ordinary People

I began to see how seriously ordinary Jai Gurudev devotees could take the imprecations to secrecy several weeks after my return from Jaipur, when I was visited by Manoj Sain and his mother Kusum. The Sains were a barber caste, one that, like those of the majority in the satsang, did not rank very high in the traditional social order. Prominent in the satsang were, for example, a tailor, a family from an old wine-trading caste, now dealing in ready-to-wear, and a number of Khateeks, former untouchables dealing in animals for slaughter, who, in economically liberalized India, had turned into spirited entrepreneurs—initiating and largely maintaining control of Jahazpur's wholesale and retail vegetable market.[25] Even the goldsmiths—many of whom, like Vishnu Soni, were quite prosperous by local standards—remained members of an artisan caste, not a particularly dignified station in traditional society. (Although I had heard that a Brahmin from the area was involved in the movement, he didn't normally come to the Jahazpur satsang.) Whatever their caste, though, most of the *satsangīs* active in the movement were generally active and hard-working people. Thus, Manoj was finishing high school as a math major and seemed poised for the modern world, while his mother had the direct, sometimes authoritative manner sometimes cultivated in village women of her caste, who have often worked as midwives.

The two had paid a call because they were worried about me, they said. I hadn't come to satsang for two Sundays, and they wondered why. Was there some problem? I had a cold and they could see it, so they didn't press the issue. But there seemed to be a little more to their visit than an inquiry after my health. They asked if I knew the names, meaning the five names heard at initiation. I nodded. Manoj and I had met briefly at the Jaipur function, so he knew I had been exposed to them. His mother, however, wasn't so sure, and asked me what they were. When I started reciting them, however, she immediately told me to be quiet: the people downstairs might hear (the floor in the covered roof courtyard we used as a sitting-room had some grating in it that helped ventilate the land-lord's flat below). The names were to be kept secret. Kusum pointed to the study and suggested that we move there for privacy. Not until after we closed the door did they ask me to start again. After they were satisfied that I knew the names, they asked if I recited them with a *mālā*, a string of rosary beads. I said no, I just repeated the names internally, which in fact I sometimes did, now that I had actually heard them from a guru. This answer had been good enough for Vishnu, who had also inquired about a *mālā*, but Manoj and especially Kusum insisted that I must have one; they would arrange it for me. Although reciting the names with a *mālā* was not a regular, or even common, practice in the Radhasoami branches with which I was familiar, it resonated with the rural traditions familiar to Baba Jai Gurudev and many of his adherents. The fact that the use of a *mālā* had been integrated into the regular prescribed practice could make some devotees very insistent about it.

The conversation that ensued began with Manoj and Kusum present-ing doctrines common within guru-centered movements, but in ways that spoke more directly to personal emotions than I usually encountered. I had come to Baba Jai Gurudev they began, because I had been chosen by him; he had called me. This struck me at the time as an affecting expla-nation of the meeting of guru and disciple—one in fact not uncommon in devotional movements[26] but never presented to me personally before (I was more used to accounts couched in abstract terms of karma, fate, or destiny). Baba Jai Gurudev, like other gurus in Radhasoami lineages, enjoins strict vegetarianism, and Kusum inquired about our dietary habits. I assured her that we hadn't eaten meat, fish, or eggs for decades— which was true—but the more usual Western dietary proclivities were well known and Kusum wanted to make sure we understood their broader ramifications. She proffered a dire warning: if we ate meat, which is very often goat meat in India, we would be born as goats in the next life and people would eat us. No talk about the virtues of nonviolence here, or the ways in which a vegetarian diet aids *surat śabd* yoga practice, but straightforward eye-for-an-eye retribution. The thought of being eaten as a goat, even though it seemed a bit fanciful, was disturbing. The down-home personal touch seemed to be working. When talk turned to Baba Jai Gurudev's prophecies, however, the millennial fear and scale of the miraculous turned out to be too much for me. There would be drought and famine, they said, but Babaji's people would be saved. When the time came, he would reveal knowledge of a special plant that could be cultivated: one leaf of it would satisfy someone's hunger for seven days! This was getting hard for me to take seriously: Baba Jai Gurudev foretold of fire and brimstone and offered manna from the earth as well.

My uneasiness was partly a matter of rational credulity. I had long before stretched the bounds of my Western common sense to take in many understandings of other gurus' devoted disciples—who most often believed not only in the metaphysical veracity of their own internal experiences, but also that gurus could intervene for them in the world, now and then effecting little miracles when they were in distress. Small marvels of the same sort, of course, also sometimes happened to Baba Jai Gurudev's devotees. A Jahazpur *satsangī*, for example, taking a late express bus from Jaipur got off at the closest town on the highway—only to find no transport for the last twenty kilometers home. He closed his eyes, thought of the guru, and as soon as he opened them a truck came driven by someone he knew, headed to Jahazpur. His ride had spontaneously materialized! Once someone accepted that gurus could have powerful psychic bonds with disciples, as my own experience has led me to do, possibilities like this seem imaginable. They are, in any event, subjective in the way of most individual religious understandings, difficult to disprove, and relatively harmless. Baba Jai Gurudev's large-scale millennial predictions, however—which had collective, outer-world ramifications—were of another order, surpassing my already stretched boundaries of belief.

My discomfiture with Baba Jai Gurudev's predictions, however, also stemmed from their rhetorical style, thus displaying my elitist prejudices.

They were presented in strong, direct language by a guru understood to say just what he thinks. That those predictions really could inspire fear in the hearts of devotees made me uneasy, even though, as in most millennial movements, that fear could motivate followers to give attention to their spiritual practice and moral behavior. Baba Jai Gurudev could also use similarly strong language to decry the uselessness of outer ritual worship, in fact making him true to the iconoclastic tradition of Kabir, remembered for his sharply spoken truths. Although I was never troubled reading Kabir's iconoclastic pronouncements on the page, hearing of the hurt and angered response of one of Jahazpur's temple priests to Baba Jai Gurudev's talks bothered my universalist sensibilities: couldn't the guru at least be a little more tactful in public? Still, Baba Jai Gurudev's direct and dramatic language, like the sayings of Kabir and some other early sants, could have a vital impact on many ordinary people in the North India countryside to which the guru was most acculturated. The appeal of his movement to more cosmopolitan town and city folk, however, seemed to derive sooner from the guru's soteriological power and the *surat shabd* yoga practice itself. When the guru's predictions and unsophisticated personal style were given less attention, Baba Jai Gurudev's satsang could occupy a niche similar to many contemporary middle-class religious movements. It was as one of these urban groups that, in Gwalior, I first encountered it.

A Middle-Class Urban Movement, Too

Baba Jai Gurudev first gave a large public presentation in Gwalior in 1972, a year taken by many there as marking the substantial beginning of his movement in the city. The satsang in Gwalior, however, had earlier roots, with a few dedicated devotees initiated elsewhere already meeting regularly in each other's houses. Much longer established in Gwalior than in Jahazpur, the satsang's early enthusiasts there were also from the more elevated strata of traditional Hindu society, including a Brahmin, a Sindhi family, and a Maratha from the old Gwalior aristocracy: the latter's house on a street named after his family long serving as a Laskhar satsang center. In contrast to many rural devotees, those from higher-class urban backgrounds tended to see Baba Jai Gurudev less as an exceptional being with a common country touch than as an accomplished guru able to lead them along an accessible esoteric path. Satsang speakers oriented to urban audiences were likely to keep quiet about the guru's prophecies and emphasize the importance and benefits of daily practice. Thus a senior devotee based in the large Rajasthani city of Ajmer could exhort a group of assembled devotees: if you let yourself become absorbed in *śabda* during the cool of the night, you'll be fresh for work in the morning. At the end of his talk he noted the existence of Babaji's prophecies—"you can read about them if you like"—but he didn't repeat any of them. He focused instead on practical, salvific aspects of the guru's teachings that city folk could readily take in. In Gwalior the regular attendees appeared to be a mostly educated, middle-class group—the sort of people one might see at meetings of many urban religious movements, if perhaps a little more *lower*-middle class and *un*cosmopolitan than at some.

Since late 2008, the regular Sunday meetings of the Gwalior satsang have been held in an ashram about twelve kilometers south of the city. Before then, the regular Sunday satsangs were held at the houses of four devotees who lived in different sections of the diffuse Gwalior urban area. Now, separate buses ply the different sections to bring devotees to the ashram outside town. The new ashram thus does more than relieve the crowding at some of the private houses (when I attended the main Lashkar satsang in earlier years, the place was often uncomfortably packed). It also brings the Gwalior Jai Gurudev community together. About 250 people showed up at the new ashram on a brisk Sunday morning in November 2010, a number consistent with estimates of normal attendance I have heard (fig. 6.4). At another satsang early the next April, held in conjunction with a movement festival and followed by a meal, the attendance was larger, about 400. At both satsangs, we gathered in an open pavilion, the only part of the ashram then built: the rest of the ashram property was land under cultivation—which, especially at harvest time, provided devotees a way to perform active service.

The general format of the program at both satsangs was similar to the ones at Jahazpur, with hymns, meditation, and readings, but there were also some differences. At the end of the Gwalior meetings, there were announcements of smaller satsangs sponsored by individual devotees, usually in conjunction with family celebrations (often weddings); slips of paper with names and addresses were handed out to those who anticipated attending. Although members of the Jahazpur satsang also socialized with one another and held special events, the small size of the group did not require formal announcements and written information: word of mouth and phone calls usually sufficed. The meditation stage of the Gwalior satsang was also longer and more relaxed than at Jahazpur, with individual *satsangīs* moving through it at their own pace, with no separate

FIGURE 6.4 Arriving at the Baba Jai Gurudev ashram outside Gwalior for Sunday satsang, 2010.

cues, as at Jahazpur, for *dhyān* and *bhajan*. Perhaps in the older and larger Gwalior satsang, members needed leeway for their different degrees of experience in meditation: for many, cues might just prove a distraction. Finally, even though Vishnu gave talks as a visiting speaker in villages, at the regular Jahazpur satsang, where people knew him well, he just concluded with readings from Babaji's sermons and other items of interest printed in movement periodicals. In Gwalior, there were a few obvious, old recognized leaders who sometimes gave talks.

Two of these leaders were distinguished through their unusual dress, part of a group of longtime *satsangīs* who habitually wore jute. In 1984, Baba Jai Gurudev announced that his disciples, as a mark of the simple life, should give up normal clothing (whether Indian or Western) and dress in items made of jute—reminiscent of the sackcloth of biblical times. This pronouncement, however, turned out to be too much to ask of most devotees—especially since wearable jute cloth, despite its simplicity, did not come cheap. Some devotees tried to reach a personal compromise by wearing regular clothes at home, but changing into jute when they went to the Mathura ashram or on other religious occasions. To Baba Jai Gurudev, however, such behavior was sheer hypocrisy, and he announced that people who couldn't regularly wear jute shouldn't wear it all. Most people then stopped doing so, but a few old devotees from those days persisted. The result was to create a sort of visible elite within the movement, of whom some have in fact occupied roles of local and national leadership.

Because the guru gave no standards for the distinctive clothing, these people wear their jute differently, sometimes as heavy burlap sewn into loose fitting Indian-style clothes, sometimes as fine-spun material crafted with a short-sleeved natty look. Although those who have come to spiritual and administrative maturity within the movement since 1984 generally bear no marks of sartorial distinction, a few ordinary devotees might have an upper garment tailored out of a jute-blend material that they wear at satsang as a sort of sectarian fashion statement—a practice now seen less as a form of hypocrisy than one of enthusiastic identification.

Wearing jute regularly while living within ordinary Indian society is not always so easy, but a few *satsangīs* ready to stand out as proud devotees have done it anyway. The unusual dress of one of the two Gwalior jute-wearing elders probably did not present much of a challenge to him. He had has own confectionary business and spent much of his time either out of sight making sweets or behind the counter selling them. New customers, when they saw him, may have noticed his unusual attire, but small-time sweet-shop owners are often dressed quite casually anyway. Distinctive clothing seems to have presented more problems to the other of the two, but not for too long. A very old and devoted disciple, he had been initiated in 1960 while still a student and spent much of his time as a retiree helping to nurture incipient satsangs in regional towns and villages. A good deal of his working life, however, had been spent at the state accountant general's office, based in Gwalior. While at the office, he said, he would wear jute every day. To my incredulous look, he responded that even though his colleagues remarked about his dress for a while, it soon lost its novelty and they kept quiet. Given the diversity of religiocultural traditions in India, people there tend to stop noticing others' harmlessly unusual ways.

Serious stress can be felt by Jai Gurudev devotees, however, who face objections from their families. More than many new religious groups emerging from Hindu traditions, the Jai Gurudev movement has been religiously dissident—with an unorthodox cosmology, caste heterogeneity, and a guru who spoke very directly; his followers, moreover, often avidly proclaim their allegiance to him. People with conventional conservative sensibilities could find all this grating when it directly touches them. Thus, for example, one young middle-class man from a mercantile caste spoke of his parents' inability to comprehend his attraction for Baba Jai Gurudev: was there something lacking in the family's regular home worship? They also disdained the social composition of the satsang itself, he said, and were unhappy that he was mixing so closely with people of all caste backgrounds. He persisted in doing so, however, regularly help-ing out at group meetings, while continuing to live in an extended family compound. Where was he to go? No doubt his parents hoped that his new religious enthusiasm would eventually pass.

It's easier, then, when whole families follow the guru. New devotees are encouraged to bring family members into the group, while established *satsangī* families often arrange marriages among themselves—a practice encouraged by Baba Jai Gurudev. At the same time though, I was told, Babaji discouraged marriages that would cross caste boundaries—which could be unnecessarily disruptive to the fabric of everyday life, especially within the less than cosmopolitan environments in which most devotees live. Tradition-minded Indians can generally abide unconventional beliefs and outspoken holy persons more easily than they can gross violations of social norms.

The Mathura Center

Although Gwalior's two jute-wearing elders spoke with authority on issues of doctrine and practice, when I had questions about the national move-ment, I was normally referred to S. K. Lulla, who was then still the long-time general secretary of the main Jai Gurudev organization at Mathura. He happened to have grown up in Gwalior, however, and continued to keep his home and accounting business there. I had looked for Lulla dur-ing several stays in the city, but he was not an easy man to find. Although his house was simple enough to identify—like Vishnu Soni's in Jahazpur, it is an upscale building with *Jai Gurudev* prominently displayed on it—Lulla himself was often out of town, on tour with the guru or at the main Mathura ashram. One day in 2010, however, I found Lulla at his office, where he was happy to talk. His family was Sindhi, he said, but they had migrated from Karachi before the 1947 partition. He had inherited the role of general secretary from his father, who like Baba Jai Gurudev was a disci-ple of Ghurelal. Lulla's father had acknowledged his fellow disciple's suc-cessorship early and had been with him from the beginning. Trained in the sciences, Lulla's father had worked at the Hindu University in Benares when Baba Jai Gurudev was active in the Gangetic plains and had later found work in Gwalior. Lulla himself had taken over the general secretary-ship when his father got too old for the job.

Having taken initiation in 1973 at the age of twelve, S. K. Lulla is one of a small proportion of devotees in his generation who grew up in a devotee family. Like many Gwalior devotees, although for reasons more readily forgiven, Lulla attended satsang irregularly. His absences, however, also sometimes brought their rewards: during a November 2007 satsang in which I participated, for example, Lulla, on tour with Baba Jai Gurudev, got the guru on the phone to offer a special blessing to the group (amplification for the satsang was provided by a cell phone on loudspeaker that was held to a microphone). Lulla's long, if then sporadic, participation in the Gwalior satsang could make its members feel privileged.

When asked about the total number of Jai Gurudev devotees and where they lived, Lulla said that they could be counted in tens of millions ("crores" in Hindi and Indian English), with the vast majority in India. There were also a few groups of Indians living abroad and a very small number of Western disciples. He also volunteered that most devotees were poor. Although tens of millions is a pretty vague number, it may have been the best he could reasonably do. It's hard to keep accurate count in a movement that has existed for decades and that includes many villagers of little means and less literacy. It's also not clear just whom to include: anyone who has come to a big meeting and heard *nām* could be considered a devotee—as well as others who profess devotion but have never heard Baba Jai Gurudev in person. Tens of millions at least gives a sense of proportion. The same sense of proportion, moreover, suggests a substantial preponderance of rural followers in the movement, with Lulla estimating only two to three thousand in Gwalior—not so many given the size of the city and the group's forty-year history within it. (One of the jute-wearing elders had given a similar figure—three to four thousand— adding that most do not regularly come to the satsangs.) Extrapolating from the Gwalior figures across North Indian cities would show Baba Jai Gurudev's devotees having a visible urban middle-class presence, but one dwarfed in his movement as a whole by his rural followers. The Jai Gurudev movement, I learned, actually had its greatest expansion among the socially and economically disadvantaged in rural areas of the Gangetic plains—U.P. and Bihar—and from there had spread among similar classes into further reaches of North India. And even as his urban centers became more solidly established, the guru continued to serve the less privileged rural world out of which he came—even in very old age bringing his tour through small towns such as Jahazpur to which people from surrounding villages could easily find their way.

The central organization at Mathura that helped give shape to the movement during the guru's lifetime was called the Jai Gurudev Dharam

Pracharak Sanstha, "the Jai Gurudev Institution for Propagating Religion," but the Hindi was used even in the organization's English-language writings.[27] Its internal structures were liable to seem rather opaque to those not actively involved in it. Outsiders looking for organizational information on its website when the guru was alive would find only Baba Jai Gurudev himself listed as its head and S. K. Lulla as general secretary, with Lulla's cell number as a contact phone.[28] When I inquired of senior Gwalior devotees, I would hear about a traditional ashram model where all matters come to the attention of the guru himself. They were presenting an ideal, of course, but perhaps they were also remembering the old days: versions of the traditional model are still common in small ashrams when gurus are strong and devotees compliant—we'll soon see one in play at Adhyatma Niketan. At the time I inquired, however, Baba Jai Gurudev was old and not in the best of health, while the Mathura ashram—the hub of a wide national organization—had about a thousand people regularly in residence. I got a clearer answer about the way things worked there from Vishnu Soni, who was then closely involved with organization work as district chairman. In a straightforward businessman's manner, he spoke of a clearly understood network of responsible devotees, if one that remained informal and unpublicized. There were about thirty "headmen"—Vishnu used the Hindi word mukhiyā—who were in charge of different fields of ashram work. These fields included not only agriculture, hospitals, schools and the like, but also the complex organizational feats entailed in the assembling of massive numbers of devotees at periodic events at the extensive Mathura grounds. State and district chairpersons from different areas knew whom to contact at headquarters to make appropriate arrangements for people from their areas.

The North India-wide organization regularly shifted into high gear to manage the principal Mathura gatherings. These were held three times a year: at spring and rainy-season Hindu festivals (Holi and Gurupurnimaa) and at the commemoration of Baba Jai Gurudev's own guru's passing in the winter. At each gathering, people might stay for up to seven days, with the organization of group transport and housing falling in good part to workers at the district level. Vishnu described his efforts for the Bhilwara district devotees: there were tents to contract and buses to hire; foodstuffs were brought from the countryside along with people to cook them. The Bhilwara pilgrims were charged a flat rate (Rs. 500 in 2011) toward their travel and lodging expenses,[29] with visitors from different districts camping separately on the very extensive land surrounding the temple. This camping arrangement was not only a practical way to handle the crowds but could also help people with little experience outside their immediate locales feel comfortable among others whose ways they understood. In doing so, further, it could lead to interactions among *satsangīs* from different parts of the district that might strengthen a sense of regional Jai Gurudev community—a practical, personalized complement to the sometimes impersonal religious vastness that could envelop a devotee when everyone came together for the guru's spiritual talks.

Indeed, the Mathura headquarters itself can still invoke awe in devotees and others, too. It was designed to be monumentally impressive (fig. 6.5). The headquarters lies along both sides of the Delhi-Agra road as it bypasses Mathura, with a sprawling (but ordinary looking) ashram to the east, where Baba Jai Gurudev lived, and to the west a temple of very ambitious scale called Naam Yog Sadhana Mandir, "The Temple of *nām-yoga* Spiritual Practice." Constructed of white marble with spires and a dome, the temple can, to the casual observer, recall the Taj Mahal, which is located about an hour to the south in Agra. Devotees, however, are likely to see the building's main claim to fame as a combination of architectural features that makes it look like a Hindu temple from one angle, a mosque from another, and a church from another; some also say it can look like a Sikh Gurudwara, too. Thus, according to a movement website "The temple belongs to the entire human race irrespective of their caste and creed."[30] Ownership here, though, just means that the temple is meant to be inclusive and open. Active support,

FIGURE 6.5 The Jai Gurudev Temple, Mathura, as seen from the ashram across the highway.

when I visited in late 2010, was not invited from everyone: a prominent sign near the donation box in the immense main hall forbade anyone who is not a strict vegetarian from contributing. Below the main hall, at basement level there were two other rooms: one referred to as a *guphā*, which can refer to a meditation "cave"; the other, a shrine to Jai Gurudev's guru. Both illuminated with colored, sometimes flashing, lights, they were not meant to appeal to those with sophisticated tastes but were likely to impress most of their intended visitors.

While the temple and crowds together could have a mighty effect on devotees during festival times, the situation of the grand temple on a main highway could also attract casual sightseers (fig. 6.6). During my visit, I encountered a small group of Russian tourists at the main gate. They had stopped because the building was so impressive, but they didn't know at first what it was (eventually they understood that it was a "church"). There were also Indian visitors who knew what it was and were exploring the expansive edifice curiously—and devotees present whose job was obviously to greet newcomers, provide explanations, and proselytize as appropriate.

Like the Mathura ashram, Gwalior's Jai Gurudev ashram, too, had been situated on a main highway—still under construction when the ashram was first developed—no doubt in part so that it could eventually catch the attention of people passing by. A Gwalior devotee, moreover, had bought some land across the way, so there would be space for further development. Situating new public buildings on main roads seems to have been a favored strategy in the movement: I was told more than once that Baba

FIGURE 6.6 Visitors taking pictures in front of the Jai Gurudev Temple, Mathura.

Jai Gurudev chose the spot for the Gwalior ashram himself. Who knows where a passerby's curious glance might lead?

In fact, when Baba Jai Gurudev was in residence at the main Mathura ashram, it was even possible for unexpected callers to get access to the guru himself. My 2010 visit to the ashram had been occasioned by a conference on Radhasoami tradition I was scheduled to attend the next day at Agra's Dayal Bagh. Time was short and I had hired a car for a few hours' excursion in the afternoon. Wandering around the temple, I was approached by a young greeter—who answered some of my questions, showed me the basement rooms, and asked if I wanted to see the ashram across the street. I readily agreed. I was immediately struck by the contrast between the ornate temple and the ashram's plain rooms and grounds. The only place that stood out was the garage, replete with a great many roomy, late-model vehicles, which were used when a large retinue accompanied the guru on tour. My greeter left me talking with some longtime devotees and then returned to ask if I wanted to have *darśan* of Baba Jai Gurudev—the "sight" or other simple interaction with an elevated being that has the potential to bestow blessings. Just as the worshippers seen in chapter 1 seek the *darśan* of their chosen deity in a temple, disciples of a guru treasure his or her *darśan*—which is often more difficult to get and experienced more palpably.[31] Baba Jai Gurudev was at a construction site a kilometer down the road, I was told, and should be able to meet people soon. We went with the car and driver I had brought from Agra and waited until the guru was ready for us: he was clearly visible in a van at the undeveloped site with a nurse tending to him.

I hadn't made the trip with even the slightest thought of getting the guru's *darśan* and wondered why it was happening. Probably, to my greeter and others, I appeared as a potentially fruitful prospect: a mature, Hindi-speaking foreigner who showed a genuine interest in the place. It also didn't hurt that, coming from Dayal Bagh, I was seen as a sectarian Radhasoami, many of whom have no great respect for Baba Jai Gurudev. Certainly, not everyone was invited to come see the guru: no uncomprehending Russian tourists or ordinary Indian visitors as far as I could see. Yet everyone present when the guru was ready was welcome to join the short line of people that formed to receive personal *darśan*. This included my shy driver from Agra, who was eventually coaxed into it. Baba Jai Gurudev was sitting in his van with the sliding side-door open and we filed up to him, one by one (fig. 6.7). When my turn came, I was introduced as a Radhasoami, and the guru nodded benevolently. Then, as

FIGURE 6.7 Baba Jai Gurudev in his van, 2010, with thanks to Adnoida and Wikimedia Commons for the original photo.

he did with most of the others, he looked me in the eye and put his hand on my head, seeming to radiate a palpable energy that elevated my consciousness for the rest of the day. I was glad I had come.

Two Lineages Converge at Adhyatma Niketan

I am also always glad to visit Adhyatma Niketan and have the *darśan* of Sant Kripal, called Maharajji by his devotees. My attitudes toward Maharajji and Baba Jai Gurudev, however, are necessarily different. My contact with Baba Jai Gurudev and his devotees was sometimes moving but was much briefer than my relationship with Maharajji, whom I have known since 1969. He was just a teenager then (I was just out of college) and few suspected that he would become a guru in his own right. About six months into my Peace Corps stay I had become a disciple of his father, Thakur Mansingh Kushwah, known to his devotees as Malik Sahib. Since then, I have had many personal interactions with them both, occasions arising less from the number of years I've known them than from the relatively small size of their followings. Although gurus' ways are different, the smaller the scale of a guru's following, the greater, generally, is the proportion of devotees that will normally be able to interact personally with him or her. And in contrast to Baba Jai Gurudev's "tens of millions" of devotees, Malik Sahib's numbered in the hundreds and Sant Kripal's number in the (mere) thousands. Thus, the story I tell about the gurus at Adhyama Niketan will be of finer grain as well as longer historical depth than the one I told about Baba Jai Gurudev. It will also betray a different sort of reverence.

A Gentleman Yogi at Home

Malik Sahib built Adhyatma Niketan as a large house on the northern outskirts of Gwalior in the 1960s after taking early retirement from a career as a middle ranked government official (fig. 6.8). The name of the place translates as "Spiritual Home." Malik Sahib would say that he gave it that name because it was a home where he lived with his family but could also serve as a spiritual home for his disciples—for whom a few rooms were also built. With increased facilities for visitors under his son Maharajji, the place now looks more like a full-fledged ashram than it did in its early days and is frequently referred to as such.

Although Malik Sahib and Baba Jai Gurudev could be considered spiritual cousins through the Radhasoami lineage, their relationships to that lineage differed substantially. Even though Baba Jai Gurudev declared that the name *Radhasoami* had been superseded by the name *Jai Gurudev* as the most potent invocation of the highest Lord, he still looks to a Radhasoami lineage alone. As far as I can tell, moreover, the *surat shabd* yoga practice and metaphysical map that he offers is basically the same as

FIGURE 6.8 Gate to Adhyatma Niketan, Gwalior, 1997.

that taught—with variations that to outsiders can only appear minor—in most Radhasoami lineages. Malik Sahib, by contrast, introduced significant new elements into the practice he offered, which for many have come to overshadow its Radhasoami aspects. These elements, further, derived from another lineage source that is also explicitly recognized.

Malik Sahib's first main guru, Shyam Lal (1872–1940)—called Guru Data Dayala, "The Merciful Giver"—was a disciple of Chachaji Maharaj, Radhasoami Maharaj's younger brother Pratap.[32] Guru Data Dayala started a residential ashram in his hometown of Gwalior, where Malik Sahib met him while a schoolboy. At his guru's passing, Malik Sahib felt called upon to carry on the latter's work. He was not recognized, however, by the ashram's managing committee—which, led for many years by the late guru's grandson, has remained in charge itself, never formally acknowledging a successor. So Malik Sahib continued on his own, gathering disciples in the small central Indian towns where he was posted while serving the princely state of Gwalior and its successors in independent India. In the early 1950s, he came into contact with a guru named Yogendra Vijnani, who saw in Malik Sahib someone qualified to carry on his own yogic tradition. Yogendra, the disciple of a guru from East Bengal, offered a type of initiation called śaktipāt, "the descent of power," that awakened the latent energy in the body that is sometimes called kuṇḍālinī śakti. Devotees are enjoined to let the divine energy thus aroused play within them, which can lead to manifestations such as rhythmic breathing or inner or vocalized repetition of mantras. Although the surat śabd yoga and the śaktipāt practice present some obvious contrasts—the first focusing on the higher realms and sometimes leading to ecstasies; the second encompassing the entire body and more likely to lead to states of clarity and peace—they could also be taken as complementary. Both psychically and intellectually, Malik Sahib managed to integrate the two. In practice, most devotees have begun with the śaktipāt practice and after some years may move on to a version of the surat śabd yoga (fig. 6.9).

Although Malik Sahib's disciples could be in awe of his spiritual achievements, their numbers were never extremely great. At once an introspective yogi and an old school gentleman—the honorific Ṭhākur in his worldly name indicates his descent from village landlords of the martial Rajput caste—he never tried to cater to a broad public. Many of his disciples came from regional villages and were often themselves Rajputs. There were also loyal devotees from some of the small towns where he had been posted over the years. A number of local people from Gwalior also

FIGURE 6.9 Meditators often pursue quiet practice at the memorial tomb (*samādhi*) of Malik Sahib, whose picture is in the background. Adhyatma Niketan, 1997.

regularly visited the ashram, and there were others from different places who had come in touch with Malik Sahib through word of mouth from family and friends. Some of the latter also brought others living in their area, so by the last years of his career as a guru, Malik Sahib had small groups of devotees in Jodhpur, Rajasthan, the Hamirpur-Banda area of U.P., and a few places in Himachal Pradesh.

These different contingents of Malik Sahib's would meet at Adhyatma Niketan during three-day functions held in conjunction with major Hindu festivals when Malik Sahib would give initiation to new disciples. As regular convocations of devotees at the guru's place—common in many Indian religious traditions—those at Adhyatma Niketan, continued by Maharajji, have been the same general type of event held at Baba Jai Gurudev's Mathura ashram. The differing scales of the events, however, could make the events themselves feel quite different: those at Jai Gurudev's ashram inevitably drawing on the excitement stemming from the very large crowd, and those at Adhyatma Niketan—especially in Malik Sahib's day—often feeling more like an extended family reunion (fig. 6.10).

The different sizes of Baba Jai Gurudev's and Malik Sahib's followings are indicative of their alternative appropriations of the sant tradition and especially of the way they seem to understand that tradition's greatest figure, Kabir. The early Hindi sants, we recall, featured some early fifteenth- and

FIGURE 6.10 Maharajji regards the author at a gathering during the festival of Holi, when revelers all over North India happily smear each other with colored powder, March, 2000. Photograph by a friend of the author.

sixteenth-century figures from the most humble sections of Indian society who used some yogic language to sing of a lord reachable within, needing no ritual mediation from Hindu or Muslim officiants. Although their message was meant for all, they spread it largely within their own milieux, sometimes using strident language against perceived religious hypocrisy. In the eighteenth and nineteenth centuries, the tradition had spread among many middle-caste devotees who emphasized its more esoteric elements. This is the tradition that Radhasoami Maharaj knew and codified for the new urban classes. Baba Jai Gurudev can then be seen as taking this codified esoteric tradition back to its early sant social roots, having worked for long periods among a poor, rural, lower-caste population, which still forms the preponderance of his mass following. Like Kabir, he could use strident language to make points about priestly hypocrisy.

For Malik Sahib, by contrast, Kabir was instead first of all a model of the complete yogi. Kabir, according to Malik Sahib, knew all there was to know about the yoga of his day, which explains the many spiritual attitudes found in his verses (the multitude of texts coming down in Kabir's name is in fact highly diverse and sometimes opaque enough to support a number of yogic interpretations). Kabir himself, according to Malik Sahib, was partial to a particular practice described in the *Śiva Saṃhitā*, a *haṭha* yoga manual, that described a path of concentration ending with absorption into *nāda*, as internal sound is usually called in Sanskrit texts.[33] Kabir saw how this practice could be animated by the force of loving devotion and simplified it for a broader audience as *surat śabd* yoga. *Surat śabd* yoga was then taken up by later Hindi sants, many of whom, including Tulsi Sahib, also integrated it with various forms of *prāṇayāma*, as *haṭha* yogic practices dealing with control of life force are called. Radhasoami Maharaj's codification of sant tradition, Malik Sahib continued, stripped away the obvious *prāṇayāma* practice to develop an esoteric path for his own generation driven solely through the power of loving devotion.[34] From this perspective, Malik Sahib's combining the *surat śabd* yoga with a *śaktipāt* initiation brought back the whole range of yogic experience.

This integration of his two lineages was also, for Malik Sahib, an integration of the *surat śabd* yoga into the wider Hindu tradition, which Malik Sahib perceived in its socioreligious wholeness, including traditional views about caste. When that subject came up, I am afraid, Malik Sahib sometimes cited Kabir as the exception that proves the rule: of course people from humble backgrounds could have profound religious insights—look at Kabir!—but usually they didn't, too burdened by their karmas and everyday work. Malik Sahib (like Radhasoami Maharaj) found it more fruitful to work among higher-caste, middle-class people. These formed the bulk of his small following, which also, to be sure, also included quite a few devotees from less elevated backgrounds. His son then repopularized the integrated practice, greatly increasing the number of devotees if not substantially altering its social composition.

The Successor Does Things Differently

When Malik Sahib died in early 1983, Maharajji—then a young-looking thirty—was soon recognized by most devotees as his successor.[35] Seen as blessed by his father's grace, he could obviously awaken psychic energies in new disciples, but from the beginning, his personal style was his own. There was a generational difference of course: Malik Sahib was a country-bred traditionalist, while Maharajji was a middle-class city boy coming of age in the 1960s and 1970s, interested in cars and popular music like many young people of the day. Just as important, however, was Maharajji's more engaging, extroverted personality. His preparation for guruhood was less in strenuous solitary spiritual practice (like his father's) than in serving at the ashram, where he honed his interpersonal skills through tactful dealings with devotees. Disciples were attracted to Malik Sahib often despite his sometimes gruff exterior, irascibility, and old-fashioned sensibilities. Maharajji is seen sooner as a modern man, competent in worldly affairs and patient with people, and he usually sports a friendly smile.

Unlike his father, moreover, Maharajji had no real career outside the ashram. In his twenties he had tried a few jobs, including a stint as an agent for the Life Insurance Corporation of India, but none had really been satisfactory. There was always work to do at Adhyatma Niketan, however, and he was good it at: business matters of greater and lesser import needed attention, while devotees in residence often needed help with practical problems. This work was all in addition to personal service to Malik Sahib, which regularly included driving him to engagements in town. Young Maharajji's responsibilities at the ashram increased exponentially during his father's last years, when the number of devotees increased just as the guru's health began to fail. When Maharajji emerged as his father's successor, he was still fairly young and ashram work was what he knew best. His development as a guru thus differed strikingly from that of his father's. Malik Sahib devoted himself to internal explorations while maintaining a career, offering initiations to devotees who came his way; he worked at being a yogi. Maharajji, whose spiritual gifts came easily to him, devoted himself with a young man's energy to sharing those gifts with ever wider circles of devotees; from the beginning, he worked at being a guru (fig. 6.11).

One of Maharajji's most noticeable departures from his father was his frequent willingness to go on long, sometimes strenuous tours. Although Malik Sahib did sometimes accept invitations to visit distant disciples, by the time he was settled at Adhyatma Niketan he was already feeling his years and didn't abide the discomforts of travel very well. He used to say that people his age should "travel restfully and rest restfully."[36] His trips were infrequent and relatively short: the only regular one was to Rishikesh at his guru Yogendra Vijnani's death anniversary, a tradition Maharajji has continued. Maharajji, by contrast, has regularly made exhausting tours to places where he had a following, sometimes making stops along the way in spots where a lone industrious disciple would introduce him to a new group. Maharajji's main tours have been to Himachal Pradesh and Rajasthan, and he has also visited the Hamirpur/Banda area. In all these areas, he has greatly expanded his father's followings, and has started visiting a growing number of disciples in Gujarat as well. There have also

FIGURE 6.11 Maharajji as a mature guru in a contemplative mood, ca. 2000.

been many trips closer to home. In particular, disciples in Guna, a Madhya Pradesh city about three hours to the south of Gwalior, had started inviting Maharajji to give multiple-day programs at a large public auditorium, which by 2010 had become a major feature of his winter event schedule (fig. 6.12). In addition to the local crowd, a large contingent from Gwalior would come, as well as a number of devotees from more distant places. Through the middle of the first decade of the twenty-first century, Maharajji was very frequently on the move, and he has continued to travel, if less often, through the beginning of the second decade.

Touring with the Guru: Himachal Pradesh, June 1997

Probably the longest and most frequent tour Maharajji makes is to Himachal Pradesh. A Himachal tour was also the first one he made as guru—about six months after his father's passing—and seems to have had a formative effect on the way he would continue to operate. By all accounts, that initial tour was a great success, with Maharajji giving programs in a number of cities, and making "more than a hundred"[37] lasting new devotees. Since then, he has usually gone to Himachal every year, sometimes more than once. In June 1997, I went along. I had never gone on a long tour with Maharajji before and was just over a month into my first long stint of formal Gwalior research, so I took notes along the way and wrote up an extensive record of the trip on returning to Gwalior. In retrospect, that record provides some interesting windows on the way Maharajji works as guru and the dynamics within his community of devotees.

FIGURE 6.12 Guna Satsang, January 2010. A cluster of devotees in the center of
the stage crowd around the guru, who is hidden, while two people are taken up in
ecstatic dance—a frequent occurrence in Maharajji's large satsangs.

The total trip lasted sixteen days—somewhat long for one of Maharajji's
tours, but not extraordinary for one to Himachal Pradesh. It takes a couple of days to get there, and devotees are spread out in towns and villages
across the small state, so Maharajji makes many stops. We left Gwalior in
three vehicles—two large vans and a smallish car—with an assorted group
of old and new devotees. For a guru's traveling party this was in fact fairly
small (remember Baba Jai Gurudev's 2003 "fifty car" procession through
Gwalior). Gurus generally travel with substantial entourages for a number
of reasons. First of all, many devotees want to go. Traveling with the guru
offers devotees a period of sustained spiritual excitement when they have
more than usual interaction with the guru. It's a time, I was told, exclusively for *bhajan* and *bhojan* "spiritual practice" and "eating"—the latter
often occurring as enthusiastic local devotees host the guru's party. It can
also be an opportunity to see an exotic new place (such as the Himalayan
foothills, where often people go on holiday) that might not otherwise come
their way. Gurus, for their part, want some people with them who can tend
to their personal needs and provide some trustworthy service at the satsangs; it can also be helpful to bring along some other devotees who will do

no more than provide assured enthusiasm at public events. Finally, traveling with a retinue indicates that the guru is a personage of some importance. For this last function, three vehicles may be about the minimum.

As we set out from Gwalior, there was a discernible hierarchy in the seating arrangements. Maharajji, of course, sat in the newest van—in the front seat next to the driver, the place of honor. He was accompanied by two government officers of some rank, both Rajputs, and A. N. Khare, a very competent man then about forty and at the time Maharajji's constant personal assistant and regular business manager. Khare in those days almost always traveled with Maharajji, and the two Rajput officers were used to some privilege. I think Maharajji also enjoyed their company. The junior and more rustic crew was in the old van: two young men from Banda who would be actively helping out and a landowner (and teacher) from a rural area not far from Gwalior who would sometimes play tabla in satsang. I sat in the middle car with some older urban devotees, two of whom (including the driver) were rather distant ones. Maharajji sometimes brought new or less active devotees along on tour to help firm up their connection with him. This was something Baba Jai Gurudev seemed to do as well, particularly if the new devotee could help: I was surprised to find that one of the people collecting money at the big Jaipur meeting had been with the guru for just three months and was traveling with the large caravan.

Sitting in the front seat of my car was Maharajji's maternal uncle, known in the satsang by the honorific form of the Hindi word for that relationship, Mamaji. A younger brother of Maharajji's mother, he lived in Gwalior but was not a frequent visitor to the ashram during Malik Sahib's day, a skinny man then whom I only remember seeing during a long critical illness of one of his brothers. Now retired and heavy, he was frequently at hand, an avuncular presence usually given fond respect. In patriarchal societies such as that of traditional India, the mother's brother often has a familiar, sometimes protective relationship with his nephews, an ally in disputes among paternal cousins. Although Maharajji didn't need Mamaji's protection, the customary familiarity between them was evident, with Mamaji also maintaining a playful, joking relationship with many devotees. (These included some women from Himachal, where intergender relationships are not as constrained as they traditionally are in the plains.) Mamaji tended to do what he liked, which I usually appreciated. Sitting closest to the dashboard cassette player as we left Gwalior, however, Mamaji jacked up the volume on the popular hymn-songs playing to a level that was uncomfortably loud for me sitting right up against a back-seat speaker. When I said something, he turned it down a little and altered the balance, but I could later see (and hear) him merrily turning the volume up and shifting the balance toward the speaker at my seat. Mamaji obviously outranked me, and these were hymn-songs, after all. I survived the trip to Delhi, where we spent the night, but the next day switched to the van with the junior crew, which had no sound system. Three more people had joined us in Delhi, which generally altered the seating arrangements in the two vehicles other than Maharajji's. In those cars hierarchical order seemed to have collapsed, practical considerations taking over in the now crowded cars. June is the peak of the hot season in North India, and driving packed into vehicles with no air-conditioning—even without blaring music—is not a particularly pleasant experience. Nerves were frayed and there was some bickering (which I was this time happily able to avoid). For most of us, I think, only some guru devotion made the drive bearable. Thus we proceeded to Bilaspur, H.P., where, arriving very late in the evening, we were most happy to see some steps leading up to a newly constructed building and a big red banner welcoming visitors (fig. 6.13). This was where we were to spend the night.

Maharajji's Bilaspur devotees had built him a permanent satsang center—as had those in Jodhpur, Rajasthan. In both cases, the project seems to have

FIGURE 6.13 The center in Bilaspur, 1997. The sign in this picture reads: Om Salutations to the guru. Adhyatma Niketan Satsang Circle Himachal Pradesh, WELCOME.

begun with a devotee who had some land he wasn't using and was ready to offer for the purpose, with other local devotees contributing for construction costs. At the Jodhpur center, when I visited it in 1993, the site was still largely undeveloped, consisting mostly of empty land in an outlying residential colony: tents could be put up when Maharajji visited. In 2007, the center opened as a large hall, with upstairs rooms for visitors, in what was now a built-up area well within the bustle of the city. (To help meet maintenance costs, parts of it are rented out as a place to celebrate and put up guests for elaborate Indian weddings.) The Bilaspur site has also seen further construction, although it hasn't changed dramatically in scale and remains in an outlying area. When we arrived that June night the small plot of land attached to it was still green and terraced into a small hill—a sharp contrast to the flat, dusty plains. We knew we were in Himachal Pradesh and appreciated it.

The next morning, as most mornings, things got off to a slow start. At Bilaspur we had been joined by many devotees from other Himachal towns—as well as a small group of Jodhpur devotees—and the strain of the large group taxed available bathroom facilities. Although the lower foothills are cooler at night in summer than are the plains, they're still pretty hot during the day, so people really do want their usual morning bath. Most were also middle-class town folk accustomed to their toilets, so finding a secluded corner in the woods was not usually an agreeable option. Throughout this and most tours, much of the morning was taken up waiting around for limited onsite facilities or searching the area for others—another recognized inconvenience of the tour, but one that could usually be alleviated pleasantly enough with small talk among the devotees. If you can't take the inconvenience (*asuvidhā*), some said, stay home!

We had a late morning satsang, which followed the general pattern long established by Malik Sahib but with some local variation. As at the ashram, one or two devotees would chant verses by the gurus in Maharajji's sant lineage. These might include verses by Radhasoami Maharaj, but were more often those by Malik Sahib's guru, Data Dayal, or by Malik Sahib himself. These would usually be followed by a reading, often of a guru in the *śaktipāt* lineage, and then by more hymn-songs from various sources. The service would always conclude with a type of song originated by Radhasoami Maharaj called an *āratī*: in Hindu worship generally an *āratī* is the worship of an image through the waving of lights before it, but the term here refers to the sequential inner worship of the lords of esoteric santism's higher worlds. During the service, some people paid close attention to the meaning of the songs and readings, others fell into meditative states, and in others the śakti was visibly awakened. With Himachal devotees doing much of the singing, the main local difference was in the selection of songs near the end, which included regional folk tunes, and in the style of the music in general, which—accompanied by the tabla player we brought—was often faster and more rhythmic than usual at the Gwalior ashram, sometimes making the play of the śakti in those who were experiencing it more intense. This regional variation in music has reverberated back to the Gwalior ashram. With Maharajji having more contemporary musical sensibilities than his father and appreciating the different tastes of his devotees, he has opened up the Gwalior satsangs to different styles of musical performance—with classical, popular, and folk styles all sometimes heard at the main Sunday gathering. According to one Madhya Pradesh singer, this all started with "the brothers and sisters from Himachal."

After lunch and a siesta we headed off. Most of the people joining us in Himachal traveled by bus—we were making mostly short trips—but our caravan also now got a little bigger: at its maximum there were six vehicles. Although the people on the bus went directly to the day's final destination, those traveling with Maharajji usually made a couple of stops along the way at the invitation of individual devotees. People liked to have their guru visit them at home. It gave them a chance to offer hospitality to the guru, and his presence gave a lasting blessing to their house. This is common in guru-centered traditions, with Vishnu Soni in Jahazpur happily mentioning to me more than once that Baba Jai Gurudev had been to his new residence. When Maharajji visited a devotee, it would be an occasion for a guru pūjan, a "ritual worship of the guru" by the host. This would sometimes entail an external āratī, as one would make to the image of divinity, and always an offering including some food—some of which would be given back to the devotee as prasād (as normally happens with food offerings to divinities through temple-priests). This was a time for devotees to explicitly acknowledge their guru as mediator of the divine. After this brief ritual there would usually be the chanting of a hymn or two together with refreshments for the guru and his party, and we would be off—sometimes to another devotee's house for more of the same. Most days followed the general pattern of the first one: a late morning satsang, lunch, a siesta if there was time, and then a drive (usually of a few hours and sometimes with stops) to the next night's resting place, where there would be a pūjan by the hosts, an evening satsang, and late dinner. Over several days, we made our way up into the higher reaches of Himachal Pradesh (fig. 6.14).

FIGURE 6.14 Stopping in Hamirpur, an Himachal Pradesh town, in 1997. Devotees crowd around Maharajji's car.

Twice, our local hosts gave our party traditional Himachal hats—simple felt brimless caps with a wide brocade band. Most of us happily put them on now and then, especially when the weather grew cooler as we ascended to higher altitudes. Wearing them in front of our hosts could be taken as a way of embracing their culture, which we were coming to appreciate, and it was clear that Maharajji thought it was a fine thing to do. One young man, however, from a family of old Rajasthani devotees, demurred: he was from Rajasthan, he said, and wearing the Himachal hat didn't feel right. Maharajji, however, pushed him to do so. There were no doubt a number of reasons for this: the young man seemed a little immature and overassertive and perhaps needed a lesson; at the same time, Maharajji genuinely seemed to like mingling his devotees' regional identities. "I bring Rajasthanis to Himachal and Himachalis to Rajasthan," he had said on that tour, and I had indeed met a few Himachalis in Jodhpur on a trip there during one of Maharajji's visits in 1993, when I was living in Rajasthan. He could also have said that he brings Madhya Pradeshis and Banda people to both places and brings them all together in Gwalior during regular functions. This personally oriented small-scale dynamic toward national integration can be especially compelling because his devotees comprise a wide range of distinct cultural types: including ethnic Tibetans originating from the Himachal district of Lahaul-Spiti who have pictures of the Dalai Lama in their living rooms, and old-family Rajputs from Rajasthan. Maharajji's devotees were from different North Indian regions and they should all embrace one another's culture.

The Himachal hats had a different meaning, however, when worn outside Himachal Pradesh. With many devotees having collected caps over successive tours, wearing one in Gwalior—where no one else does—can be a sign of affiliation to Maharajji. You don't even have to go to Himachal to get a Himachal cap: they are usually available for purchase at the bookstand that is set up during the large Sunday satsang. They're not expensive and sell nicely in the winter, when a wool felt hat can be useful. As a token of visible self-identification, the caps present a contrast to the more explicit signs sometimes displayed by Jai Gurudev devotees, who may have the name Jai Gurudev emblazoned not only on caps but also on houses and motorcycle banners as well. These displays appear as a proud proclamation with at least a latent missionary intent. The Himachal caps are sooner a sign to the knowing that the wearer is proud to be a member of the Maharajji-disciples' club. Although a great many people in Gwalior know of Maharajji, most don't immediately connect someone wearing a Himachal cap with him, even though he himself wears one frequently.

Indeed, although most devotees who have caps wear them sometimes in the cold weather or at the ashram, Maharajji himself wears one in public much of the time when it is not too hot. It is an element of his distinctive sartorial style. While people who have taken formal Hindu vows of renunciation are likely to wear generic orange robes, Indian holy men in less orthodox traditions often develop their own individual modes of dress. Many—particularly those not married—favor white robes, the traditional dress of the Brahmachari, the celibate practitioner who has not taken formal vows of renunciation. Baba Jai Gurudev's attire in his later years was a variation of this, with very full white robes and a broad cloth headcovering that seems particularly distinctive. Maharajji's distinctive style of dress seems to derive from his father's, which was simply a mode of decorous North Indian attire in his day. For most of his adult life, Malik Sahib had a regular job in addition to disciples as a guru, and didn't particularly want to stand out. At home, Malik Sahib usually wore a *tahmat*—the staid Northern counterpart to the often colorful South Indian *lungī*—a piece of cloth, normally white, that was wrapped around the waist, reaching to the ankles. He wore this with a kurta, the long Indian tunic, also usually white. If he used a wool vest or shawl in winter it was most often muted beige or khaki. When he went out, he normally exchanged his *tahmat* for the loose

Indian white pajama. Maharajji wears a *tahmat*—which now seems something of an archaism—all the time, with kurtas often in brighter hues than his father's. His Himachal cap covers hair reaching down to his neck, and his jewelry—beads and rings—is often quite noticeable. The beads, of the sort sometimes worn by sadhus, are usually made of berries, wood, or polished stone, all of which can have various religious significances; the rings—often worn on multiple fingers by Indian men—have semiprecious gems with different astrological significances said to be beneficial when worn. His look is not that of an ascetic like Baba Jai Gurudev, but of the individual householder guru that he is. Each has dressed for his role as an unorthodox holy man in his own distinctive way.

Traveling with Maharajji through Himachal, we usually stayed with devotees. Most were middle-class town folk, but there were others as well. Once we stayed in the village home of an avid disciple who was obviously not very prosperous, but who had a cozy house and some friends who helped out. We also stayed at the estate of a former minister in the state government. Located outside Manali, a vacation spot at an altitude high enough to be temperate in June, the estate provided a place for satsang with clear Himalayan views (fig. 6.15)—as well as a look at how Maharajji deals with devotees whose explicit political views run counter to his own.

FIGURE 6.15 Satsang in Manali, 1997, with Himalayas in background. Many of the men are wearing Himachal caps.

Although Maharajji welcomes people of any political persuasion, his own broad views are closer to the inclusive vision of Gandhi and Nehru ("India is a secular country that has room for people of all religions") than to the Hindu nationalism that is its main alternative ("it's important to remember that the culture of India is Hindu"—a proposition that can have less than salubrious implications for India's many minorities). Our hosts however, were prominent regional members of the main Hindu nationalist political party, the BJP, with the former minister's son then the chair of the BJP youth wing. Noticing a placard in the house reading "All we Hindus are one" ("*Hindu ham sab ek haiṃ*"), Maharajji gently suggested that instead of *Hindu* perhaps this should read *Hindustani*, a religiously neutral term that can refer to all Indian nationals. The son, with the father present, countered that there was a philosophy behind the slogan. Maharaji persisted a bit, but not much, and kept smiling. Eventually the conversation drifted to other topics. Although it is unlikely that Maharajji immediately changed anyone's established philosophical views, speaking as a family guru he might have made some of its members think a bit, and in any event made clear to the *satsangīs* present that the slogan on the wall was not one he endorsed. He spoke out, but in a gentle way that ruptured no personal relations. The former minister and his wife added their vehicle to our caravan as we left Manali.

Coming down from the higher hills, we stopped in some places different from those where we did on the way up, and were finally on the road to Delhi. Before we got there, however, the car in which I was riding developed an obvious steering problem and we pulled over. It was already well into the night and our other two vehicles were ahead and out of sight. Because driving in India can be an adventure, we tried to look out for one another on longer trips by staying more or less together—the lead car stopping periodically to let all the vehicles reassemble. (This was in the days before cell towers had spread through the rural areas). It was late, we were alone, and the driver didn't know quite what to do: he thought the problem might need a major repair, but that could leave us stranded for a day or two; a minor repair might work, but that could lead to further mishaps soon. We were in a dilemma and feeling uneasy. About half an hour after we stopped, we saw Maharajji's car heading back in our direction—after waiting a while for us to join the rest of the pack, he had come looking. What was the matter? One reassuring aspect of going on tour with Maharajji was that his years of serving his father as chauffeur had turned him into an experienced driver (he had taken the wheel a couple of times in Himachal this trip) and, like many who regularly ply Indian roads and need to be able to make minor repairs on the fly, had a decent knowledge of auto mechanics. If he gave an opinion in a situation like ours, people would understand that it wasn't based solely on psychic intuition (although there might be that, too) and would accept it without cavil. Maharajji had a look under the hood, conferred with the driver of our car, and the two concluded that the situation was in fact not so serious—a problem with a bearing—and a temporary repair should be enough to get us home: practical experience meets spiritual authority on the road.

Changing Ashram Life

During the decades I've known the Gwalior Ashram, it has gone through a number of changes. There has been physical development to be sure, and technological advances with the times: TVs accessible for the family and regular residents; computers (with a designated room when there was just one); and a couple of difficult-to-procure landlines giving way to multiple cell phones. These changes made life more comfortable for everyone but didn't seem much noticed by the largely middle-class devotees: the ashram was just keeping pace with increasingly high-tech India.

More deeply felt were changes in the tenor of life that most people with longtime experience in the ashram have recognized. Some of these changes have clearly been due to the personalities of the two gurus. In Malik Sahib's day there was generally more tension in the air. He was stricter with his children and his disciples than Maharajji is, and there would sometimes be public scoldings (I was not spared). His relationship with his oldest son was difficult, and it seemed to weigh on him, coming up heatedly in general conversations at unexpected times. Money was usually pretty tight. Maharajji, by contrast, has had a generally more relaxed personality, which makes everyone more at ease. With increasing middle-class prosperity in India and a much larger number of devotees, there is also less financial stress. During the first few years after Maharajji's establishment as a guru, returning visitors might remark on the difference in the way things felt. The tenor of ashram life changed again for a while around the beginning of the new millennium, when Maharajji maintained some prominent political connections.

Toward the end of the 1990s, Maharajji had actively caught the eye of Digvijay Singh, a politician in the secularly oriented Congress party, and then chief minister of Madhya Pradesh. By that time Maharajji was a well-known public figure in the Gwalior region, frequently called upon to say a few words as special guest at local civic functions of all sorts: the dedication of a patriotic statue by a youth organization, a national Hindi Day event, or the distribution of prizes at a statewide high-school science exhibition. His cultivation of the irenic virtues of patience and calm, for which his Rajput caste brothers are *not* well known, also helped him achieve positions of leadership in local and national Rajput caste organizations. Rajputs from the surrounding districts with no active spiritual connection to Maharajji were still able to think of him as their man. For Digvijay Singh, a Rajput himself with a fondness for holy persons, he could seem worth cultivating—perhaps even someone to field as a candidate from one of the regional electoral districts. Maharajji was ready to play along: as a householder-guru he was necessarily involved in the world and ready to see where it took him. Although I had first met Digvijay Singh briefly at the ashram in early 1993, when he was still a member of Parliament in Delhi, it wasn't until the end of the 1990s—well into his second term as Madhya Pradesh chief minister—that I heard frequent reference to him there: usually as the "C. M. Sahib," who could be contacted when appropriate favors were needed.

Thus, for several years around the turn of the millennium, Maharajji was a man of recognized political influence. This greatly increased the pace of public life at the ashram. Before then, in the absence of one of the ashram's major seasonal festivals, life there could often feel rather slow. There were some chants in the early morning for people who lived at the ashram or nearby, and a satsang in the evening to which some people from the city also came. The few sadhus who lived at the ashram, and maybe some visitors, spent time meditating, while the family and longer-term resident helpers would pursue their everyday work. Maharajji would usually come into the public area for a while a few times a day, paying particular attention to visiting devotees—but he was regularly invited to public functions and frequently off in town. Even though I participated in aspects of ashram life when I stayed there over the years of my research, I was glad to be able to get out into the city to investigate other traditions: at the ashram, there was usually not much going on. By the beginning of the 2000s, however, the pace picked up considerably. Maharajji would come out regularly at 9:00 a.m., and people would frequently be there waiting for him. Could he help them with some particular practical matter? Sometimes he could and sometimes he couldn't, but he was almost always ready to listen.

The numbers of people who came for matters clearly of worldly import and the amount of time Maharajji was giving to them could be dismaying to some of the older devotees: shouldn't Maharajji be engaged in more elevated pursuits? The ashram seemed not only much busier, but also more mundane. Maharajji himself often complained about how much work it was to deal with so many ordinary petitioners, but he obviously thought that expanding his networks in this way was worth the effort. It's also true that his influence could help his devotees in ways that were more than mundane, particularly those in government service who faced regular transfers around the state. These he was sometimes able to keep (or bring) close by, and living near the guru is usually seen as spiritually beneficial for a disciple. These sorts of more spiritually understandable interventions, however, were only a small proportion of those that were sought.

The ashram's ambience as the abode of a busy man of influence probably peaked when Maharajji's name was publicly mentioned in the local media as a possible nominee for a regional parliamentary seat in the 2004 national elections. For several days, workers from more than one political party flocked to the ashram. Although most people, of course—considering Maharajji's relationship to Digvijay Singh—thought of him then as a Congress man, perhaps he could be persuaded to see the benefits of running on another party's ticket: such turnarounds are not at all uncommon in Indian politics. After all the fuss, however, no nomination for Maharajji ever materialized, and about the same time Digvijay Singh led the Congress to a decisive defeat in a state election in Madhya Pradesh. Although the now-former chief minister survived well enough politically, soon assuming an important Congress party post in Delhi, he had little influence on the new BJP government in his home state, and neither did Maharajji. A phase in Maharajji's career as a guru—and in the life of the ashram—was over.

Ashram life, however, didn't quite return to the way it was before. Experience with the vagaries of political life and age itself seems to have had an effect on Maharajji, and the ambience at the ashram has become more like it was Malik Sahib's day. Indeed, Maharajji is roughly the same age as Malik Sahib when the latter first started the ashram and may be feeling some of the same dissatisfactions with life in the world that Malik Sahib often explicitly expressed. More than before, his attitude seems inward and religiously serious. Earlier, he used frequently to miss the daily evening satsang to attend outside events. He still does, but by 2005 he had instituted a regular morning satsang at 11:00, with time for silent meditation, which he makes a point of attending regularly. Maharajji is now a little less accessible, sometimes not coming out until shortly before the morning satsang, and maybe a little less cheerful: he still most often seems warm and smiling, but not quite as much as before. He always lights up, though, when playing with his grandchildren.

The Guru for Community and Practice: Contrasting Images

Many devotees of Maharajji have a chance to see him as a person who has much to give but who also changes and has some normal human limitations. They sense something special in him, which they take as divine, but as they spend time around him they are also likely to develop an everyday sense of what it can mean for that divine to be embedded in a living person. It's a way of coming to terms with a paradox frequently met in religious traditions—the infinite in a finite form—which for the pious can appear as an eternal religious mystery. Those disciples of Baba Jai Gurudev who spent much time around him when he was alive were also likely to resolve that paradox in something like the same way that many of Maharajji's devotees do, giving due weight to the finite, human side of the mysterious equation. Those disciples, however, have been proportionately few, and most of his great many devotees have always probably resolved the paradox somewhat differently, giving more weight to the superhuman ideal image than to the limited human embodiment. All disciples, of course, tend to idealize their gurus to some extent (as may be evident in some of my writing in this chapter), but just as the number of Baba Jai Gurudev's devotees has been of another order of magnitude than Maharajji's, so does the idealization of their image of him seem to be.

The information publicly disseminated about Baba Jai Gurudev's early life even in his lifetime was sparse and archetypal, often presented through narrative conventions familiar from diverse Indian sources that describe larger-than-life personalities. The "About Swamiji" page at what was once one of the principal movement websites (jaigurudeo.org), for example, sketched the outline of an individual who had simple rural roots but was in no way ordinary. We are told that Baba Jai Gurudev was born in a small Uttar Pradesh village, there unnamed, with a father who was a "talented person" and a "landlord." The future guru was soon orphaned, however, and his mother, before her death, "asked him to search out and realize God." Leaving home at age seven, he "visited temples, mosques and churches and did what their heads told him." When he finally met his guru from "a Brahmin family in Chirauli village in Aligarh district," he started meditating intensely—"more than twelve hours a day" while taking just one daily meal. When he eventually felt ready to teach, in 1952, he went to Benaras; there "he started with only five disciples and now the number is in billions."

That a great renunciate should have good parentage and actually possess something to give up is a common theme in Indian lore,[38] but these traits of Baba Jai Gurudev are presented in a way with which many of the guru's rural, less privileged devotees could still feel comfortable: many village landowners are not particularly rich and good parentage here is described in terms of individual talent, not caste. While the lack of any mention of the guru's birth caste in this description (or any written source I have found) is consonant with ideas about the renunciate's status beyond the norms of ordinary society, it also lets more of his devotees easily imagine him as one of their own—a democratizing strategy similar to one used by many mid-twentieth-century writers of Hindi short fiction, who often took pains to avoid specifying the caste origins of their main characters.[39] A narrative convention that may be more familiar to most of Baba Jai Gurudev's devotee's however, is suggested in the mention of his dying mother's request to him to search out God, which is easily imaginable in the world of classic Hindi film melodrama, where the mother is regularly taken as the fount of all good and truth.[40]

More specific echoes of stories of familiar holy persons—modern, ancient, and generic—also find resonances in the short sketch. Like the well-known Sri Ramakrishna mentioned in chapter 5, Baba Jai Gurudev stayed in temples, mosques, and churches, in good faith exposing himself to a number of different religions and, like the Buddha, began his career as a spiritual teacher with five disciples in Benaras. A period of intense askesis, moreover—comparable to the future guru's twelve hours of daily meditation with little food—is familiar from many holy persons' biographies. While this public story of Baba Jai Gurudev's early life leaves much to devotees' imaginations, it guides their conceptualization of him through some obvious narrative moves that suggest a very extraordinary personage—albeit one with fairly ordinary rural roots.

When considering Baba Jai Gurudev's actual life course, two points in the spare website biography stand out. The first is the specific reference to village birth and a village guru—both in Western Uttar Pradesh. By the time we first hear of a city, Banaras, Baba Jai Gurudev would have been well into middle age (however we understand the claims of his extremely long life). His formation as a person and a sadhu, we might infer, took place in rural U.P., where he still has very large numbers of devotees. Baba Jai Gurudev's style remained simple and straightforward—and his tastes, if sometimes appearing to tend toward the grandiose, did not seem highly sophisticated. The second point to note is Baba Jai Gurudev's early loss of a parental home and subsequent wandering. In those days, young boys (for a variety of reasons, including becoming orphaned)[41] sometimes found their way into small-scale village monastic establishments where they might be raised as sadhus and possible successors to the monk in charge. Sometimes child-sadhus found a rooted home in a particular ashram, but the future guru seems to have stayed unsettled for some time—remaining his own person, not happy in the conventional religious establishments through which he moved. Although he eventually did find a guru with whom he was most satisfied, it wasn't any of the ones at his early, establishment-oriented spiritual homes. It was, instead, an individual, somewhat unconventional person—a Brahmin carrying on a non-Brahminic lineage. Whatever this says about the young sadhu's powers of spiritual discrimination, it also speaks to his independence of spirit and willingness to reject what he took as imperfect authority. This independent nature is consistent with some of Baba Jai Gurudev's best-known activities during his life as a guru, including his oppositional stance during Indira Gandhi's emergency years, for which he was jailed, and his bold millennial prophecies, which often predict the destruction of those in power in ways that suggest an Old Testament prophet. (Perhaps the reference to churches that the guru stayed in as a boy indicates more than an implied universalism!)

The contrast between Baba Jai Gurudev's spiritual personality and that of Maharajji is striking: one a lone sadhu since childhood who doesn't mince his words, the other very much his father's son and known for his tactful ways; one presenting his *sant mat* path as the only effective means of salvation for the times, the other presenting something like that path as an elevated option within a broad-based, liberally understood Hindu tradition. A corresponding contrast is evident in the forays of both into the world of politics. Baba Jai Gurudev's Doordarshi party, if never electorally triumphant, was at least broad-scale and ambitious: in the 1989 national polls, for example, it fielded 298 candidates in thirteen states and territories (none of whom won). The party was also oppositional in its platform, taking uncompromising positions that had no chance of becoming national policy: the banning of all animal slaughter, for example, and of liquor sales. Enthusiastic devotee-volunteers chanted rhymed slogans espousing moral and religious ideals.[42] Maharajji's years as a person of recognized political influence, by contrast, had longstanding roots in the practice of Indian rulers working with charismatic religious figures to further their normal establishment ends.[43] One was the thundering, idealistic visionary, able to galvanize candidates, if not enough voters; the other, a personally engaging practical man moving effectively between spiritual and temporal authority.

Thus, even as Baba Jai Gurudev and Maharajji have drawn on some of the same Radhasoami lineages sources, they exemplify alternative kinds of spiritual leadership, playing different roles for their devotees. Baba Jai Gurudev was the larger-than-life guru of innumerable disciples, personally distant from the vast majority of them but offering them a definite path. Maharajji, by contrast, has been able to personally present many fewer devotees with different elements of an expansive yoga not easy to grasp as a whole. As gurus, then, they have differed as sources of practice and as foci for religious community. It is worth looking more closely at how they have done so.

Practices Differently Packaged

When giving *nām* to thousands of people at a time Baba Jai Gurudev presented a single set of codified instructions, including words to repeat, aniconic internal sights to contemplate, and sounds to listen for. There is some scope for personal choice in just which aspects of the practice an individual might emphasize to start with—but, with the objects of meditation offered as a sequence, a definite path for advancement. At all stages, moreover, greater concentration will bring increasing intensity of experience. Methods are presented and a course is set. The guru, drawing on a version of sant tradition, has outlined the path to travel and given devotees the means to do so.

Devotees vary, of course, in how far they travel on the path. *Sant mat* language speaks of practitioners catching the sound, merging into it with loving devotion, and letting it pull them up. Many devotees who give time to their practice have experiences along this line that are ecstatic and personally fulfilling; their success in practice keeps them regular in it and heightens their enthusiasm about the movement. But not all are so fortunate. Later stages of practice demand tenacity in concentration to the point of absorption. It is not hard to imagine that many among the tens of millions counted as Baba Jai Gurudev's devotees don't get much beyond repetition of divine names. They may still feel a strong if straightforward devotion toward their recently passed guru, however—a feeling taken as valuable in itself and leading to further stages of experience, if not in this life, then in future ones. In their own way, they remain his avid devotees.

For some avid devotees, moreover—whatever the extent of their practice—a good deal of their fervor of comes from the belief that not only has the path of the sants long provided a direct route to the highest divine, but to travel it successfully today the particular divine name that was taught by their guru is also necessary. "Jai Gurudev," the concluding paragraph of the web page cited above begins, "is the name of GOD. This is the only name at present which would liberate the soul from the rotation of birth and death. This name shall soon spread not only throughout India but it shall take over the entire world." Enthusiastic devotees are at the forefront of a global spiritual renewal!

Maharajji's devotees, while not usually thinking about global spiritual renewal, have their own reasons to think they are special. As disciples of someone carrying forward Malik Sahib's psychic synthesis of *sant mat* and *śaktipāt* initiations, they feel they have access to the full breadth of Hindu yogic experience. Experientially, the two practices clearly do work in different areas of the body and call on different attitudes of devotion. The *sant mat sādhana* demands calm attention at the point between the eyebrows (and places above it) to meet the lights and sounds that will pull the devotee toward the loving Lord. Particularly in its Radhasoami versions, the practice demands a self-effacing devotion and leads to rapturous aniconic visions. The *śaktipāt* initiation awakens force active in the whole of the body, to which devotees are told to surrender. As the devotees let the force purify their minds and bodies, they are likely to have experiences of the power of the divine, which once quietened, can lead to a sense of profound peace. Theologically, Malik Sahib talked about the goal of *sant mat sādhana*, reached through concentrated love and ecstasy, as "the true Vishnu" and the surrender to divine power possible through the *śaktipāt* initiation as leading to "the true Shiva," taken as the essence of peace and clarity. His disciples could thus feel they had access to a complete package of inward experience in the Hindu tradition.

In practice, most devotees begin by experiencing the energies that *śaktipāt* awakens in the bodily chakras most strongly, but they often experience it together with a version of the rapturous devotion more typical of Radhasoami experience. During satsang, they regularly hear poetic descriptions of (or at least references to) the *sant mat* sounds and lights in the *āratīs* of Soamiji Maharaj and others. They are told that when they are ready, these phenomena will open up to them. For some, they do. Before then, however, as devotees learn to surrender to the divine energy playing within them, they undergo diverse somatic and sometimes emotional experiences. These depend on a devotee's individual personal history and psychological makeup, and there is much room for the unexpected. If problems or confusions arise—as they may, especially at the beginning— some personal communication with the guru usually resolves them. For this kind of intervention, not an extremely common event, Maharajji always finds time. Baba Jai Gurudev, by contrast, with his tens of millions of devotees, understandably offered a single straight path that does not have the potential to disrupt the psychic balance of the body.

Communities of Different Shapes

As a distant guru, moreover, Baba Jai Gurudev was the head of a religious community that was itself more organized, with authority more practically diffused, than in the community of Maharajji's devotees, which has no formal organization to speak of. Although Maharajji's devotees sometimes forge warm informal bonds with one another, there's not much in place institutionally to encourage interaction among them when the guru is not present. The satsang halls in Himachal and Jodhpur serve mostly as bases for Maharajji when he visits. Although a few devotees do regularly meet at these places, I have been told, substantial groups do not often congregate. Busy householder disciples engaging in their own meditation at home may feel that their individual practice is sufficient. In fact, even though group singing and meditation may be recommended practices, a guruless satsang is often not much of a draw: Maharajji is an accessible figure who visits these places regularly and the de facto local leaders have not usually been seen to carry much religious weight. This situation, however, has recently begun to change, at least in Himachal. Some time around the beginning of 2009 Maharajji explicitly granted a measure of authority to a longtime disciple then in his seventies, someone living in a town fairly distant from the Bilaspur satsang hall and not specifically connected to it.[44] He accepts invitations to speak to (and meditate with) gatherings of devotees throughout the area and is treated reverentially by them. Maharajji, it seems, has begun to feel greater formal diffusion of religious authority could be helpful among his more far-flung groups of disciples but hasn't found many qualified to provide it. In the Jai Gurudev movement, by contrast, recognition of local leaders is normal, if qualifications less stringent.

The local branches of the Jai Gurudev movement in Gwalior and the Jahazpur area have active local satsangs that meet regularly, usually led by people who are given an extra measure of respect by their fellow devotees. They may be old disciples wearing burlap, or younger enthusiastic organizers who have personally helped to bring many of the current group into the fold. Although most of the movement activists I met were at least moderately well off, even someone of very ordinary socioeconomic status can gain a new sense of self-worth as a local movement leader. At a regional event in Jahazpur, for example, a senior devotee from a nearby town was introduced to me by another devotee from the same place as his "guru." Although the term here obviously did not refer to an exalted religious personage such as Baba Jai Gurudev, it still carried weight in the sense of a respected religious teacher. The man referred to as guru, a fruit seller with a stand at a small-town bus station, accepted the title with a calm smile. Beyond any eventual boosts to self-esteem, moreover, the organizational and missionary work done by local activists offers them a means of religious fulfillment beyond their internal practice. They are able to contribute to the communitarian spirit of the Jai Gurudev movement through zealous proselytizing.

Also contributing to the communitarian spirit of the movement have been independent devotee publishers, whose hymn-books and broadsheets enrich collective religious life. The existence of these publishers is in fact a testament to the organic way in which the movement has grown. Although most large religious establishments have had substantial in-house publishing operations, the Jai Gurudev movement has not. It instead seems satisfied with the work done by devotee entrepreneurs, some of whom began their businesses when the movement was young. These independent publishers have offered both inexpensive collections of sant verse, including verses by Baba Jai Gurudev, and movement-related lithographs of different sorts—all of which are sold in part by very small-scale independent dealers such as those seen at the large Jaipur satsang. Just as important, some devotees have published ongoing periodicals. The current most popular one, *Śākāhārī Sadācārī Bāl Sangh* ("The Union of Vegetarian, Right-Acting Children"), originally aimed at young readers, uses simple, vivid language appropriate for reading out at satsangs. It contains summaries of Baba Jai Gurudev's discourses on spiritual experience and sayings on various topics; while the guru was alive it also published new messages he gave while on tour. Fresh insights from the distant guru were (and still are) regularly provided without the guru being present. With continuous new material and some religiously authoritative leaders, the weekly satsangs outside Mathura find regular attendees.

In addition to attending local satsangs, Baba Jai Gurudev's devotees are enjoined to spread the word about their guru. Not everyone does so with enthusiasm, of course, but local leaders generally do. In contrast to Maharajji's lone authoritative disciple in Himachal, whose job seems largely to serve the established satsang there, local leaders in the Jai Gurudev movement try actively to expand it. The importance of this was brought home to me after a long and fruitful talk with one of the old Gwalior jute-wearing devotees. He knew I would be going back to the United States soon but asked me to please come back in December for the big annual festival at Mathura. Not only should I come myself, but I should also bring some friends with me. "Sometimes you have to spend money in spiritual work," he added, "but it will be returned to you tenfold." Although the Gwalior elder's pronouncement did not have the effect he desired on *me*, it might have on a devotee living not too far from Mathura who had much faith and a bit of cash on hand.

Indeed, one of the main jobs of the local leaders has been to help bring people to major festivals at the Mathura ashram. These were occasions for a renewed *darśan* of the guru when Baba Jai Gurudev was alive and remain times for experiencing his extremely extensive community of devotees. For those enthusiastic about the idea of their guru being at the forefront of global spiritual renewal, the large numbers present at these occasions could bring reassurance. They could also, for some, add to the exhilaration of the event. "I'm really very, very happy," said one devotee who had been visiting the Mathura ashram at festivals for three years, "when I see my guru sitting in front of more than a hundred thousand people and giving them best wishes."[45] The guru's blessing seemed even bigger because there were so many people gathered to receive it.

The gatherings at Maharajji's place are nothing like this. Not everybody knows one another (sometimes several hundred people show up) but people who have been devotees for a while usually meet others from different places whom they are happy to see. Some of the same kind of interregional and interpersonal dynamics among middle-class devotees described on the Himachal tour take place, but more of them. An architect from Delhi talks to a shopkeeper from a Madhya Pradesh village whom he has long respected for his wisdom and sincerity. A bank manager from Jodhpur (now posted in Gujarat) mingles with a confectioner from Banda, Uttar Pradesh. His wife is catching up with an ethnic Tibetan woman from Himachal. This sort of easy cross-regional familiarity may not be too common in modern Indian religious groups—perhaps the mark of one that has spread to a few diverse places but hasn't got too large. And at the major festivals of the yearly cycle, the gathering has grown uncomfortably big for some distant devotees, who would rather attend the smaller-scale events. Instead of the collective effervescence of the crowd, these prefer the personal intimacy of a cozier gathering of devoted familiars around the guru.

The emphasis on organization, mission, and collectivity seen among Jai Gurudev's devotees—marks of a consciously expansive movement— are not so commonly found in Radhasoami groups, even those that have become quite large. They have certainly not been particularly prominent in the mainline Radhasoami satsang based at Beas, most comparable to the Jai Gurudev movement in size and with branches throughout North India. That satsang, long established in the Punjab, does not advertise itself publicly to the same extent as the Jai Gurudev movement, and although attracting local people wherever it takes root, has spread in part through networks of Punjabis and Sindhis, many of whom have been born into the tradition. Its gurus have been presented as personages less like Baba Jai Gurudev than like Maharajji—indeed, often more like Malik Sahib: people dressed in an unobtrusive traditional style and unashamed to have had regular jobs. They have appeared, for the most part, as relatively modest figures, not spiritual extroverts. Even as the followings of gurus in Beas lineages have expanded, some gurus have cautioned about developing too much organization: it could interfere with devotees' individual spiritual growth.[46]

The official local associations that have developed with the growth of the Beas lineage have thus tended to be quieter than those found among Baba Jai Gurudev's devotees. The Beas Satsang in Gwalior, for example, has officers and a president, but the concern of these men is largely with the affairs of the ashram outside town; they don't seem to spend much time organizing people to go to seasonal functions in Beas. Indeed, there is less emphasis here than there has been in the Jai Gurudev movement on regular large-group contact with the guru, or even to getting initiation instructions from the guru himself. In some Beas lineages, as long as an inner contact is made, the instructions can be taught by a qualified intermediary.

Socioreligiously, this lineage seems like a more straightforward development of the path taught by Radhasoami Maharaj to nineteenth-century
office workers than that of either Baba Jai Gurudev—with its conscious
turn toward an expansionist movement—or of Maharajji, with its radical
change in practice and perspective.

Say *Jai Gurudev!*

Despite the different turns their traditions have taken, devotees of both
Maharajji and Baba Jai Gurudev all understand that when you meet a
fellow devotee, the most appropriate words of greeting are *Jai Gurudev*.
Members of many religious groups in India and elsewhere have a particular phrase of greeting that they use among themselves, a mutual acknowl-
edgement of community identity. For several Radhasoami groups, the
greeting has been simply "Radhasoami," a divine name but also by now a
sectarian affiliation. Devotees of Malik Sahib's guru, Data Dayala, still say
Śabd Pratāp, which has a special significance for the group: *śabd* refers
to the divine sound current, Pratap was the given name of Data Dayala's
guru and means "glory." The residential colony where many of them live
is called Shabd Pratap Ashram. As Malik Sahib and Baba Jai Gurudev both
moved away from their previous sectarian identification, they adopted the
salutation *Jai Gurudev*, a generic phrase used in many groups of devotees.
They gave it different significances, however, and their devotees have even
tended to say it in different ways.

For Malik Sahib and then Maharajji, *Jai Gurudev* has remained basically a friendly greeting among members of a group, words recalling the
nature of their spiritual bond. For Baba Jai Gurudev's disciples the phrase
has also been a friendly salutation, but it is at the same time a divine name
signaling a new spiritual dispensation with which they remain strongly
identified. The words are regularly affirmed within group meetings and
announced to the world as well.

Among Maharajji's devotees, then, the phrase *Jai Gurudev* is used
mostly as a conventional hello among a group of largely middle-class folk
restrained in their public enthusiasms. It is usually spoken in a normal
tone of voice, often accompanied by the Hindu palms-together gesture
of greeting, and sometimes with a warm smile. Within the Jai Gurudev
movement, by contrast, even when the phrase is used as a salutation, it
carries the residual force of its emphatic repetition in satsang—where it
proclaimed loudly, with *Jai*, a word that means "victory," distinctly stressed

and elongated. Spoken with gusto in public by disciples of a populist spiritual leader out to transform the world, it carries a greater illocutionary force. Thus, before local movement meetings, we might hear devotees greeting each other with a rousing *"JAAII Gurudev!* Have you heard about the special *satsang* next week? See if you can get your brother-in-law to come!" At Adhyatma Niketan, by contrast, one is likely to be met with a quiet *"Jai Gurudev. . .* how are you doing? Maharajji should be out soon." In provincial Hinduism as in much religious culture, when related traditions develop in substantially different ways, their surface similarities are not always what they seem.

Afterword: Personal Religious Identity in a Pluralist Society

FOR DEVOTEES OF Maharajji, Baba Jai Gurudev, and other charismatic Indian teachers, their gurus are likely to be the most important focus of their religious lives—but usually not the only one. Most Indian devotees have grown up in full religious worlds, replete with envisioned divine beings and different varieties of ritual practice. If new devotees come to gurus in part because familiar forms of divinity and practice have not been entirely fulfilling, few give up their previous ways entirely. Shared with family and caste-fellows, old observances may still have cherished personal meanings, while helping maintain valued familial bonds and important social networks.

At the same time, *any* powerful new religious focus is likely to alter the significances given to old ones, sometimes diminishing them, but sometimes also enhancing them with a borrowed spiritual radiance. Verses of the Radhasoami gurus, for example, display both types of attitude: in some verses, major Hindu divinities are subordinated to the supreme Lord, their abodes located at different stages on the path toward the highest goal; in others, traditional Hindu festivals have been revalued, imbued with esoteric meaning. People in the subcontinent with traditionally grounded pieties (whatever their attitudes toward gurus) are likely to recognize several objects of reverence arrayed together in their inward religious worlds. These have different relationships to one another and elicit different responses—emotionally, ritually, and for contemplative practice. To the extent that people respond individually to particular sets of religious objects recognized as their own, we can talk about them as having distinctive personal religious identities.

For ordinary middle-class Hindus, these inward religious identities are sometimes expressed outwardly in personal altars. Here let's imagine the altar set up on a table in the corner of a bedroom by an older woman, the matriarch in a successful family from an artisan community. In Gwalior, if chapter 1's general temple survey is any guide, that altar might well be centered on Durga, represented here by a particularly fine old image sitting at the back of the table right between the corner walls. In front of Durga on either side are smaller images of Shiva and Ganesha, both divinities with a familial connection to the goddess in well-known lore and often receiving attention from her serious devotees. On the wall to the right is a framed lithograph of the youthful Krishna with his flute. He isn't closely connected to the goddess in story, but our matriarch likes to go to the hymn-singing parties for Krishna to which she is often invited by higher-caste women in her neighborhood, and she thinks the picture itself is very beautiful. At the same time, she is proud of her own caste origins, so on the opposite wall she has hung a lithograph of Vishvakarman, "the maker of the world," a figure revered in several artisan castes. Because she is from a family rooted in the area, she doesn't have a regional god on display, as a Sindhi or Gwalior Maharashtrian might.

These lithographs are surrounded by some photos of holy persons, including one of Ramakrishna. She used to go to Gwalior's Ramakrishna Ashram, where they regularly sing hymn-songs to the nineteenth-century saint. She stopped going to the ashram as she got older, but she still reveres Ramakrishna as a great devotee who can continue to give blessings. Across from the picture of Ramakrishna there's one of Asaram Bapu, a contemporary media guru whom our matriarch has long been fond of watching on television. She feels his discourses really speak to her and—even though people have started speaking ill of him—he is still her favorite holy person.[1]

Below Asaram's photo is one of Maharajji. Our matriarch was given the picture by a sister who is an enthusiastic devotee of his, and she went to his ashram with her a few times. On the sister's altar, a photo of Maharajji stands front and center, and our matron put one up in her own shrine room partly to please her. While never bonding closely with Maharajji herself, she still sees him as a genuine holy person with whom she has personally connected; the picture, when she looks at it, might help link her to his grace.

Opposite Maharajji's photo but a bit below it and to the side is a picture of Rashid Sahib from the Khwaja Khanoon Sufi shrine. She had gone to

Rashid before her last pregnancy, when she wanted a son after bearing three daughters. Her wishes fulfilled, she suspected that Rashid's benevolent intercession with Khwaja Khanoon had helped grant them. Even though she has never had occasion to go back to the shrine, she keeps Rashid's picture up. While recognizing the forces he mediates as powerful, she feels that she doesn't really understand them, and she certainly doesn't want anything to happen to her only son: it's prudent to demonstrate continued respect.

Our matron thus recognizes a number of sources of divine grace (or at least otherworldly powers) as ones she is linked to, but in various ways and to different degrees. She likes to commune with them daily in her own shrine space. Although she reveres all the Hindu divinities and most Indian holy persons in a general way, these are particularly *hers*.

Our matron's chosen divine beings represent different aspects of her fluid religious sensibilities. They accumulated with new religious interests and enthusiasms, and, once installed, tended to remain even as her enthusiasm waned. They reflect widespread convention (the images of Shiva and Ganesh alongside the central Durga) and individual encounters (especially the local holy persons Maharajji and Rashid Khanooni). They indicate personal predilection (the beautiful picture of Krishna in addition to the image of Durga) and social significance (especially the caste deity Vishwakarma). The picture of Krishna actually has both social and personal meanings for our matriarch: it indicates her integration into a middle-class neighborhood's mixed-caste social network, but it is also a token of the very deep devotion she feels for the deity when she meets with the neighborhood ladies to sing hymn-songs to him.

The holy persons with whom she finds a connection are not all the same to her either. Ramakrishna and Asaram Bapu, facing each other above the rest, she sees as the most deserving of her respect: the first as a well-known saint of the modern age whom everyone should venerate; the second, recently very popular, as her still current personal favorite. The regional guru Maharajji, below them, is not as widely revered as those two or especially close to her heart, but she respects him as an authentic saint who has a connection with her family. The local Sufi Rashid, set apart from the rest, was once important for her personally and remains a figure she recognizes as her own.

Our matriarch's shrine space has evolved over time, but mostly around the edges. Devout Hindus tend to maintain a central religious focus—a chosen deity *(iṣṭadevtā)* or perhaps a guru with whom they strongly identify—while having some other religious affinities, too, differing in type and depth, any one of which may on occasion preoccupy them. To the extent that an element of someone's personal religious identity has active social implications at a given time, it can affect the way that person moves in the world.

In many traditionally envisioned Indian worlds, particularly in rural areas, the dominant factor of social identity has been and continues to be caste, although in contemporary urban environments it often seems to be trumped by class, generally marked by economic status and educational attainment. Caste is not lost in the city, but in India's booming metros, filled with people from all over India, an individual's caste origin is often not easily determinable or its significance understood—and is anyway claimed to be unimportant by many with cosmopolitan sensibilities. Here wealth and educational qualifications become more crucial social identifiers. In a village, a rich person from a farming caste is still usually first of all seen as a member of his particular farming community; acculturated in a metro, he is more likely to be treated first of all as just a rich man. In a provincial city such as Gwalior, where people come largely from the surrounding regions and few have cosmopolitan outlooks, caste and class are both very vital, playing out against other social factors such as regional origin (usually not a factor in villages) and broad Hindu and Muslim identity (significant wherever populations are mixed).

The chapters of this book have examined some intersections between inward religious and outward social identity in Gwalior along a number of socioreligious axes: the economic classes of chapter 1's temple-goers; the meanings of the Muslim other for Hindus visiting chapter 2's Sufi shrines; the realities of neighborhood caste and class interactions and the complications of regional ethnicity in chapters 3 and 4, respectively; and, in different ways in chapters 5 and 6, the formation of new communities around socially oriented charismatic individuals, salvation-oriented holy persons, and the institutions they both foster.

The chapters together suggest some basic patterns of change that occur in personal religious identity as individuals participate in the public religious life of a provincial Indian city. Although radical conversions happen—particularly when gurus are involved—for most mainstream Hindus, the old is more often assimilated to the new unselfconsciously. Thus, a Gwalior Shiva-devotee requesting practical help at a Sufi shrine is likely to find a place for its powers somewhere within his established religious world without much thought—perhaps seeing them as something like those at the Bhairava shrine at his grandfather's village.

Among minority groups, natal religious identities need to be affirmed within the larger communities in which they live. This was particularly true for the Muslim image-makers of chapter 3, who—however much they participated in Hindu ritual life professionally and sometimes personally—felt the need to make it clear to me that they were Muslims first of all. Related dynamics of conscious assertion are also found among regional Hindu ethnic groups in town. Many Sindhis and Maharashtrians work to keep up the traditions of their homelands and show them off to their Gwalior neighbors: Sindhis sometimes worrying about appearing too different; Maharashtrians feeling the loss of their former privilege.

Socioreligiously, things have been easier for Hindus from regional villages settling in the city's poorer neighborhoods. They find immediate religious continuities in the many goddess temples there, often more similar to those they left behind than are those frequently met in the city's wealthier areas. Religious change can come quickly for new migrants, though, as it can to anyone, if they encounter a modern religious organization. And it is likely to come eventually if they simply achieve some economic success. For in all neighborhoods, as class divisions overtake caste boundaries, people discover lasting personal affinities with neighbors from different caste-communities. And as the upwardly mobile emulate middle-class devotional ways, people may become more comfortable worshipping together, too. For everyone in urban areas, new opportunities for socioreligious change, together with the availability of modern gurus and organizations, create the potential for some highly individualized personal religion.

There has long been room for individualized religious sensibilities, if not practice, in older Hindu tradition. In many previous eras, the relative stability of a social identity grounded in caste in fact gave great leeway to inward religious life. Presuming that everyday ritual practice was more or less maintained, a religious attitude that was questioning or curious did not normally lead to serious social marginalization. As long as hierarchies remained intact, moreover, rituals themselves could be quietly adjusted (and were regularly adjusted anyway as hierarchies changed). Particular caste groups had outwardly normative religious traditions—usually more flexible than they seemed—while individuals could quietly explore other options. Caste provided a place where a commonly recognized social identity converged with an outwardly constrained but inwardly malleable religious one.

In contemporary urban India, the same malleability of inward religious life remains, but there is no simple convergence of social and religious identity. As individuals juggle multiple social identities—professional, caste, regional, civic, some with specific religious implications, some with decidedly nonreligious ones—they may have to struggle to keep their inner worlds unified. Encountering different, twenty-first-century forms of Hinduism while maintaining some of their old ways, they can develop personal religious identities that become quite complex. In the contemporary Indian world this complexity is often salutary—at least more so than its opposite: the easy convergence of modern religious and social identities at their most frequent lowest common denominator, Hindu and Muslim—bases for movements of religious nationalism.

Religious nationalism, giving emotionally driven clan solidarity the infinite dimensions associated with the divine, easily becomes toxic in whatever community it is found, but it is the Hindu variant that has sometimes come into view in Gwalior. Although the Hindu rightist organizer met above Hippopotamus Street seemed fairly ineffectual, he has many colleagues in the broader movement who are better at their jobs. We've seen one of them working for the Vivekananda Kendra, promoting an homogenized national program to rival the Vivekananda Needam's flowering local garden. The rise of Ram temples in Gwalior emerges from similar ground, the old Ram as exemplar of virtue now also shadowed by his image of the warrior defending his birthplace from the infidel. Many individuals caught up in the spirit of Hindu nationalism have managed to avoid its communal excesses, and the sincerity and higher religious aims of many of the Vivekandsa Kendra workers and Ram-temple builders are patent and worthy of respect. But religious nationalism in principle demands an other against which to stand, and impulses stemming from it, as we see in South Asia and elsewhere, can readily degenerate into violent conflict. It is likely to be the basis of a religious identity that is too dangerously simple for complicated times. With many things religious—prayer, ritual, contemplation practice—simpler often seems better, but not, in contemporary India, with religious identity. Complex religious identities are often the best to be had in a complicated socioreligious world. They deserve our respect, if not our admiration.

Notes

INTRODUCTION

1. Classic studies based in villages from earlier decades include Mysore N. Srinivas, *Religion and Society among the Coorgs of South India* (London: Oxford University, 1952); G. M. Carstairs, *The Twice-Born: A Study of a Community of High-Caste Hindus* (Bloomington: Indiana University Press, 1961); and Susan Snow Wadley, *Shakti: Power in the Conceptual Structure of Karimpur Religion* (Chicago: Department of Anthropology, University of Chicago, 1975). Newer city-oriented work includes Smriti Srinivas, *Landscapes of Urban Memory: The Sacred and the Civic in India's High-Tech City* (Minneapolis: University of Minnesota Press, 2001); Joanne Punzo Waghorne, *Diaspora of the Gods: Modern Hindu Temples in an Urban Middle-Class World* (New York: Oxford University Press, 2004); and Jacob Copeman, *Veins of Devotion: Blood Donation and Religious Experience in North India* (New Brunswick, N.J.: Rutgers University Press, 2009).

2. Colonial writers used *provincial* as a translation into standard English of the Indian English *mofussil*, a relative term that referred to the hinterland of an urban point of reference: in Calcutta, the *mofussil* was all the rest of Bengal, but someone in a district headquarters could use the term to mean the surrounding towns and villages: see Henry Yule, A. C. Burnell, and William Crooke, *Hobson-Jobson: A Glossary of Colloquial Anglo Indian Words and Phrases, and of Kindred Terms, Etymological, Historical, Geographical and Discursive*, 2nd ed. (Calcutta: Rupa & Co., 1990 [1903]), p. 570. The contrast to the cosmopolitan implicit in this sense of *provincial* has been articulately expressed by Nita Kumar, who uses the term to describe contemporary Banaras, among other places: "Provincialism in Modern India: The Multiple Narratives of Education and Their Pain," *Modern Asian Studies* 40, no. 2 (2006): 397–423. I follow her usage.

3. On middle-class anxiety in Kathmandu, see Mark Liechty, *Suitably Modern: Making Middle-Class Culture in a New Consumer Society* (Princeton, N.J.: Princeton University Press, 2003); Liechty also ties the cosmopolitan extremes to economic disparity. For a more relaxed provincial attitude, see Kathinka Frøystad, *Blended Boundaries: Caste, Class, and Shifting Faces of "Hinduness" in a North Indian City* (New York: Oxford University Press, 2005), who presents it throughout her book on middle-class life in Kanpur.

4. Long recognized as a distinct cultural area, Chhatisgarh has great mineral wealth together with a large and mostly poor tribal population. The creation of Chhatisgarh was part of a broader reorganization of large northern states that saw the emergence of the new states of Jharkhand and Uttaranchal Pradesh (now Uttarakhand).

5. Newer work on the topic includes Leela Fernandes, *India's New Middle Class: Democratic Politics in an Era of Economic Reform* (University of Minnesota Press, 2006); Christiane Brosius, *India's Middle Class: New Forms of Urban Leisure, Consumption and Prosperity* (Delhi: Routledge India, 2010); Amita Baviskar and Raka Ray, eds., *Elite and Everyman: The Cultural Politics of the Indian Middle Classes* (New Delhi: Routledge, 2011); Minna Saavala, *Middle-Class Moralities: Everyday Struggle over Belonging and Prestige in India* (New Delhi: Orient Blackswan, 2012).

6. See Waghorne, *Diaspora of the Gods* and Srinivas, *Landscapes of Urban Memory*.

7. Figures for greater Gwalior based on preliminary 2011 census data put its population at over 1,100,000.

8. Baba Jai Gurudev died on May 18, 2012, and—as is often the case when a guru passes on—there were fractious issues over his succession. I have offered some initial reflections on these issues at the end of an article on some of the movement's rural dimensions: "Bābā Jai Gurudev in the Qasbā: The Ruralization of a Modern Religion," *International Journal of Hindu Studies* 17, no. 2 (2013): 127–52.

CHAPTER 1

1. B. D. Misra, *The Forts and Fortresses of Gwalior and Its Hinterland* (Delhi: Manohar, 1993), pp. 28–59, discusses the complicated political and military history of the fort. For an early history of temple architecture in the broader Gwalior region, see Michael D. Willis, *Temples of Gopakṣetra: A Regional History of Architecture and Sculpture in Central India AD 600–900* (London: British Museum Press, 1997).

2. Maharaja Madhav Rao Scindia, a former railway minister in Delhi, was an important player in the Congress party—still the principal secularist force on the Indian national stage. He died at fifty-six during the 2001 crash of a private airplane taking him to a political rally. His mother, Vijaya Raje Scindia, was a major force in Madhya Pradesh state politics in the 1960s and a cofounder of the rival Hindu Nationalist Bharatiya Janata party. She also died in 2001, of old

age. The political and personal estrangement between the Rajmata and her son—who lived in separate wings of Jai Vilas Palace—has an air of epic tragedy about it. But the two seemed to have come closer during the Rajmata's final years, when she grew physically weak just as her political party gained ascendancy over Madhav Rao's for the first time.

3. On the religious topography of Banaras, see Diana L. Eck, *Banaras: City of Light* (Princeton, N.J.: Princeton University Press, 1982).

4. For the *cār dhām* taken to encompass the Indian subcontinent, see Diana L. Eck, *India: A Sacred Geography* (New York: Harmony Books, 2012), pp. 29–31. For their replication on the borders of a particular village, see Ann Grodzins Gold, *Fruitful Journeys: The Ways of Rajasthani Pilgrims* (Berkeley: University of California Press, 1988), pp. 34–36.

5. On the sixteenth-century leader Shivaji, taken as the fount of the Maratha military renaissance, see James William Laine, *Shivaji: Hindu King in Islamic India* (New York: Oxford University Press, 2003). On Tulja Bhavani and contemporary worship of her at her main shrine in Tuljapur, Maharashtra, see Kiran A. Shinde, "Re-scripting the Legends of Tuljā Bhavānī: Texts, Performances, and New Media in Maharashtra," *International Journal of Hindu Studies* 17, no. 3 (2014): 313–37.

6. Even though family members now use Bhelsavali as a surname, they are still considered Parles and Brahmins, like their military forebear who built the Bhelsavali temple. In contrast to Brahmins in many parts of India, who until modern times were engaged predominantly in priestly professions, Maharashtrian Brahmins performed a range of professional activities, including administration, trade, and the military (see chapter 4 below). Brahmin generals were not uncommon in the armies of imperial Maharashtra.

7. The decisive change in the duty seen by Gwalior's military officers actually came in 1843. Although Maharaja Daulat Rao Scindia was compelled to come to terms with the British in 1818, he was still able to keep an army that defended the boundaries of his expansive domains and kept his own feudatories in check. After long-simmering discontent with the British led to an uprising and defeat at the 1843 Battle of Maharajpur, Gwalior and its army was definitively subjugated. See Amar Farooqui, *Sindias and the Raj: Princely Gwalior c. 1800–1850* (Delhi: Primus Books, 2011), pp. 65–92. A detailed account of the relationship of the Scindias to their subordinate Rajput feudatories is given in Hindi by Anand Miśra, *Gvāliyara Rājya ke Rājapūta Jagīradāra* (Bhopal: Bhāratīya Itihās Saṃkalan Samiti, 1996).

8. The signboard at the temple announces that it is the "Holy Place of the Honored Goddess Great Kali Mandare Mother, the Slayer of Mahishasura" (*Devasthān Śrī Mahākālī Devī Māṃdaṛe kī Mātā Mahiṣāsura Mardanī*). In most traditions, it is the form of the goddess as Durga who slays Mahishasura, not Kali. The image in the temple of a goddess on a mount is anomalous: it presents neither Kali's customarily horrific guise nor Durga's normal Mahishasura-slaying pose (standing with leg raised, spear in hand).

9. This section is based largely on interviews with Ashok Rao Mandare on November 25, 2010, and with Babu Rao Mandare and devotees on the temple steps on August 13, 2008. I later heard the stories told by the devotees from a number of other popular sources.

10. Although the shape suggests a phallus, the word *lingam* can also mean a sign or emblem, so the term *Shivalingam* can also be read more prudently as "a sign of Shiva."

11. Zealous religious enthusiasm among active businessmen is especially common in Jain tradition. See James Laidlaw, *Riches and Renunciation: Religion, Economy, and Society among the Jains* (Oxford: Clarendon Press, 1995).

12. Interview with Devendra Gupta, November 23, 2007.

13. Said to have lived six hundred years ago, Kunwar Sahib's shrine is in Roli, M.P. He is taken as a descendent of the Rajput warrior Prithvi Raj Chauhan (1149–92 C.E.).

14. "Kailā Maiyā Kā Jāgaraṇ," *Mahā Śakti kī Lalkār* 5, nos. 3–4 (2011): 31. This short article in a sectarian journal obtained at the Karauli shrine describes how the goddess first came to a devotee named Sukhdev Paṭel and now comes every night to Bharosā Lāl Mīṇā from Karaulī village.

15. With Hiralal's children still small when he died, Kunwar Sahib first started coming to his maternal nephews. In 2011, the medium was Chandraprash, Hiralal's youngest and only living son. When asked about the inheritance of the mediumship, he said that it was the place that was powerful (*siddha*), not the person.

16. For some less than savory perceptions of spirit possession in urban Indian contexts see Veena Das, "The Dreamed Guru," in *The Guru in South Asia: New Interdisciplinary Perspectives*, ed. Jacob Copeman and Aya Ikegame (New York: Routledge, 2012), pp. 133–55; and Jonathan P. Parry, *Death in Banaras* (New York: Cambridge University Press, 1994), esp. ch. 7: "Spirit Possession as 'Superstition.'"

17. These headings follow the phases of the ritual: before the medium is possessed; after the medium is possessed; garlanding the possessed medium; after garlanding; and making requests at Kunwar Sahib's court.

18. On pilgrimage to the Himalayan Vaishno Devi, see Kathleen M. Erndl, *Victory to the Mother: The Hindu Goddess of Northwest India in Myth, Ritual, and Symbol* (New York: Oxford University Press, 1993), pp. 61–83.

19. The Himalayan Vaishno Devi is represented aniconically through three *piṇḍīs*, naturally formed rising stone formations, to which a small image of Durga has been added. The Gwalior cave, by contrast, has a large image of Durga with three small artificial *piṇḍīs* below.

20. The most visible suggestion of a new wave of attraction-laden, reduplicative temples is no doubt the Swaminarayan sect's Akshardham Temple, which has made a very big splash outside Delhi—the most elaborate of several complexes of similar name erected by the sect in recent decades. Its planners visited Disneyland and Universal Studios to get ideas for an audio animatronic

diorama presenting the life of the sect's founder, a boat ride past monuments to Indian culture, and much more. Like Sharad Sharma at Gwalior's Kaila Devi, a monastic manager at the Akshardham complex speaks frankly about its "attractions": see Sanjay Srivastava, "Urban Spaces, Disney-Divinity and Moral Middle Classes in Delhi," *Economic and Political Weekly* 44, nos. 26–27 (2009): 338–45.

21. Temples as public spaces—sometimes of sorts not met in Gwalior—have been examined in some detail. Enduring studies of large South Indian temple complexes include Arjun Appadurai, *Worship and Conflict under Colonial Rule: A South Indian Case* (New York: Cambridge University Press, 1981) and C. J. Fuller, *Servants of the Goddess: The Priests of a South Indian Temple* (New York: Cambridge University Press, 1984). Some interesting newer developments have been treated in a special issue of the *International Journal of Hindu Studies* (13.3, 2009) "Temple Publics: Religious Institutions and the Constructions of Contemporary Hindu Communities."

22. The authorities at the temple interpret the meaning of *kheṛā* in a more extended sense, suggesting that their establishment was given that name when the Scindia armies arrived and found a small mandir in the jungle between their camp and the old city that offered a ritual center encompassing them both as a single "settlement." Kherapati is one of Hanuman's less frequent epithets.

23. According to a newspaper report describing the mass wedding, the Achaleshwar priests spent all day in ritual activities, and the temple trust organized a wedding feast for the relatives, making gifts to the couples of household essentials such as utensils, cupboards, and blankets: Ashok Pal, "Over 1200 Couples Nuptial Knot in Mass Marriage in Gwalior [*sic*]," *SIFY News*, February 17, 2010.

24. *Pancāyat* is a general term for a community's governing body. In contemporary rural India, it usually refers to the village council selected through regular government elections. In urban areas it can refer to the governing body of an organized caste community, which in this case seems to stand for the small cohesive caste community itself. The official name for the *deśi* Agrawals is the Gwalior Agrawal Valan Panchayat, Lashkar Residents (*Śrī Gvāliyar Vālān Agrawāl Pancāyat, Laśkar Nivāsī*).

25. There are twenty-one members on the Ram Mandir temple committee: ten officeholders and eleven others. Elections are held every two years.

26. Group interview with Santosh Kumarji Agraval, the general secretary, Yogesh Garg, a past general secretary, and Dipak Agrawal, the festivals chair, November 23, 2010.

27. The major yearly events organized at Ram mandir are two widely celebrated festivals to important Vaishnava divinities—Ram Navami and Krishna Janmashtmi—and two festivals particularly dear to the hearts of the temple's membership: Vivah Panchmi, commemorating the marriage of Ram and Sita, and Ganga Dusshera, the celebration of the emergence of the Ganges. The last is important for the temple because it takes place on the day of the Hindu calendar when the temple's new images were consecrated in 1953.

28. On the Arya Samaj and other movements of the era, including the Sanatan Dharm movement, see Kenneth W. Jones, *Arya Dharm: Hindu Consciousness in 19th-Century Punjab* (Berkeley: University of California Press, 1976) and Kenneth W. Jones, *Socio-religious Reform Movements in British India, The New Cambridge History of India* 3:1 (Cambridge: Cambridge University Press, 1989). These movements are discussed briefly toward the beginning of chapter 5 below.

29. Group interview with Sanatan Dharm Mandir officers including Satyendra Gupta, the joint vice president, Girraj Kishore Goyal, the joint secretary, and Lakshman Das Vaishya, the secretary, September 4, 1997.

30. Conversation with Ashok Jain, September 4, 1997. In 1997 there were two classes of members at the Sanatan Dharm Mandir, paying Rs. 5001 and Rs. 3,000 each. Most of the service is performed by a thirty-member board of directors with two-year terms, which meets once a month. (The general membership meets twice a year.) There is in addition an office staff of about six or seven, which includes a manager, an accountant, a caretaker, and cooks (including cooks for the food offered to temple deities).

31. The most cogent interpretation of personal ritual encounters with Hindu deities remains Diana L. Eck, *Darśan: Seeing the Divine Image in India*, 3rd ed. (Chambersburg, Pa.: Anima Books, 1998).

32. Although many ordinary temple-goers do not have well-formed ideas about the nature of a temple image, most do see the deity somehow present in it in a special way: why shouldn't a powerful, potentially omnipresent divinity be able to manifest itself effectively anywhere? Popular understandings of the relationship between image and deity (including the significance the image's eyes) are discussed at length by C. J. Fuller, *The Camphor Flame: Popular Hinduism and Society in India* (Princeton, N.J.: Princeton University Press, 1992), pp. 59–62. See also Eck, *Darśan*, pp. 48–51, who in addition presents some theological perspectives. Different particular Hindu understandings of embodied divinity are explored in Joanne Punzo Waghorne, Norman Cutler, and Vasudha Narayanan, eds., *Gods of Flesh, Gods of Stone: The Embodiment of Divinity in India* (New York: Columbia University Press, 1996).

33. The sense of the temple as the home of an embodied divinity is especially evident in sectarian traditions such as the *puṣṭimārg*, a Vaishnava lineage originating in Vraj country but now most prominent in western India. In this tradition, a temple is often referred to as a *havelī*, a large manor house. For a description of the elaborate worship performed to Krishna as Śrīnāthjī eight times a day in the *puṣṭimārg* center at Nathdvara, Rajasthan, see Rajendra Jindel, *Culture of a Sacred Town* (Bombay: Popular Prakashan, 1976), pp. 62–67. The eight viewings are called *darśans*.

34. The extremes of our neighborhoods' economic categories could be distinguished without much difficulty: the relatively few upper-class ones —featuring largish well-maintained houses with nice new cars in their driveways—were obvious

and well known; much more frequently met were clearly lower-class neighborhoods, where many people shared little space and less private transport. The distinctions among upper-middle-, middle-, and lower-middle-class neighborhoods were less clear, but we tried to be consistent by paying attention to some regularly occurring cues. Thus, in general, families in upper-middle-class areas had houses that they kept up and cars that didn't look too old. Families in lower-middle-class had at least a few rooms to live in, but these might be shabby or not quite finished and too often crowded; many relied on public transportation to get around town, although some might ride an old motorcycle. Families in middle-middle-class neighborhoods ranged somewhere between these two, with decent, if sometimes cramped housing—perhaps in government flats— and usually access to a motorbike in good repair or an older car.

35. When we began our survey, we weren't quite sure how long we would have to work to get results that seemed significant to us. We started by simply going from neighborhood to neighborhood in the city, making conscious efforts to visit the city's three historic areas of settlement—Old Gwalior, Lashkar, and Morar. Our intent was to include samples from neighborhoods of all economic classes in each area, although consideration of the three historic areas did not turn out to be crucial for our analysis. At mandirs with officiants present, we talked to them and left offerings; in other places we spoke with attendees or people nearby who felt like talking; sometimes we just made our own observations. In each of the neighborhoods we visited, we were anxious about being thorough. We ended our survey when, for each combination of class and area, the kinds of temples we saw started looking overly familiar. This point of apparent redundancy had been reached, we later estimated, when our sample of the city's places of worship was at about 10 percent of the whole.

36. Of the 381 places of worship included in the thirty-nine neighborhoods of our sample, 111 (29 percent) were to the mother goddess, the largest total number by a substantial margin.

37. There were eighty-one mandirs to Hanuman (21 percent) and seventy-three to Shiva (19 percent). The total number of mandirs to these two divinities and the mother goddess (in the note above) is 69 percent of all those in our sample.

38. Of the sites dedicated to other prevalent Hindu deities in our sample, none represented more than 5 percent of the total, and this 5 percent (nineteen sites) was dedicated to Bhairava, generally seen as an active force of Shiva. The next most numerous were fourteen to Krishna (4 percent), ten to Ram (2.5 percent), and seven to Ganesh (2 percent).

39. 53 percent of mandirs to the goddess and 52 percent of those to Hanuman were in lower- or lower-middle-class neighborhoods.

40. For a perceptive insider's edition of the Devi Mahatmyam, a central text of devotion to the goddess as Durga, see Devadatta Kali, *In Praise of the Goddess: The Devimahatmya and Its Meaning* (York Beach, Me.: Nicolas-Hays, 2003). On the lore

of Hanuman in contemporary India, see Philip Lutgendorf, *Hanuman's Tale: The Messages of a Divine Monkey* (New York: Oxford University Press, 2007).

41. For a treatment of Shiva lore that insightfully explores the deity's ambivalent nature, see Wendy Doniger O'Flaherty, *Siva: The Erotic Ascetic* (New York: Oxford University Press, 1981).

42. About two-thirds of the relatively few sites (nineteen) in our sample dedicated to Bhairava are simple shrines. On Bhairava in Hindu and Buddhist tantra, see David Gordon White, "At the Mandala's Dark Fringe: Possession and Protection in Tantric Bhairava Cults," in *Notes from a Maṇḍala: Essays in the History of Indian Religions in Honor of Wendy Doniger*, ed. Laurie L. Patton and David L. Haberman (Newark: University of Delaware Press, 2010). The same author deals with Bhairava's relation to dogs in *Myths of the Dog-Man* (Chicago: University of Chicago Press, 1991), pp. 100–106.

43. The phenomenon may also have local roots: I've heard it said that there are a large number of Shiva temples in Gwalior because Shiva was the patron deity of the Scindias. If this patronage did in fact somehow lead to the construction of a substantial number of less-than-grand neighborhood Shiva temples, these would still nevertheless be largely in the better parts of town.

44. There were twenty-eight mandirs to Shiva in the lower- and lower-middle-class neighborhoods of our sample, compared to fifty-nine to the goddess and forty-two to Hanuman. Of Shiva's mandirs, a little over half (54 percent) were small temples and shrines, a proportion about the same as Hanuman (57 percent) though quite a bit smaller than those of the goddess (73 percent).

45. Upper-middle-class neighborhoods had nine out of the fourteen Krishna temples in our sample. (Three of the others were in middle-class neighborhoods, with one each in lower and lower middle-class locales.) Middle-middle-class neighborhoods had five of the ten Ram temples. (Two others were in lower-middle-class neighborhoods with one each in upper-, upper-middle, and lower-class ones.)

46. See Max Weber, *The Religion of India: The Sociology of Hinduism and Buddhism*, ed. and trans. Hans H. Gerth and Dan Martingale (Glencoe, Ill.: Free Press, 1958), pp. 314–16 and Max Weber, *Economy and Society: An Outline of Interpretive Sociology*, ed. Guenther Roth and Claus Wittich, trans. Ephraim Fischoff et al. (Berkeley: University of California Press, 1978, pp. 478–79).

47. See Philip Lutgendorf, *The Life of a Text: Performing the Rāmcaritmānas of Tulsidas* (Berkeley: University of California Press, 1991) for important textual and socioreligious contexts of Ram worship in North India, esp. ch. 6. For the significance of Ram in turn-of-the-twenty-first-century Hindu nationalism, see Peter van der Veer, *Gods on Earth: The Management of Religious Experience and Identity in a North Indian Pilgrimage Centre* (London: Athlone Press, 1988).

48. On songfests to the Mother Goddess, see Erndl, *Victory to the Mother*, pp. 84–134. On Maharashtrian-style devotional singing (still practiced in Gwalior) see Christian Lee Novetzke, *Religion and Public Memory: A Cultural History of Saint Namdev in India* (New York: Columbia University Press, 2008), pp. 80–90.

49. *Small* temples could generally accommodate just a few people easily for occasional worship or daily *āratī*; a *medium-sized* temple could comfortably accommodate a group of regular worshippers of about fifteen (and more uncomfortably);
a *large* temple could easily seat twenty-five or more for special religious talks
and performances of devotional music by local groups. Freestanding *shrines*
were functionally diverse. Not really built for people to enter, they could nevertheless serve a small crowd given enough surrounding space. In the tight urban
spaces in which they were most often found, however, they were functionally
similar to small temples.

50. In upper- and upper-middle-class neighborhoods, the number of large and
medium-sized temples was 83 percent of the number of small temples and
shrines; in middle-class neighborhoods the same proportion was 74 percent;
and in lower and lower-middle class neighborhoods 49 percent.

51. Of Ram's ten temples two were large and eight were medium-sized. Of
Krishna's fourteen sites, eight were large or medium-sized temples and there
was only one shrine, and that in a lower-class neighborhood.

52. The Ram temples in our sample included eight that were old, one that was *new*—
in a modern style or of obviously new construction—and one that was *renovated*,
with major parts clearly old and new. Those to Krishna included seven old temples, four renovated ones (together 77 percent), and three new ones.

53. The mostly smaller goddess and Hanuman mandirs outnumbered the large Ram
and Krishna temples by almost two and a half times in upper- and upper-middle
class areas and more than seven times in middle-middle-class ones!

54. Our sample included a temple to Shyam Baba, a deity prominent in Sikar district, Rajashtan, which was started by migrants from that area; a temple to Sai
Baba, the early twentieth-century saint from Shirdi, Maharashtra; a place of
worship used by members of the Arya Samaj, a Hindu reformist group dating
from the nineteenth century; three temples to deities worshipped primarily by
members of specific local caste communities; a temple in the name of a local
holy man; and a neighborhood Sikh *gurudwara*.

55. Of these four mandirs, three were medium-sized temples and one was a shrine.
There were also two other medium-sized temples in colonies that contained
other mandirs, but no large temples at all.

56. House temples comprised 10.5 percent of all sites in our sample and were well
represented in all classes of neighborhoods. (In our survey, the house temple
was a category of *public situation*, together with freestanding *buildings*, the large
majority of cases, and places of worship in *ashrams*, and *institutions*, both very
small percentages).

57. An extended example of temple exclusion and its consequences is presented
by Diana Mines *in Fierce Gods: Inequality, Ritual, and the Politics of Dignity in a
South Indian Village* (Bloomington: Indiana University Press, 2005). On page
109 above, a middle-class Gwalior Valmik gives an angry diatribe about his own
experience of temple exclusion.

58. Of Mataji's fifty-nine sites, twenty-four were shrines (41 percent); of Hanuman's forty-two, just nine were (21 percent).

59. In the poorer neighborhoods of our sample, Hanuman had fifteen small temples to his nine shrines, 40 percent *more* small temples; the goddess had nineteen to her twenty-four shrines, 21 percent *less*.

CHAPTER 2

1. For a definition of Sufis that distinguishes them from dead saints, see Nile Green, *Making Space: Sufis and Settlers in Early Modern India* (New Delhi: Oxford University Press, 2012), pp. 1–5; this book gives some valuable insights into the ways in which Sufi traditions spread in the subcontinent. For a broader phenomenology of Persianate Sufism in society, see Shahzad Bashir, *Sufi Bodies: Religion and Society in Medieval Islam* (New York: Columbia University Press, 2011). On Sufi tradition generally, see Nile Green, *Sufism: A Global History* (Malden, Mass.: Wiley-Blackwell, 2012).

2. Common Urdu terms for Sufi shrines are *dargāh*, a "portal," which can refer to a royal court; and *maqbarāh*, a burial site, or tomb.

3. In recent years a family that claims a long lineage as shrine attendants at Muhammad Ghawth's tomb has made its presence felt there and begun arranging some religious events.

4. Interesting religious dimensions of saints' shrines are explored by Scott Alan Kugle, *Sufis and Saints' Bodies: Mysticism, Corporeality, and Sacred Power in Islam* (Chapel Hill: University of North Carolina Press, 2007), pp. 46–48.

5. Carla Bellamy gives a thorough exploration of the significances of the power at a Sufi healing shrine for Hindus and Muslims in *The Powerful Ephemeral: Everyday Healing in an Ambiguously Islamic Place* (Berkeley: University of California Press, 2011).

6. An *'urs*—literally a wedding—celebrates the death of a Sufi saint in South Asia, when he goes to live with his beloved lord. It is normally held at the death anniversaries of historical Sufis when the dates are known. In other cases, a different appropriate date is set. An *'urs* is customary at all active South Asian shrines.

7. The estimate of the Muslim population of Gwalior as "6 or 7 percent" is an informed judgment by Rashid Khanuni of Khwaja Khanun: interview, June 11, 1997. The 2011 Census of India shows Muslims as 13.4 percent of the country's total population, suggesting that Gwalior's percentage is about half the national average.

8. From 1232 to 1389 a series of Muslim rulers were in control of Gwalior fort. In 1394, the fort was taken by Vir Singh, an ancestor of Mansingh Tomar (r. 1486–1516). By the last years of his reign, Mansingh had begun to face aggression from Delhi, and the Tomars lost the fort soon after his death, with Islam Shah

Suri (r. 1545–54) reported to have actually shifted his capital to Gwalior: B. D. Misra, *The Forts and Fortresses of Gwalior and Its Hinterland* (Delhi: Manohar, 1993), pp. 32–50.

9. Baba Kapur is remembered as having supplied water to the poor and also having regularly enjoyed a particular opium brew of his own invention, which the Catalan Jesuit Antonio de Montserrat describes in detail but finds despicable: Antonio Monserrate, John S. Hoyland, and S. N. Banerjee, *The Commentary of Father Monserrate, S. J., on His Journey to the Court of Akbar* (London: H. Milford, Oxford University Press, 1922), pp. 24–25, including note 58. The existence of a distinct Baba Kapur cult in Gwalior in the early twentieth century is recorded in the *Imperial Gazetteer of India*, new ed., ed. James Sutherland Cotton and William Meyer (Oxford: Clarendon Press, 1908), vol. 9, p. 354.

10. Khwaja Khanun is said to have left his native Nagaur at the age of twenty-one for Ajmer, where he received a command from the spirit of that city's great Muinuddin Chishti to seek teachings from a Sufi named Ismail near Orchha, southeast of Gwalior. Ismail then directed him to Gwalior to be "a pillar of light for all humankind": Kumvar Rājendra Singh Sīkarwār "Yātrī," "Tum Āo to Mere Pās," 469vāṃ 'urs Sharīf, Dargāh Hazrat Khvājā Khanūn Sāhab (1988), p. 2. An Urdu compendium of lore on Khwaja Khanun, with some Persian originals as appropriate, is given in Sayyad Aziz Ahmad, ed., *Gulzār-e-Khānūn* (Gwalior: Rūhānī Akadamī, Hazrat Khwājā Khānūn, 1987).

11. The BJP stands for the Bharatiya Janata Party, the "Indian People's Party." Although clearly rooted in earlier Hindu nationalist political formations, the BJP itself was founded in 1980.

12. Veer Savarkar's *Hindutva*—a pamphlet smuggled out of prison in 1923 and regularly reprinted—offers a classic statement of Hindu nationalist doctrine: Vinayak Damodar Savarkar, *Hindutva: Who Is a Hindu?* (Bombay: Veer Savarkar Prakashan, 1969). Over the last decades, much has been written about Hindu nationalism. For a substantial introduction to two long-lived Hindu nationalist organizations with attention to their socioreligious dimensions, see my "Organized Hinduisms: From Vedic Truth to Hindu Nation," in *Fundamentalism Observed*, ed. Martin E. Marty, and R. Scott Appleby (Chicago: University of Chicago Press, 1991). Peter van der Veer, *Religious Nationalism: Hindus and Muslims in India* (Berkeley: University of California Press, 1994) examines the broad cultural ramifications of Hindu and Muslim nationalism in India. For a focus on Hindu nationalism's political aspects with reference to Madhya Pradesh, see Christophe Jaffrelot, *The Hindu Nationalist Movement in India* (New York: Columbia University Press, 1996). For a competent critical overview, see Chetan Bhatt, *Hindu Nationalism: Origins, Ideologies and Modern Myths* (New York: Berg, 2001).

13. A classic modern confrontation is the Shah Bano controversy, a complicated case in which an elderly Muslim woman, Shah Bano, challenged her traditional

Islamic divorce settlement in Indian Civil Court. The case exploded in 1985 when a Hindu justice of the Indian Supreme Court, quoting the Quran, ruled in Shah Bano's favor, to general outrage in the Muslim community. Mainline secularists, whatever their personal views, thought it best to support the precedence of Muslim traditions here. On the other side were Hindu nationalists, arguing for a uniform civil code, in an unaccustomed alliance with Indian feminists, who argued for justice for women. See Asghar Ali Engineer, ed., *The Shah Bano Controversy* (Hyderabad: Orient Longmans, 1987).

14. On the concentration of Muslims in particular urban areas and its socioeconomic consequences, see Laurent Gayer and Christophe Jaffrelot, *Muslims in Indian Cities: Trajectories of Marginalisation* (London: Hurst & Company, 2012).

15. See Veena Das and Ashis Nandy, "Violence, Victimhood, and the Language of Silence," in *The Word and the World: Fantasy, Symbol and Record*, ed. Veena Das (New Delhi: Sage Publications, 1986), pp. 178–79.

16. The most influential article in this vein has been Sheldon Pollock's "Rāmāyaṇa and Political Imagination in India," *Journal of Asian Studies* 52, no. 2 (1993): 261–97, but he has had predecessors in his general line of argument: Kamil Zvelebil, *Two Tamil Folktales: the Story of King Matanakama, the Story of Peacock Ravana* (Delhi: Motilal Banarsidass, 1987), p. xlvi; and Hans Bakker, "Reflections on the Evolution of Rāma Devotion in the Light of Textual and Archeological Evidence," *Wiener Zeitschrift für die Kunde Südasiens* 31 (1987): 19–22. Pollock has been criticized for reading fixed modern communal collectivities back into to a medieval world of diverse ethnic identities, changing state formations, and shifting political loyalties that extended beyond religious communities. Yet once granted this more fluid medieval world, even those ready to offer critiques will acknowledge, with varying degrees of enthusiasm, that members of Muslim groups were liable to be depicted as demonic others when perceived as a threat to Hindu regimes: Cynthia Talbot, "Inscribing the Other, Inscribing the Self: Hindu-Muslim Identities in Pre-colonial India," *Comparative Studies in Society and History* 37, no. 4 (1995): 701–6; Phillip B. Wagoner, *Tidings of the King: A Translation and Ethnohistorical Analysis of the Rāyavācakamu* (Honolulu: University of Hawaii Press, 1993), pp. 50–69; Carl W. Ernst, *Eternal Garden: Mysticism, History, and Politics at a South Asian Sufi Center* (Albany: State University of New York Press, 1992), p. 31.

17. Violent repercussions of the new politicization of the story of Ram occurred in December 1992, when a mass Hindu nationalist demonstration went out of control and destroyed the Babri *masjid*, at the site of Ram's traditional birthplace in Ayodhya. This was a turning point in contemporary intercommunal relationships and, with nothing reconstructed there, remains an unresolved issue. Jitendra Bajaj, *Ayodhya and the Future India* (Madras: Centre for Policy Studies, 1993) offers thoughtful articles on the then-fresh Ayodhya crisis from both secular and Hindu nationalist viewpoints. Vijay Mishra, *Bollywood Cinema: Temples of Desire*

(New York: Routledge, 2002), ch. 7, draws out the implications of this politicization of Ram for current representations of Muslims in Indian popular culture.

18. Thus Ravana, the king of the *rākṣasas*, is motivated in part by lust in his capture
of Sita, as is his sister Surpankha more thoroughly in her attempted seduction
of Ram. Yet when Ravana has Sita in captivity, he does not immediately ravish
her, but instead waits unsuccessfully for her willing submission. Ravana's brother
Vibhishana, moreover, is an exemplar of a redeemed *rākṣasa*—recognizing Ram's
virtue, going over to his side, and helping him in battle. See also the analysis in
Robert P. Goldman and Sally J. Sutherland Goldman, *The Rāmāyaṇa of Vālmīki: An
Epic of Ancient India*, vol. 5 (Sundarakāṇḍa) (Princeton, N.J.: Princeton University
Press, 1984), pp. 5–70.

19. R. S. McGregor, *The Oxford Hindi-English Dictionary* (New York: Oxford
University Press, 1993), p. 859.

20. On some significances of the good demon in Hindu mythology, see Wendy
Doniger O'Flaherty, *The Origins of Evil in Hindu Mythology* (Berkeley: University
of California Press, 1976), ch. 5.

21. Alf Hiltebeitel, in the introduction to his edited volume *Criminal Gods and Demon
Devotees: Essays on the Guardians of Popular Hinduism* (Albany: State University
of New York Press, 1989), offers a general discussion of these shady spirits and
godlings. Some Central Indian examples are discussed by Lawrence A. Babb in
The Divine Hierarchy: Popular Hinduism in Central India (New York: Columbia
University Press, 1975), pp. 227–29.

22. See Peter Gottschalk, *Beyond Hindu and Muslim: Multiple Identity in Narratives
from Village India* (New York: Oxford University Press, 2000), ch. 5.

23. See Diane Coccari, "The Bir Babas of Banaras and the Deified Dead," in
Hiltebeitel, *Criminal Gods*, pp. 251–56.

24. Most stories of Tansen have him born in a Brahmin family and studying with
the Hindu teacher Haridas, but living as a Muslim under the influence of
Muhammad Ghaus and the emperor Akbar, in whose court he served. He is
frequently referred to as "Mian Tansen," using an honorific normally applied to
Muslims. A contemporary novelization of his life has him being given as a child
to Muhammad Ghaus to raise: he was made impure in the eyes of his community by chewing some betel that had been in the Muslim saint's mouth: Girish
Chaturvedi, *Tansen*, trans. Sarala Jag Mohan (New Delhi: Roli Books, 1996).

25. By the time Madhav Rao died in 2001, he was one of the most experienced of
the younger senior politicians in the Congress and a close confidant of Sonia
Gandhi, the party president (at the time of his death Madhav Rao, at fifty-six,
was the party's deputy leader in Parliament). Contemporary political commen-
tators saw his passing as a serious loss for the Congress.

26. The swing of Gwalior to the Hindu right in the 1990s can be traced in Madhav
Rao's fortunes in parliamentary elections in the city. In 1984 he won a landslide
victory over the future BJP prime minister, Gwalior's own A. B. Vajpayee, who

thenceforward ran from a safer seat in Lucknow. But by 1998, Madhav Rao barely managed to win and in 1999 decided to run from a safe seat within his old principality, effectively ceding the city to Vajpayee's BJP. Madhav Rao's political legacy, however, remains active in the old Scindia domains. In the BJP's 2004 national defeat—to which BJP-ruled Madhya Pradesh did not significantly contribute—Gwalior was one of only four Congress seats (out of M.P.'s twenty-nine); one of the others was Madhav Rao's old seat, won by his son Jyotiraditya.

27. Although Mansur himself stayed in Beed, Maharashtra, he sent his son Habib to Mahadji. For many generations the name of the Gwalior lineage successor alternated between Mansur and Habib. For Beed as a Sufi center, see Green, *Sufis and Settlers*, pp. 188–93, who gives a short account of the shrine of "Mansur Ali Shah (d. after 1720?)" and its patronage by the Scindias, whom he refers to by their Marathi name, Shinde. He also writes of the patronage of Sufi shrines by other Maratha rulers (p. 192).

28. My assistant Giriraj told me another version of the story that circulated in Gwalior. Obviously less informed, it is perhaps for that reason more dramatic: Mahadji was an officer from Maharashtra, a strong man. When he realized that all his brothers had died in battle, he started crying on the battlefield. A poor Muslim saw him, gave him water, and carried him away in a bullock cart so that the enemies wouldn't see him. Mahadji, now saved and cured, later met a fakir in the jungle in Gwalior: this was really a miraculous appearance of Mansur. Mahadji said he was hungry, so the fakir made seven thick chapatis for him. Mahadji ate with gusto. The fakir then took his hand and said, "Enough! You've eaten seven chapatis, and your rule will last seven generations." The bit of chapati that is left from when he was eating is what is kept.

29. The ceremony was explained to me after the fact by Nafeez Qureshi, a local sociologist interested in Sufism (interview, September 30, 1997). Qureshi added that Mahadji's mother was a devotee of Mansur.

30. Jayaji Rao, who reigned from 1843 to 1886, was the great Scindia monarch of the nineteenth century, but Bhonsle's taking him as a mature ruler in his story is inconsistent with his own understanding of the date of Mir Badshah's death. According to Bhonsle's reckoning, the festival of Mir Badshah he inaugurated in 1958 was the 114th, which would put the saint's death in 1844. Jayaji inherited the throne in 1843 at age nine, which would be just a year before the saint's passing. Preceding Jayaji Rao was Jankoji Rao (r. 1827–43), who died in his prime. For a fine study of the early history of the Scindias in Gwalior, see Amar Farooqui, *Sindias and the Raj: Princely Gwalior c. 1800–1850* (Delhi: Primus Books, 2011).

31. Although *qāzī* means "judge," the term *city qāzī* (*śahar qāzī*) seems to be an honorific with no legal significance. When I inquired about it, I was told (by no friend of the *qāzī*) that it might have been bestowed upon him by Madhav Rao during days when they were local political allies.

32. None of Ramjilal's stories, alas, were available. The story is from an interview with Ramjilal on October 8, 1997, when he further claimed that the name Mir Badshah came from a stone found at the site—although he doesn't know who dug it up.

33. Interview with Bhonsle, October 13, 1997.

34. Although our 1997 survey of the city's temples revealed several small shrines to Bhairav—a strong earthy figure associated with Shiva—it showed none to named local deities. These do seem to be present, however, around urban Banaras (Coccari, "Bir Babas"). For a survey of named local deities in a Rajasthani village see Ann Grodzins Gold, *Fruitful Journeys: The Ways of Rajasthani Pilgrims* (Berkeley: University of California Press, 1988), pp. 34–58.

35. One of the Agrawal houses, in an older part of the city, was bought from a Muslim family by the current residents' grandfather. The other, in a new development on the edge of the city, was rescued from a hut at the site that had belonged to someone from a tribal caste. In both cases, a place for the spirit was preserved through reconstruction and successive renovations.

36. Claudia Liebeskind, *Piety on Its Knees: Three Sufi Traditions in South Asia in Modern Times* (Delhi: Oxford University Press, 1998); Richard Maxwell Eaton, *The Rise of Islam and the Bengal Frontier, 1204–1760* (Berkeley: University of California Press, 1993); Carl W. Ernst and Bruce B. Lawrence, *Sufi Martyrs of Love: The Chishti Order in South Asia and Beyond* (New York: Palgrave Macmillan, 2002); Green, *Sufis and Settlers*.

37. Complaining about the couple's loss of active interest in the shrine, Pyarelal said, "If they had come more they would have gotten a boy." They seemed happy with their baby girl.

38. Classic works on Sanskritization include Mysore N. Srinivas, *Religion and Society among the Coorgs of South India* (London: Oxford University, 1952) and Milton Singer, *When a Great Tradition Modernizes* (New York: Praeger, 1972). The term *Urduized* is occasionally used informally by Hindi scholars to refer to language of a Hindi-speaker that uses Urdu forms—sometimes in an artificial way and not always correctly. Terms like *Persianized* or *Islamicized*, more commonly used by scholars, do not seem quite right to talk about the romantic evocation of a particular Indo-Islamic cultural style.

39. The first word should actually read *tabarruk*, ending with the *k* common to both Hindi and Urdu instead of the more exotic Urdu *q*, written on the banner in Devanagari transcription. The error is no doubt the result of overcompensation of a sympathetic Hindi-speaker somewhere in the sign-making process.

40. This term most properly refers to a celebration of the prophet's birthday. At the celebration at Mir Badshah's festival, I was told, stories of the prophet were narrated and a Quran reading held.

41. This amount, about 2,300 1997 US dollars, might be as much as an ordinary working person earned in a couple of years.

42. See my *The Lord as Guru: Hindi Sants in North Indian Tradition* (New York: Oxford University Press, 1987), pp. 98–104.

43. Rashid Khanuni mentioned having been vice president of an All India association of Sufi successors. Much more than Mir Badshah, it is Khwaja Khanun that bears comparison with Sufi establishments with charismatic heads discussed by Arthur F. Buehler, *Sufi Heirs of the Prophet: The Indian Naqshbandiyya and the Rise of the Mediating Sufi Shaykh* (Columbia: University of South Carolina Press, 1998) and Katherine Pratt Ewing, *Arguing Sainthood: Modernity, Psychoanalysis, and Islam* (Durham: Duke University Press, 1997).

44. Rashid Khanuni suggested that the old shrine committee had not been making proper accounts to the board or paying them the regular 7 percent charge on income as Rashid himself did (interview, February 7, 2011).

45. The wedding was described in leading stories in all the major local newspapers on May 7, 2009. These included the Hindi dailies *Dainik Bhāskar* and *Nai Duniyā*, from which I take the description.

46. S. Mayaram, "Coexistence between Communities in Everyday Culture: A Study of Ajmer," Report for the Multiculturalism Project of the International Centre for Ethnic Studies (1997). On the shrine itself see P. M. Currie, *The Shrine and Cult of Muin Al-din Chishti of Ajmer* (New York: Oxford University Press, 1989).

47. On factors that contribute to ethnic calm, see Ashutosh Varshney, *Ethnic Conflict and Civic Life: Hindus and Muslims in India* (New Haven, Conn.: Yale University Press, 2002). Varshney emphasizes the importance of vital civic organizations. By contrast, Jonathan Parry and Christian Struempell, "On the Desecration of Nehru's 'Temples': Bhilai and Rourkela Compared," *Economic and Political Weekly* 43, no. 19 (2008): 47–57, point to the importance of functionally effective (as opposed to dysfunctional) modernization.

48. Sagir Ahmed Ansari, "Madhyakālīn Gwāliyar ke Sūfī Sant evam Paramparā," PhD diss., Jiwaji University, 1987.

49. Regula Qureshi, *Sufi Music of India and Pakistan: Sound, Context, and Meaning in Qawwali* (Chicago: University of Chicago Press, 1995), p. 60.

50. Ibid. Indeed, in Mughal India the potential of Sufi music to excite listeners into loss of self-control was a cause for its disapproval not only among many of the strictly orthodox, but in some more refined Sufi circles as well. On disapproving attitudes toward music among conservative Sufis see Ian Richard Netton, *Sufi Ritual: The Parallel Universe* (Richmond, England: Curzon Press, 2000), pp. 81–84. For a survey of Muslim attitudes toward Sufi music in medieval India, see Muhammad Umar, *Islam in Northern India during the Eighteenth Century* (New Delhi: Munshiram Manoharlal and Aligarh Muslim University, Centre of Advanced Study in History, 1993), pp. 124–31.

51. On the relationship of qawwali to Sufi chanting (*dhikr*), see Jean During, *Musique et extase: L'audition mystique dans la tradition soufie* (Paris: Albin Michel, 1988), pp. 21–23 and Qureshi, *Sufi Music*, pp. 82–84.

52. For Sufis as intercessors, see P. Lewis, *Pirs, Shrines and Pakistani Islam* (Rawalpindi, Pakistan: Christian Study Centre, 1985), pp. 23–43 and Qureshi, *Sufi Music*, p. 81.

53. On Hanuman as an intercessor with wide regional popularity, see Philip Lutgendorf, "Monkey in the Middle: The Status of Hanuman in Popular Hinduism," *Religion* 27 (1997): 314–15; on Hanuman's strength see the same author's "My Hanuman Is Bigger Than Yours," *History of Religions* 33, no. 3 (1994): 211–45. The import of both these articles have been integrated into Lutgendorf's *Hanuman's Tale: The Messages of a Divine Monkey* (New York: Oxford University Press, 2007).

54. Posed here as a logical query, the question of Hindus visiting Sufi shrines can be a contentious one during phases of active communal aggressiveness. For a discussion with reference to the cult of Ghazi Miyan in U.P. in the 1920s and 1930s, see Charu Gupta, *Sexuality, Obscenity, Community: Women, Muslims, and the Hindu Public in Colonial India*, 1st Palgrave ed. (New York: Palgrave, 2002), pp. 281–98. For the situation in post-2002 Gujarat, see Caroline Heitmeyer, "Religion as Practice, Religions as Identity: Sufi Dargahs in Contemporary Gujarat," *South Asia: Journal of South Asian Studies* 34, no. 3 (2011): 485–503.

55. See Goldman and Goldman, *Rāmāyaṇa (Sundarakāṇḍa)*, pp. 84–86.

56. See Lutgendorf, "Monkey in the Middle," p. 327.

57. Think of the young Gandhi's secret meat-eating: Muslims, if impure like the English, are often perceived as strong, and somehow the two qualities are linked, just as they are in the *rākṣasas* of the Ram myth: M. K. Gandhi, *An Autobiography, or, the Story of My Experiments with Truth*, trans. Mahadev Desai, 2nd ed. (Ahmedabad: Navajivan Pub. House, 1940), pp. 31–38.

58. Ann Grodzins Gold, "Jātrā, Yātrā and Pressing Down Pebbles: Pilgrimage within and beyond Rajasthan," in *The Idea of Rajasthan: Explorations in Regional Identity*, ed. Karine Schomer, Joan L. Erdman, Deryck O. Loderick, and Lloyd I. Rudolph, (Columbia, Mo.: South Asia Publications, 1994), p. 101.

59. Qureshi, *Sufi Music*, p. 12.

60. Barbara Metcalf, "Presidential Address: Too Much and Too Little: Reflections on Muslims in the History of India," *Journal of Asian Studies* 54, no. 4 (1995): 962–63.

CHAPTER 3

1. Although caste in some form seems to have a long history in the Indian subcontinent, caste and caste-like groups now seem to have been more fluid than was once thought, with current scholarship pointing to the transformations of caste institutions under different political and economic conditions: see Susan Bayly, *Caste, Society and Politics in India from the Eighteenth Century to the Modern Age*, The New Cambridge History of India, 4:3 (New York: Cambridge

University Press, 1999) and William R. Pinch, *Peasants and Monks in British India* (Berkeley: University of California Press, 1996). Dipankar Gupta's *Caste in Question: Identity or Hierarchy* (Thousand Oaks, Calif.: Sage Publications, 2004) collects a number of interesting essays treating social and political dimensions of caste at the turn of the twenty-first century. The classic structural study of caste by Louis Dumont is still influential: *Homo Hierarchicus: An Essay on the Caste System* (Chicago: University of Chicago Press, 1970). It has been critiqued effectively from a postcolonial perspective by Nicholas B. Dirks, *Castes of Mind: Colonialism and the Making of Modern India* (Princeton, N.J.: Princeton University Press, 2001). Helpful digests of contemporary thinking on caste are Diane P. Mines, *Caste in India* (Ann Arbor, Mich.: Association for Asian Studies, 2009), written from an anthropological point of view; and Surinder S. Jodhka, *Caste* (New Delhi: Oxford University Press, 2012), who takes a sociological perspective. Both books have substantial bibliographies.

2. The colonial folklorist William Crooke, for example, tells the story of "a poor Brahmin who used to get his living by begging" and had a friend who was a goldsmith of some means. In pursuit of more wealth, the goldsmith tempted fate and was eaten by a tiger. The Brahmin had wisely fled the scene. See Crooke's "The Tiger, the Brahmin, and the Covetous Goldsmith" in his *North Indian Notes and Queries* 3, 61, p. 29 (Allahabad: Pioneer Press, 1893).

3. Mark Liechty gives a book-length treatment of tensions between class and caste among the urban middle classes of Kathmandu, Nepal—a South Asian city about the same size as Gwalior, but as a national capital with a large tourist industry, somewhat more cosmopolitan: *Suitably Modern: Making Middle-Class Culture in a New Consumer Society* (Princeton, N.J.: Princeton University Press, 2003).

4. "Hippopotamus Street" translates the Hindi *gendevālī saṛak*. Although there are no hippopotamuses in India (they are found in Africa), rhinoceroses are native to the subcontinent, and the same word, *gendā*, is used for both. Perhaps in the old days, when the street was on the outskirts of the city, rhinoceroses sometimes came to the area. When I asked local people what the name meant, however, they all told me "hippo," a trendier expression than rhinoceros (or even rhino) in common North Indian usage, so I adapted the popular term.

5. On Valmik history and community organization, see Vijay Prashad, *Untouchable Freedom: A Social History of a Dalit Community* (New York: Oxford University Press, 2000).

6. I was told that the temple—which also serves as a community center—was built in 1953 with the help of some government aid to low-caste groups.

7. On the use of alternative surnames by upwardly mobile members of formerly untouchable castes, see Gyanendra Pandey, *A History of Prejudice: Race, Caste, and Difference in India and the United States* (New York: Cambridge University Press, 2013), pp. 207–10. Pandey gives an extended example of multiple surnames in the same family, as seen here.

8. The other major temples in the cluster, like the Jain temple, also have regular support from local sources outside the neighborhood. The temple to Bhairava for many years drew plentiful donations from admirers of a well-respected sadhu who lived there until his death at the beginning of the 2000s, and it still receives regular modest support from a Scindia foundation. The Satya Narayan temple is actually new, constructed by a prosperous builder to house an old image of the deity whose previous abode not far away was in a state of disrepair. The builder continues to sponsor religious events such as Ramayana readings there.

9. For an insightful discussion of the film and the scholarly literature about it, see Philip Lutgendorf, "A Superhit Goddess: Santoshi Maa and Caste Hierarchy in Indian Films," *Manushi* 131 (July–Aug. 2002), pp. 10–16, and "A 'Made to Satisfaction Goddess': Jai Santoshi Maa Revisited," *Manushi* 131 (July–Aug. 2002), pp. 24–37.

10. It is worth comparing Arjun's attitude toward *mālās* and *sahrās* to that that of the Agrawals of chapter 2 (in the section *Local Spirits and their Transformation*). They both recognized *mālās* as Hindu and *sahrās* as Muslim, but the Agrawals had a place for each.

11. For a strikingly illustrated account of a similar story of industrial decline and unemployment distress in Ahmedabad, see Jan Breman and Parthiv Shah, *Working in the Mill No More* (New Delhi: Oxford University Press, 2004).

12. "Illegal Structures Leveled," *Dainik Bhaskar*, Gwalior, August 14, 2002, p. 7.

13. "They Kicked and Punched Then Dragged Us Out," *Dainik Bhaskar*, Gwalior, August 17, 2002, p. 8.

14. The local newspaper accounts agree on the substance of what happened, although details differ. The *Nav Bharat* gives forty-two arrests and mentions the rumor that the police in charge wanted to fire into the crowd ("Battle between the Police and the People: Satya Narayan Tekri, 16 Wounded," Gwalior, August 15, 2002, p. 1). The *Dainik Bhaskar* noted forty arrested, twenty-four women and sixteen men ("Stoning of a Force Come to Level Illegal Structures," August 15, 2002, p. 1).

15. Attributed to Wasim Akhtar, district magistrate, in "Who Saw What," *Dainik Bhaskar*, Gwalior, August 15, 2002, p. 2.

16. "They Kicked and Punched."

CHAPTER 4

1. Studies of South Asian diaspora focusing on Hindu traditions include Paul Younger, *New Homelands: Hindu Communities in Mauritius, Guyana, Trinidad, South Africa, Fiji, and East Africa* (New York: Oxford University Press, 2010), which gives an historical treatment of Hindus' different patterns of settlement, and Steven Vertovec, *The Hindu Diaspora: Comparative Patterns* (New York: Routledge, 2000), which examines socioreligious issues that have developed in different diaspora communities. Ron Geaves, *Saivism in the Diaspora: Contemporary Forms of Skanda Worship* (Oakville, Conn.: Equinox, 2007) looks specifically at the transplantation of regional

Shaivite traditions in Britain. Valuable edited volumes include John R. Hinnells, *Religious Reconstruction in the South Asian Diasporas: From One Generation to Another* (New York: Palgrave Macmillan, 2007), which focuses on Western diaspora communities, and Deana Heath and Chandana Mathur, *Communalism and Globalization in South Asia and Its Diaspora* (New York: Routledge, 2011). On cultural issues of Indian diaspora in the Anglo-American world, see Sandhya Shukla, *India Abroad: Diasporic Cultures of Postwar America and England* (Princeton, N.J.: Princeton University Press, 2003).

2. Different characteristics of diaspora are given by J. Milton Yinger, *Ethnicity: Source of Strength? Source of Conflict?* (Albany: State University of New York Press, 1994), pp. 3–4, and George A. DeVos, "Ethnic Pluralism: Conflict and Accommodation," in *Ethnic Identity: Creation, Conflict, and Accommodation*, ed. Lola Romanucci-Ross and George A. De Vos (Walnut Creek, Calif.: AltaMira Press, 1995), pp. 18–23.

3. The seminal article on caste associations by Lloyd I. Rudolph and Susanne Hoeber Rudolph, "The Political Role of India's Caste Associations," *Pacific Affairs* 33, no. 1 (1960): 5–22 was recently reprinted in the same journal (85, no. 2 [2012]: 335–53), together with an update by them: "Caste Associations to Identity Politics: From Self-Help and Democratic Representation to Goonda Raj and Beyond" (pp. 371–75). Accompanying these are related articles by James Manor, "After Fifty Years of Political and Social Change: Caste Associations and Politics in India" (pp. 355–61) and Ronojoy Sen, "The Persistence of Caste in Indian Politics" (pp. 363–59). Most of the scholarly writing on caste associations was done in the 1960s and 1970s. Two interesting monographs from the period are R. S. Khare, *The Changing Brahmans: Associations and Elites among the Kanya-Kubjas of North India* (Chicago: University of Chicago Press, 1970), which focuses on the social and economic issues caste associates; and Ghanshyam Shah, *Caste Association and Political Process in Gujarat: A Study of Gujarat Kshatriya Sabha* (Bombay: Popular Prakashan, 1975), which focuses on their political aspects. More recently, interesting studies on specific groups have been done by Lucia Michelutti, "'We (Yadavs) Are a Caste of Politicians': Caste and Modern Politics in a North Indian Town," in *Caste in Question: Identity or Hierarchy*, ed. Dipankar Gupta (Thousand Oaks, Calif.: Sage Publications, 2004), pp. 43–71; and Ramesh Bairy T. S., "Brahmins in the Modern World: Association as Enunciation," *Contributions in Sociology* (n.s.) 43, no. 1 (2009): 89–120.

4. B. D. Misra, *The Forts and Fortresses of Gwalior and its Hinterland* (Delhi: Manohar, 1993), pp. 51–52.

5. V. S. Krishnan, *Gwalior*, Madhya Pradesh District Gazetteers, vol. 1 (Bhopal: Government Central Press, 1965), p. 33.

6. On the Maratha movements, see Susan Bayly, *Caste, Society and Politics in India from the Eighteenth Century to the Modern Age*, The New Cambridge History of India, 4:3 (New York: Cambridge University Press, 1999), pp. 239–42; and

K. K. Verma, *Changing Role of Caste Associations* (New Delhi: National, 1979), pp. 20–21, 26. For parallel instances of the social mobility of soldiering classes, see William R. Pinch, *Peasants and Monks in British India* (Berkeley: University of California Press, 1996), ch. 3.

7. For caste composition in pre-partition Sindh, see U. T. Thakur, *Sindhi Culture* (Bombay: University of Bombay, 1959), pp. 207–23. Thakur gives a valuable picture of Hindu Sindhi life in its prepartition homeland and as it developed in the early years of its internal Indian diaspora.

8. Claude Markovits, *The Global World of Indian Merchants, 1750–1947: Traders of Sind from Bukhara to Panama* (New York: Cambridge University Press, 2000), pp. 46–47.

9. Mark-Anthony Falzon, *Cosmopolitan Connections: The Sindhi Diaspora, 1860–2000* (Boston: Brill, 2004), p. 35.

10. Thakur, *Sindhi Culture*, pp. 194–206.

11. The total value of the aid—about Rs. 200 ($5.00 or so in 2005)—could represent a substantial proportion of a small household's monthly costs for basic foodstuffs, the prices of which Indian governments try to keep low.

12. These were the committees charged with overseeing welfare, justice, education, health, and ritual reform.

13. Prakash Chaudhary, interview, July 18, 2005.

14. Group meeting, August 3, 2005.

15. Sardar P. K. Kadam, interview, July 17, 2004.

16. Shantaram Moghe, interview, July 17, 2004.

17. On the Ganesh puja in Maharashtra in its socioreligious and political contexts, see Raminder Kaur, *Performative Politics and the Cultures of Hinduism: Public Uses of Religion in Western India* (Delhi: Permanent Black, 2003).

18. On the emergence of modern Sikh identity, see Harjot Oberoi, *The Construction of Religious Boundaries: Culture, Identity, and Diversity in the Sikh Tradition* (Chicago: University of Chicago Press, 1994).

19. On the 1950s emergence of the Jhulelal movement in Bombay, see Falzon, *Cosmopolitan Connections*, pp. 58–63.

20. Ibid., p. 38. Falzon quotes an unnamed *āmil* informant.

21. I am grateful to Steven Wesley Ramey for making me suspicious about the presence of Sikh themes in the Jhulelal festival and suggesting the probable reason why this is so. On Hindu Sindhis in India, see his *Hindu, Sufi, or Sikh: Contested Practices and Identifications of Sindhi Hindus in India and Beyond* (New York: Palgrave Macmillan, 2008).

22. On syncretic characteristics of Maharashtrian religion, see Maxine Berntsen and Eleanor Zelliot, *The Experience of Hinduism: Essays on Religion in Maharashtra* (Albany: State University of New York Press, 1988), pp. xviii–xix.

23. Sai Baba of Shirdi lived in the first half of the twentieth century and was probably born a Muslim: he dressed like a Sufi and lived in a mosque. He has many Hindu

devotees who worship him in dedicated temples, however, including at least two in Gwalior. On Shirdi Sai Baba himself, see Antonio Rigopoulos, *The Life and Teachings of Sai Baba of Shirdi* (Albany: State University of New York Press, 1993). Kiran A. Shinde and Andrea Marion Pinkney discuss his modern movement in "Shirdi in Transition: Guru Devotion, Urbanisation and Regional Pluralism in India," *South Asia: Journal of South Asian Studies* 36, no. 4 (2013): 554–70.

24. The historical details about the Dholi Buwa lineage in this chapter are from a five-page Hindi article in an unpaginated 1980 pamphlet commemorating the twenty-fifth year of the reign of the late Dholi Buwa Vasudev Nath by the latter's youngest brother: Śrīkānt Gopālnath Purandare, "Maṭh kā Itihās: Ek Vihaṅgāvalokan (the History of the Math: A Bird's-Eye View)," in *Smārikā: P(aram) P(ūjya) Śraddheya Vāsudevnāth Dholī Buva Mahārāj Pīṭhārohaṇ Rajat-Mahotsav San 1980*, ed. Kṛṣṇa Murārī Miśra, Y. N. Moghe, and Anant Moghe (Gwalior, India: Dholi Buwa Math, 1980). For a substantial English summary of the article including legendary material see my "Different Drums in Gwalior: Maharashtrian Nath Heritages in a North Indian City," in *Yogi Heroes and Poets: Histories and Legends of the Naths*, ed. David N. Lorenzen and Adrián Muñoz (Albany: State University of New York Press, 2011), pp. 51–61. That volume is a helpful collection of essays on various aspects of Nath tradition.

25. For early Nath lore, see David Gordon White, "The Exemplary Life of Mastnāth: The Encapsulation of Seven Hundred Years of Nāth Siddha Hagiography," in *Constructions Hagiographiques dans le Monde Indien: entre Mythe et Histoire*, ed. Françoise Mallison (Paris: Champion, 2001), pp. 139–61; on contemporary householder Naths, see my "Nath Yogis as Established Alternatives: Householders and Ascetics Today," *Journal of Asian and African Studies* 34, no. 1 (February 1999): 68–88.

26. Santosh Purandare, interview, July 12, 2004.

27. Santosh Purandare speaks of this style as being in the sage Narada's performance tradition, which includes the three divisions of music—singing, playing instruments, and dance—and is performed standing up. It contrasts with a parallel tradition attributed to the sage Vyasa, in which storytelling greatly predominates (interview, March 8, 2003). For more on the Maharashtrian traditions of religious performance, see Christian Lee Novetzke, *Religion and Public Memory: A Cultural History of Saint Namdev in India* (New York: Columbia University Press, 2008), pp. 80–90.

28. As an attempt at socioreligious integration, the Sindhis' procession here differs from many presented in recent studies of South Asian processions, which—in making claims to public space—often seem more overtly political. See Kaur, *Performative Politics*, ch. 4, and especially Diane P. Mines, *Fierce Gods: Inequality, Ritual, and the Politics of Dignity in a South Indian Village* (Bloomington: Indiana University Press, 2005), pp. 35–46 and *passim*.

29. On globalization and the homogenization of Hinduism see Meera Nanda, *The God Market: How Globalization Is Making India More Hindu* (Noida: Random House India, 2009). On the role of processions and public display in South Asia generally see ibid., pp. 62–64, and K. A. Jacobsen, ed., *South Asian Religions on Display: Religious Processions in South Asia and in the Diaspora* (New York: Routledge, 2008). On the increase of public display in small-town India see Ann Grodzins Gold, "Sweetness and Light: The Bright Side of Pluralism in a North Indian Town," in *Religious Pluralism, State and Society in Asia*, ed. Chiara Formichi (New York: Routledge, 2013).

CHAPTER 5

1. Although groups in the past usually seem to have become part of the Hindu fold through a long process of assimilation, politically motivated efforts by Hindu nationalist groups since the beginning of the twentieth century have speeded up the process: Yoginder Sikand and Manjari Katju, "Mass Conversions to Hinduism among Indian Muslims," *Economic and Political Weekly* 29, no. 34 (1994): 2214–19. Individual conversion to Hinduism, though rare, is possible: J. F. Seunarine, *Reconversion to Hinduism through Śuddhi* (Madras: Christian Literature Society, 1977). The term *reconversion* in the title here conveys the Hindu missionary's sense that non-Hindu Indians are returning to their natural roots.

2. On the debates surrounding early Indian history and the dating of the Vedas, see Edwin F. Bryant and Laurie L. Patton, eds., *The Indo-Aryan Controversy: Evidence and Inference in Indian History* (New York: Routledge Curzon, 2004).

3. On the Arya Samaj, see Kenneth W. Jones, *Arya Dharm: Hindu Consciousness in 19th-Century Punjab* (Berkeley: University of California Press, 1976). This is an enduring study that still remains the best work on the subject.

4. A sense of Ramakrishna's spiritual presence can be gleaned from Ramakrishna, Mahendra Nath Gupta, and Abhedānanda, *The Gospel of Ramakrishna* (New York: Vedanta Society, 1947). This voluminous work presents detailed descriptions of some of the saint's interactions with his disciples based on diary notes of a longtime devotee.

5. This karma yogic interpretation of Vivekananda's organizational aims is one I heard from members of the Vivekananda Kendra. It does, though, seem rooted in Swami Vivekananda's teachings: Vivekananda and Nikhilananda, *Karma-yoga and Bhakti-yoga*, rev. ed. (New York: Ramakrishna-Vivekananda Center, 1955).

6. The basic story of Swami Swaroopananda and the Ramakrishna Ashram is outlined in N. N. Tandon, "Ramakrishna Ashram, Gwalior: A Plant in Blossom," *Svarṇ Jayaṃtī Smarikā Viśeṣānk: Golden Jubilee (2008–2009)* (Thatipur, Gwalior, 2008), pp. 115–17.

7. See ibid.

8. The size of the tract as fifty-two acres comes from an interview with Swami Swaroopananda on August 12, 2008; Binoo Sen, however, a retired government officer, writes of 104 *bīghas* provided by the state: "Sarada Balgram and Sneh Kutir," *Svarṇ Jayaṃtī Smarikā Viśeṣānk*, pp. 118–19. A *bīgha* is a unit of land measurement that in fact refers to different measures in different parts of India, and here we see the Swami making a simple two to one conversion of *bīghas* to acres. A recent survey done by a local NGO, though, reports 2.5 *bīghas* to the acre, a figure I have also frequently heard: this would make the Balgram about forty acres— still quite sizable: *Draft Report of a Study on Watershed Development in Sunari Watershed (Semi-ravine Area) of Datia District of Madhya Pradesh* (New Delhi and Gwalior: Society for Promotion of Wastelands Development [SPWD], 2004).

9. When I visited ROSHNI in 2009, I ran into members of two prominent Maratha families whom I had previously met while researching the Maharashtrian community.

10. The only scholarly research on the Vivekananda Kendra of which I am aware is that of Gwilym Beckerlegge. See his " 'An Ordinary Organization Run by Ordinary People': A Study of Leadership in Vivekananda Kendra," *Contemporary South Asia* 18, no. 1 (2010): 71–88; and "Eknath Ranade, Gurus, and Jīvanvratīs: The Vivekananda Kendra's Promotion of the 'Yoga Way of Life,' " in *Gurus of Modern Yoga*, ed. Mark Singleton and Ellen Goldberg (New York: Oxford University Press, 2014), pp. 327–50.

11. http://www.vkendra.org/mission, June 25, 2010.

12. http://www.vknardep.org, June 27, 2010.

13. The RSS is the commonly used abbreviation for the Rāṣṭrīya Svayamsevak Sangh, which means the "National Volunteer Association." Insiders also simply call the group "the Sangh." The Sangh Parivar is the "family" (*parivār*) of the RSS. On the RSS in relationship to some of its predecessors, see my "Organized Hinduisms: From Vedic Truth to Hindu Nation," in *Fundamentalism Observed*, ed. Martin E. Marty and R. Scott Appleby (Chicago: University of Chicago Press, 1991), pp. 531–93. On Hindu nationalism in general, a good starting place is Christophe Jaffrelot, *Hindu Nationalism: A Reader* (Princeton, N.J.: Princeton University Press, 2007), which offers a clear introduction, plentiful source materials, and a detailed bibliography.

14. Gwilym Beckerlegge notes, however, that the Vivekananda Kendra "is not strictly a constituent of the [Sangh] parivār. Its activities, for example, are not recorded in the RSS's database of the sangh parivār's sevā projects" (Beckerlegge, "Eknath Ranade," p. 329).

15. http://www.vKendra.org/vki, June 28, 2010.

16. The extremely valuable land for the Kendra International building in Chankayapuri, the diplomatic enclave, was originally awarded during the (secular) Congress government of Narasimha Rao, and financial help for the organization's mammoth

rock memorial to Vivekananda off Kanyakumari drew support across the board in the Lok Sabha (interview with Mukul Kantikar, Delhi, August 19, 2008).

17. http://www.vkendra.org/rashtriyaYajna, June 26, 2010.
18. www.karna.org/KARNA_utkarsha_project.pdf.
19. vknardep.org, July 16, 2013.
20. Like most large ethnic communities, the Gwalior Maharashtrians are not politically homogenous, but people do talk about political tendencies within it. The common local understanding is that its Brahmins frequently have sympathies for the Hindu right. The Marathas, by contrast, at least during Madhav Rao Scindia's late twentieth-century ascendancy in the Congress, have often given strong support to that secular party.
21. In his "An Ordinary Organization," Gwilym Beckerlegge mentions in passing that marriages between lifeworkers are encouraged. He later reports, however, that further interviews with his sources offer a picture consonant with what Mukul told me (personal communication, December 10, 2010).
22. On the priority of loyalty to the organization over that to any guru in the Vivekananda Kendra, see Beckerlegge, "Eknath Ranade."

CHAPTER 6

1. For the Brahma Kumaris as a modern religious movement, see Lawrence A. Babb, *Redemptive Encounters: Three Modern Styles in the Hindu Tradition* (Berkeley: University of California Press, 1986), pp. 93–155.
2. For an insightful analysis of the diversity of modern Indian religious gurus and the dynamics of their movements, see Jacob Copeman and Aya Ikegame, "The Multifarious Guru," in *The Guru in South Asia: New Interdisciplinary Perspectives*, ed. Jacob Copeman and Aya Ikegame (New York: Routledge, 2012), pp. 1–45. The essays in that volume largely present different *types* of gurus.
3. Famous examples of gurus' tests of disciples abound in Indic traditions. For an extended example from classical Hindu tradition, see the separate trials inflicted by Dhaumya Āyoda on his three students, Upamanyu, Āruṇi, and Veda: J. A. B. van Buitenen, *The Mahābhārata: The Book of the Beginning*, vol. 1 (Chicago: University of Chicago Press, 1973), pp. 45–53. Sikh tradition reveres the extreme devotion of the Panj Pyare, "the five beloved," to the tenth Sikh guru, Gobind Singh: Max Macauliffe, *The Sikh Religion: Its Gurus, Sacred Writings, and Authors* (Delhi: S. Chand, 1963), vol. 5, pp. 91–93. And Indo-Tibetan Buddhists are familiar with the lengthy travails of the Tibetan yogi Milarepa: W. Y. Evans-Wentz et al., *Tibet's Great Yogi Milarepa: A Biography from the Tibetan*, 2nd ed. (New York: Oxford University Press, 1969), pp. 93–135.
4. *Śive ruṣṭe gurus trātaḥ; gurau ruṣṭe na kaścana;* the line can be found in verse 88 of the Guru Gita, a section of the Skanda Purana often excerpted for popular devotion: Narayanananda, *Sri Guru Gita* (Shivanandanagar: Divine Life

Society, 1972), p. 36. Another frequently met version of the text gives close variants of this line in verses 44 and 79: Vrajavallabha Dwivedi, *Śrī Guru Gītā* (Varanasi: Shaiva Bharati Shodha Pratishthanam, 1999), pp. 36, 53.

5. *Guru Gobind doū khaṛe, kāke lāgauṃ pāy? Balihārī guru āpne, jin Gobind diyo milāy.* This verse, attributed to Kabir, is cited as an oral tradition in L. B. Ram (Anant)'s introduction to the couplets on guru devotion in his edition of Kabir's sayings: *Kabīr Granthāvalī* (Delhi: Regal Book Depot, 1968), p. 99. It is not found among those couplets themselves or in the sections on guru devotion in any other scholarly edition of old Kabir texts that I have seen.

6. Daniel Gold, *The Lord as Guru: Hindi Sants in North Indian Tradition* (New York: Oxford University Press, 1987) and *Comprehending the Guru: Towards a Grammar of Religious Perception* (Atlanta: Scholars Press, 1988). Monographs devoted to the Radhasoamis include Mark Juergensmeyer, *Radhasoami Reality: The Logic of a Modern Faith* (Princeton, N.J.: Princeton University Press, 1991) and David Christopher Lane, *The Radhasoami Tradition: A Critical History of Guru Successorship* (New York: Garland, 1992).

7. Eighteenth- and nineteenth-century sants from mercantile backgrounds include Charandas of Delhi, Ramcharan of the Ramsnehi sampradaya, and Paltu Sahib of Ayodhya.

8. On the *sants'* popular ways, see Charlotte Vaudeville, *Kabīr* (Oxford: Oxford University Press, 1974), pp. 97–110. The introduction to this volume remains one of the finest scholarly introductions to *sant* tradition. For an article on late *sant* use of everyday metaphor, see my "What the Merchant Guru Sold: Social and Literary Type in Hindi Devotional Verse," *Journal of the American Oriental Society* 111, no. 1 (1992): 22–35.

9. See, for example, David Lorenzen, *Praises to a Formless God* (Albany: State University of New York Press, 1996); and Milind Wakankar, *Subalternity and Religion: The Prehistory of Dalit Empowerment in South Asia* (New York: Routledge, 2010).

10. This is most notably the case of the fifteenth-century poet Rai Das (or Ravi Das), by caste a tanner: Winand M. Callewaert, Peter G. Friedlander, and Ravidāsa, *The Life and Works of Raidās* (New Delhi: Manohar Publishers & Distributors, 1992). In parts of North India, tanners refer to themselves, and are referred to politely by others, as Raidasis. Religious groups oriented toward old and new *sants* have been important channels of low-caste political mobilization in some parts of India, especially the Punjab: see Vijay Prashad, *Untouchable Freedom: A Social History of a Dalit Community* (New York: Oxford University Press, 2000); and Lionel Baixas, "The Dera Sacha Sauda Controversy and Beyond," *Economic and Political Weekly* 42, no. 40 (2007): 4059–65.

11. See Juergensmeyer, *Radhasoami Reality*, pp. 24–31; and Gold, *Lord as Guru*, p. 113.

12. As a word for the individual being, the Hindi *surat*, which can also mean "recollection" in Hindi, probably derives from the Sanskrit *smṛti*, a common word for memory. But for practitioners, *surat* can also suggest the Sanskrit *śruti*, "hearing" and the Arabic *sūrat*, "face," a word commonly used in Urdu.

13. Early Radhasoami doctrinal writings in English include a frequently reprinted compendium of discourses by Maharaj Saheb, an important figure in the main Agra lineage: Brahm Sankar Misra, *Discourses on Radhasoami Faith* (Benares: B.P. Dey., 1909). Less readily available is a narrative treatment by Guru Data Dayala of Gwalior: Shyam Lal, *Retransformation of Self* (Lashkar, Gwalior: G. S. Niwas, 1923). In both cases, the volumes were first published under the gurus' legal names.

14. Thomas Dahnhardt, *Change and Continuity in Indian Sufism: A Naqshbandi-Mujaddidi Branch in the Hindu Environment* (New Delhi: D.K. Printworld, 2002), pp. 335–83, pays attention to the Kayastha origins and development of another late esoteric sant sublineage—one offering practices similar to the Radhasoamis but with a more explicit Sufi orientation. On the Kayasthas in general see Karen Isaksen Leonard, *Social History of an Indian Caste: The Kayasths of Hyderabad* (Berkeley: University of California Press, 1978).

15. Lane, *The Radhasoami Tradition*, discusses six successors to Soamiji Shiv Dayal; in addition to the four discussed here, he mentions Soamiji's wife Radhaji and a sadhu named Sanmukh Das.

16. The Beas groups see Soamiji as a disciple of Tulsi Sahib, and thus as a *sant* among *sants*, while the Agra groups take him as a special guruless divine incarnation—one no doubt influenced in his earthly life by Tulsi Sahib, but actually the unique source of a new religious movement.

17. The Delhi-based Ruhani Satsang founded by Sant Kirpal Singh (1894–1974), at this writing led by his grandson Sant Rajinder Singh, continues to have a large international following. There are also small sublineages descending from Jaimal Singh in the Punjab in addition to his main Beas lineage.

18. *Jai Gurudev nām kis kā? Prabhu kā. Kyā hai prabhu kā pāvan nām? Jai Gurudev! Kyā hai prabhu kā pyārā nām? Jai Gurudev! Kyā Jai Gurudev nām insān kā? Nām bhagvān kā.*

19. The remark about the guru as father to his children is a direct quote from a Jahazpur satsang talk, January 31, 2011.

20. For reflective sketches of two other unbelievably old gurus, see Lawrence Cohen, *No Aging in India: Alzheimer's, the Bad Family, and Other Modern Things* (Berkeley: University of California Press, 1998), pp. 278–86.

21. On Yadav identity in Western Uttar Pradesh, see Lucia Michelutti, " 'We (Yadavs) Are a Caste of Politicians': Caste and Modern Politics in a North Indian Town," in *Caste in Question: Identity or Hierarchy*, ed. Dipankar Gupta (Thousand Oaks, Calif.: Sage Publications, 2004), pp. 43–71.

22. I was told at the Mathura Ashram that Ghurelal's older brother was a direct disciple of Garib Das, reasonable given that Garib Das died in 1917.

23. I have come across different years for the passing of Ghurelal, most often 1947 or 1948; the main Wikipedia article on Baba Jai Gurudev (on January 10, 2013), however, gave a more precise time of December 1950.

24. *"Anevāle musibatoṃ se kaun bacāyegā? Jai gurudev!"* Although millennialist thought is not common in Hindu tradition, Baba Jai Gurudev is not the only modern guru

to have taken it up. On the Brahma Kumaris, with a well worked-out millennialist theology, see Babb, *Redemptive Encounters*, pp. 93–155. On the Mumbai-based millennialist guru Aniruddha Bapu, see Jacob Copeman, *Veins of Devotion: Blood Donation and Religious Experience in North India* (New Brunswick, N.J.: Rutgers University Press, 2009), pp. 143–46. As a guru reaching out to the rural masses and initiating them into a modern form of religion, Baba Jai Gurudev also resembled what Copeman calls a gateway guru, opening his devotees to modern ways (pp. 139–47). In particular, the emphasis in the Jai Gurudev movement on experiencing the guru's presence at large gatherings pushes village people to travel and mix with others in ways they may not have done otherwise.

25. On Khateek enterprise, see Kaveri Gill, *Of Poverty and Plastic: Scavenging and Scrap Trading Entrepreneurs in India's Urban Informal Economy* (New Delhi: Oxford University Press, 2010), which examines the Khateeks' crucial role in the Delhi scrap-trading business.

26. See Tulasi Srinivas, *Winged Faith: Rethinking Globalization and Religious Pluralism through the Sathya Sai Movement* (New York: Columbia University Press, 2010), p. 51.

27. An institution with this name no longer appears to be active. After Baba Jai Gurudev passed away there was a major succession dispute. Gatherings are still held in Mathura, but the organizational structures of the movement have undergone transformation. I have written about some of the changes occurring in the movement in the first months after the guru's passing as an epilogue to "Bābā Jai Gurudev in the Qasbā: The Ruralization of a Modern Religion," *International Journal of Hindu Studies* 17, no. 2 (2013): 127–52. This article deals with some ways in which the movement has developed in the countryside.

28. That website, Jai Gurudev.org, was very lively during Baba Jai Gurudev's final years and was vital for a while after his passing, with the phone number of an untitled person other than Lulla as contact. By summer 2013 it seemed to have become defunct.

29. Though a significant sum in rural Rajasthan, Rs. 500 (then about US$12) was still manageable for most working people and reasonable considering the distance and time spent.

30. The quote was taken from the "About Swamiji" page at the now defunct website www.jaigurudeo.org, July 23, 2010. When I tried to pin people down on which religion's house of worship the temple looked like from any particular angle, they would most often say that it is up to the eye of the observer.

31. For a description of the potentially surprising effects of *darśan* on the spiritually curious, see Amanda J. Lucia, *Reflections of Amma: Devotees in a Global Embrace* (Berkeley: University of California Press, 2014), p. 25. That book offers a very sensitive treatment of a major Indian movement centered on a female guru who gives personal *darśan* with hugs. In so doing it presents some interesting

reflections on the guru's *darśan* in general, giving brief descriptions of *darśan* practices of several modern gurus (pp. 41–45).

32. Shyam Lal was born within a mercantile caste in a village in Etawah district, Western U.P., the same district in which Baba Jai Gurudev's birth village is located. He came to Gwalior for higher education and later served there as a high-school headmaster. (Shyam Lal's honorific as guru, Data Dayala, was also used for Shivbrat Lal, a better-known Radhasoami guru who lived about the same time and with whom he is liable to be confused; the latter was a disciple of Soamiji's successor Rai Saligram and has a lineage continuing in Dinod, Haryana.) Although I write of Shyam Lal as Malik Sahib's first main guru, Malik Sahib acknowledged a guru prior to him: a sadhu named Lochan Das from Morena district, where Malik Sahib's family had roots. Lochan Das, Malik Sahib would say, taught him a version of the same *sant mat* practices offered by Shyam Lal.

33. Malik Sahib specifically refers to the *svapratīkopāsanā* in the Shiva Samhita, with verse numbers: Sant Mansingh, *Divya Rahasya Prakāś: Adhyātmparak Nibamdhom kā Samgrah* (Gwalior: Divine Charitable Society, Adhyatm Niketan, 1976), p. 67. The passage referred to is presented clearly in James Mallinson's translation of that text, ch. 5, vv. 29–45—*The Shiva Samhita: A Critical Edition and an English Translation* (Woodstock, NY: YogaVidya.com, 2007), pp. 110–14.

34. Sant Mansingh, *Divya Rahasya Prakash*, pp. 67–69. The meditation practices presented by Malik Sahib are treated in greater detail in my "Two Yogic Paths to the Formless Lord: The Hindi Sants' Ways Out of the Body," in *Meditation and Culture: The Interplay of Practice and Context*, ed. Halvor Eifring (London: Bloomsbury Academic, 2015).

35. For more on the succession itself, see my "Continuities as Gurus Change," in Copeman and Ikegame, *The Guru in South Asia*, pp. 243–54.

36. This phrase sounds more ironic in Hindi: *ārām se safar karnā aur ārām se ārām karnā*.

37. This number comes from R. G. Agraval, a trusted old disciple who went along on the trip. He first said *saimkrom*, which suggests an indefinitely great quantity, but later restrained himself (interview, November 6, 2007).

38. Thus, Gautama Buddha and the Jaina Tirthankara Mahavira were both said to have been born princes, although their realms may not have been very large.

39. Because surnames in India normally suggest a caste identity, Hindi short story writers have sometimes only referred to their characters by their first names.

40. Rosie Thomas, "Melodrama and the Negotiation of Modernity," in *Consuming Modernity: Public Culture in a South Asian World*, ed. Carol Appadurai Breckenridge (Minneapolis: University of Minnesota Press, 1995), pp. 157–72.

41. In addition, parents might give their children to a sadhu out of economic hardship, devotion to the sadhu, or fulfillment of a vow. A boy in an unhappy home situation might prefer to live with a sadhu who invites him. For more on child sadhus see my *The Lord as Guru*, pp. 101–2.

42. J. P. Rathore, an old Gwalior *satsaṅgī*, recalled a number of these from memory, for example: *Dūrdarśī kā ādhār, sārā jīvan ūṃc vicār* (The basis of Doordarshi: high thoughts throughout life); *Dūrdarśi ka elān, yah svarg banegā hindustān* (Doordarshi announces: this India will become heaven).

43. For one of the most famous instances of a guru working with a maharaja, see Padmaja Sharma, *Maharaja Man Singh of Jodhpur and His Times (1803–1843 a.d.)* (Agra: Shiva Lal Agarwala and Company, 1972).

44. R. G. Agrawal, speaking in Gwalior in early 2011, said the Himachal disciple was invested with authority two years before. He called him a *mukhiyā*, "leader."

45. This is a comment taken from a devotee posting about the Mathura temple on the Internet: wikimapia.org/384500/Yog-Sadhna-Mandir-Temple, found March 20, 2011.

46. Charan Singh, *Divine Light* (Beas, India: Radhasoami Satsang, 1967), pp. 291, 327. This book is a collection of discourses and letters by one of the most prominent modern gurus of the Beas lineage.

AFTERWORD

1. Asaram was born in Sindh (now Pakistan) to a Hindu family that after Partition settled in Ahmedabad, Gujarat. In 1971, he started an ashram in that city that has affiliates all over India, including Gwalior. There have been accusations of land encroachment against some of the ashrams and, in 2013, allegations of sexual assault that led to Asaram's imprisonment. It can take much more than allegations of serious impropriety, however, to disabuse a guru's convinced devotees of their faith. After all, they may surmise, great souls often provoke hostility from bad people, and even if some of what these detractors say is true, who can actually see the real inner significance of a guru's acts? Gurus often survive scandals with much of their following intact.